A Transactional Perspective on Teaching and Learning

A Framework for Adult and Higher Education

ADVANCES IN LEARNING AND INSTRUCTION SERIES

Series Editors:
Andreas Demetriou, Erik DeCorte, Stella Vosniadou and Heinz Mandl

Published

VAN SOMEREN, REIMANN, BOSHUIZEN & DE JONG
Learning with Multiple Representations

DILLENBOURG
Collaborative Learning: Cognitive and Computational Approaches

SCHNOTZ, VOSNIADOU & CARRETERO
New Perspectives on Conceptual Change

BLISS, SÄLJÖ & LIGHT
Learning Sites: Social and Technological Resources for Learning

KAYSER & VOSNIADOU
Modelling Changes in Understanding: Case Studies in Physical Reasoning

Forthcoming titles

COWIE, AALSVOORT & MERCER
Social Interaction in Learning and Instruction

ROUET, LEVONEN & BIARDEAU
Integrating Text and Graphics in Computer-Supported Learning Environments

Other titles of interest

REIMANN & SPADA
Learning in Humans and Machines: Towards an Interdisciplinary Learning Science

Computer Assisted Learning: Proceedings of the CAL series of biennial Symposia 1989, 1991, 1993, 1995 and 1997 (five volumes).

Related Journals - sample copies available on request

Learning and Instruction
International Journal of Educational Research
Computers and Education
Computers and Human Behavior

A Transactional Perspective on Teaching and Learning

A Framework for Adult and Higher Education

by

D. Randy Garrison and Walter Archer

2000

PERGAMON
An imprint of Elsevier Science
Amsterdam – Lausanne – New York – Oxford – Shannon – Singapore – Tokyo

ELSEVIER SCIENCE Ltd
The Boulevard, Langford Lane
Kidlington, Oxford OX5 1GB, UK

First edition 2000 by Pergamon (An imprint of Elsevier Science Ltd) in association with the European Association for
Research and Learning (EARLI)

Library of Congress Cataloging-in-Publication Data

Garrison, D. R. (D. Randy), 1945-
    A transactional perspective on teaching and learning / by D. Randy Garrison and Walter Archer.
    p. cm. -- (Advances in learning and instruction series)
    ISBN 0-08-043780-X (hardcover)
    1. Adult education. 2. Education, Higher. 3. Learning, Psychology of. 4. Teaching. I.
Archer, Walter. II. Title. III. Series.

    LC5201 .G27 2000
    374--dc21

                                                                    00-029343

British Library Cataloguing in Publication Data

A catalogue record from the British Library has been applied for.
ISBN: 0 08 043780 X

⊚ The paper used in this publication meets the requirements of ANSI/NISO Z39.48-1992 (Permanence of Paper).
Printed in The Netherlands.

Table of Contents

Acknowledgement

Producing this book would not have been possible without the support of the European Science Foundation, Strasbourg. The European Science Foundation is an association of 62 major national funding agencies devoted to basic scientific research in 21 countries. The ESF assists its Member Organisations in two main ways: by bringing scientists together in its Scientific Programmes, Networks and European Research Conferences, to work on topics of common interest; and through the joint study of issues of strategic importance in European science policy. The scientific work sponsored by the ESF includes basic research in the natural and technical sciences, the medical and biosciences, the humanities and social sciences. The ESF maintains close relations with other scientific institutions within and outside Europe. Through its activities, the ESF adds value by cooperation and coordination across national frontiers and endeavours, offers expert scientific advice on strategic issues, and provides the European forum for fundamental science. This book is one of the outcomes of the ESF Scientific Programme on "Learning in Humans and Machines".

Preface

The primary aim of this book is to provide a comprehensive and coherent perspective on the process of adult and higher education. Our focus is on the teaching-learning transaction; therefore, most of our discussion is about the educational *process*, rather than the selection of *content*. This is not to denigrate the latter — we are quite aware that acquiring knowledge and wisdom is the ultimate goal of education. However, this book is about the means to that ultimate end.

We assume a "collaborative constructivist" perspective for examining meaningful and worthwhile educational experiences. Within this overall perspective, we examine the conceptual models of critical thinking and self-directed learning, which have been central to the study and practice of adult and higher education. The twin themes of responsibility and control are carried throughout the book. Together, these foundational concepts and themes frame a discussion of the design and implementation of teaching methods and learning activities.

Audience

While the primary audience for this book is individuals involved in adult and higher education, the relevance of the essential concepts and framework discussed in the book is not confined to a particular educational subgroup. Therefore, this book will be of interest and value to all educators who wish to inquire into the theory and practice of teaching and learning. In particular, it will be a useful text in college and university classes studying teaching and learning in a variety of contexts.

Overview of the Contents

The book proceeds from the conceptual to the pragmatic. Part I begins by exploring the transactional relationship between the personal reflective world of the learner and the collaborative shared world of the educational setting. It does this through the identification of the themes of responsibility and control and the concomitant development of critical thinking and self-directed learning models. The second part of the book moves into the practical issues of responsible teaching, design, and meaningful learning activities. These issues are addressed from the perspective of desired goals and intended outcomes which make it necessary to address the question "why" before discussing the issue "how".

The first chapter provides an overview of the themes and concepts explored in the subsequent chapters of the book. Complementary concepts, which parallel the reciprocal nature of the teaching and learning transaction, are identified and described. An integration of the concepts concludes the chapter and foreshadows the ongoing concern with teaching as a professional practice.

The second chapter explores the works of Dewey, Rogers and Habermas. The purpose here is to provide a foundation for discussions to follow. The key themes and concepts that frame the book are identified and discussed.

Chapter 3 provides a general overview of three contrasting perspectives of learning. Particular attention is given to the distinction between surface or reproductive learning and deep or meaningful learning. The influence of sociocultural context on meaningful and worthwhile learning experiences is also examined.

The next two chapters present the core conceptual models of the educational process. In Chapter 4 we argue that critical thinking is the cornerstone of the process of higher education. This chapter begins with Dewey's concept of reflective thinking and builds a comprehensive view of critical thinking by incorporating creative and intuitive thought processes. The chapter also discusses the facilitation of critical thinking within the educational curriculum.

Chapter 5 shifts to the cognitive and social dynamics of the teaching-learning transaction. A model of self-directed learning is provided which integrates contextual, cognitive and conative issues. Self-direction is defined in terms of self-management (contextual), self-monitoring (cognitive), and motivational (conative) concerns. The inherent challenge is to maintain a dynamic balance amongst management, monitoring and motivational concerns.

In Chapter 6 the focus shifts to effective and responsible teaching. The chapter opens with a critical review of effective teaching. Next, emerging conceptualizations of responsible teaching are explored from a collaborative constructivist perspective. It is emphasized that responsible teaching cannot be prescriptive; instead, it is based upon professional judgement in the context of changing needs and expectations.

Chapter 7 complements the overview of responsible teaching in the previous chapter with a pragmatic discussion and organization of meaningful learning activities. Consistent with the general approach of this book, the strategy is to first understand the purpose and function of various learning activities. The discussion focuses on four key learning activities — listening, reading, talking and writing. Through a discussion of these learning activities, specific practical issues are identified and their application for educational purposes is anticipated. Activities addressing these issues, in practical educational settings, are discussed in the following chapter.

Chapter 8 provides practical strategies and suggestions for facilitating a meaningful and worthwhile learning experience. The chapter moves from a discussion of how to organize an educational experience to specific techniques and suggestions associated with the major learning activities discussed in the previous chapter. The chapter ends with a discussion of the importance of modelling learning strategies and approaches.

In Chapter 9 the crucial issue of assessing learning and achievement is discussed. The point is made that assessment directly influences approaches to learning and the quality of learning outcomes. Discussion focuses on feedback and evaluation for guiding learning and measuring achievement respectively. Specific assessment techniques and test design suggestions are presented.

Chapter 10 discusses the role that technologies of educational design and delivery play in the teaching-learning transaction. Placing technological issues in perspective is crucial if learning is to be seen as more than simply accessing and acquiring information. This is particularly relevant to discussion of the Internet and other learning networks. The message is that technology must be used not only to enhance access in order to expand the intellectual creativity and freedom of the students, but also to enhance communication in order to facilitate the teaching-learning transaction.

The final chapter concludes the book with a systemic analysis of the teaching-learning transaction. A discussion of the forces limiting responsible teaching and meaningful learning is presented. Issues related to teacher development are also explored. Finally, the themes and general thesis of the book are revisited.

Acknowledgements

This book represents the culmination of a decade of work concerning the teaching and learning transaction in a variety of contexts. However, before I could finish the manuscript I was pulled away by administrative responsibilities. During the hiatus from writing, I shared the unfinished manuscript with a colleague and golfing companion, Dr. Kris Magnusson. He provided valuable feedback and gave me confidence that it was a worthwhile project. I thank Kris for his support and input. Ultimately, the credit for completing the manuscript and constructing a form worthy of publication goes to my friend, colleague and co-author — Walter Archer.

At this point in my career, my greatest satisfaction in seeing this book published is that my young daughters will be able to read it one day. I hope they will find it of some interest, if for no other reason than daughterly curiosity. I would also like to note that it was an insight of my daughter Nadine, when she was seven years old, that triggered the analogy between the practical inquiry model to the seasons of the year. While we were out walking one day, she noted how winter and summer were opposites and spring and fall were similar. This immediately made me think of the analogy between the phases of inquiry and the seasons. Inspiration was also provided by my youngest daughter Sabrine, who at two years old, was so aware and consumed with making sense of her experiences. She personified practical inquiry.

I dedicate this book to Nadine and Sabrine.

Finally, I wish to acknowledge that a significant portion of the article described subsequently was reprinted with permission in Chapter 5.

Garrison, D.R. (1992). Critical thinking and self-directed learning in adult education: An analysis of responsibility and control issues. *Adult Education Quarterly*, *42*, 136–148.

D. Randy Garrison, December, 1999.

PART I: Conceptual Framework

1

A Transactional Perspective

There are many excellent books and articles that provide practical guidance for educators, including effective methods and techniques. These can be very valuable, as compendia of craft "know-how." This book is intended to complement these valuable compendia of good practice by providing a coherent theoretical framework on the basis of which reflective practitioners of education can select one method or technique over another. We refer to this theoretical framework as the transactional perspective on teaching and learning.

The first five chapters of this book are devoted to discussion of the background and rationale for the transactional perspective, and explaining its features. The final six chapters provide theories of the mechanisms (i.e. approaches and strategies) by which this theoretical perspective of learning can be applied in various educational situations, including face-to-face classroom instruction, learning enhanced through various technologies, and distance education.

Characteristics of Adult Learning

The learning theories that have inspired education to date are based, directly or indirectly, on studies of how children learn. However, adults now do most of the intentional learning that takes place in modern western societies. The purpose of this learning and the contexts in which it occurs differ markedly from the purposes and contexts of childhood education. For adult learning, our current models are, therefore, more or less unsatisfactory, despite efforts by many educators to modify them to give a better fit with typical adult learning situations. In contrast with these current models, the transactional perspective proposed in this book is based directly on adult learning — though it has application to learners of all ages.

We have not arrived at our perspective inductively, on the basis of a sampling of actual learning situations, because these actual situations are the sum of many factors, some of them quite unrelated to learning. Instead, we have arrived at this perspective through reflection on an ideal learning situation. The various practical and political factors that impact upon actual learning situations can be addressed as the perspective is applied in specific contexts.

The ideal learning situation that we have in mind might be described as follows:

1. all of the learners have life experience relevant to the learning task at hand, so are able to engage in constructivist creation of knowledge;

2. the group constitutes what may be referred to as a collaborative community of learners;
3. the learners are all capable of assuming responsibility for their own learning;
4. the learners have, or can acquire, a capacity for critical thinking;
5. the balance of control in the learning situation is congruent with the educational goals and learner capabilities;
6. the learning situation includes a purpose which gives students substantial motivation to master and manage their own learning — that is, they have incentive to be self-directed.

The transactional perspective follows from these six ideas that can be identified in the ideal learning situation. Figure 1.1 is an attempt to illustrate how these ideas are related. The transactional perspective is built upon two foundational concepts — that a constructivist approach is necessary for learners to create meaning, and that collaboration is essential for creating and confirming knowledge. On the basis of this philosophical foundation we examine two themes that run through all learning activities — responsibility for learning, and control of the educational transaction. From examination of these themes we proceed to consideration of two processes which are essential for the achievement of the goals of education, particularly higher education — critical thinking (CT), and self-directed learning (SDL).

Understanding the educational process requires not only a synthesis of the cognitive and social worlds but also complementary theories of learning and practice (i.e. mechanism). The theories associated with critical thinking and self-directed learning are synergistically connected and provide, respectively, an explanation of higher-order learning and a mechanism for implementing such learning. This is consistent with Schoenfeld (1999) who states, in regard to constructing educational theory, that "… no theory of learning is complete without a theory of mechanism — an elaboration in detail of the processes by which learning takes place" (p. 6). The theory of mechanism (i.e. practice) is elaborated in the second part of this book.

The dotted line that bisects Figure 1.1 is intended to indicate that each of these three pairs of concepts is actually a unity being considered from two different viewpoints — the cognitive and the social. That is, constructivism refers to the creation of knowledge and meaning "from the inside," while collaboration is the "outside" or public face of this process. Similarly, the teacher and student are linked to the public and personal face of the educational transaction, respectively. Finally, the spiral form of the figure is intended to indicate that each of these concepts is linked to its mate, as well as to other levels of the figure, through the transactional nature of the educational experience.

The Transactional Perspective

We should emphasize that in our discussion of the six points listed above we have been describing an *ideal* learning situation. *Actual* learning situations approximate

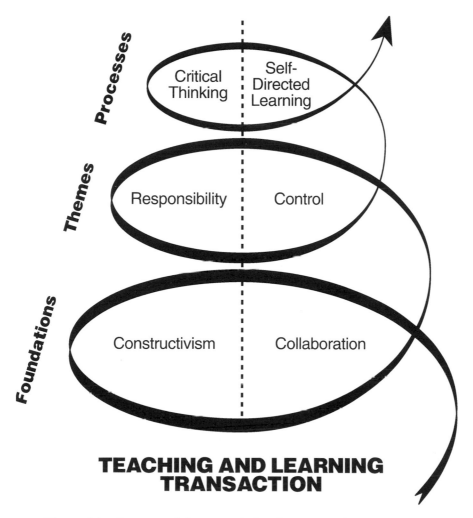

Figure 1.1: Conceptual framework for the transactional perspective.

this ideal to a greater or lesser extent. The ideal is often approached rather closely in adult and continuing professional education. Our perspective, then, should be of particular interest to facilitators of this form of education.

Another context that often approximates the ideal is the everyday work situation of modern knowledge workers, whose work involves constant learning. Modern knowledge work, in fact, shades almost imperceptibly into continuing professional development. Our perspective applies almost equally well to the everyday context of knowledge work as to those situations in which the knowledge workers have stepped back from their daily work in order to take part in continuing professional education. It should, then, be of interest to knowledge workers who reflect on the process through which they carry on their work.

Other contexts approximate the ideal learning situation to a lesser extent. In typical college or university classes, for example, the balance of control may be tilted away from the students in a manner not at all congruent with their capacities. However, we believe that our transactional perspective of learning has much to say to educators working in formal higher education since it focuses attention on the ideal learning situation for adults. By reflecting upon this ideal, educators in institutions of higher education may be able to alter their practice so as to approximate this ideal as closely as possible.

In typical grade school classes few of the characteristics of our ideal learning situation may be present, for various practical reasons having to do with the age of the students, their relative lack of life experience, and the non-educational functions of the school (e.g. the custodial function). Both of the authors of this book have taught in grade schools and carried out research in that context, so are well aware of the practical difficulties faced by educators in grade schools. However, we believe that the perspective proposed herein can be applied to the education of children as well, with appropriate allowances for the practical realities of the learning context. This book, therefore, should also be of some interest to educators working at this level of the education system.

Preliminary Remarks on Learning

Learning is a process of constructing meaning from raw information and confirming knowledge. This includes personal meaning-making, in which individuals make connections between facts and create coherent knowledge structures from the information available to them. It also involves social validation, in which information is applied in a social context. Thus education, when viewed from a knowledge construction perspective, is an iterative process of personal meaning-making and the social validation of this meaning.

In the context of a knowledge society, the process of learning becomes one of constructing shared meaning and understanding (i.e. knowledge structures). Although such a process assumes the acquisition of facts and information as the building blocks, it relies on critical and constructive thinking about how this information can form a pattern or structure to which additional information may be integrated. Sharing carries with it the added requirement of being able to explain personal meaning and understanding. This process moves learners iteratively between the shared world of experience and the private reflective world of ideas. In a knowledge society, systems of education must employ processes in which information and experience are reconstructed to create meaning for the individual while concomitantly confirming understanding and validating knowledge in a collaborative manner.

A great deal of intentional learning, particularly among adults, is organized autonomously by the individual. As Alan Thomas has pointed out, "education floats in a sea of learning" (1987, p. 109). However, a significant and socially crucial fraction of all learning occurs in educational settings, in which some agency or person (school, university, training department, teacher, etc.) attempts to arrange circumstances so as to efficiently promote worthwhile learning. Therefore, it is necessary to reflect on some current practices in educational settings that tend to promote learning or, in far too many cases, prevent learning.

Incongruent Practices in Education

The stated purposes of education are not always reflected in its actual practices. The declared goal of educators, particularly in higher education, is usually something like "to develop critical thinking and higher-level communication skills". Their actual practice, however, often belies this stated goal. There are a number of reasons for this discrepancy.

Information addiction. Institutions of higher education, in practice, often employ approaches to learning designed for the efficient transplantation of information into the minds of supposedly receptive students. This has commonly been referred to as a transmission model of learning. It is typified by an all too common practice in which a professor lectures to a group of hundreds of students. The lecturer dispenses, at a rapid rate, fragmented facts and information that the students will be expected to reproduce during an examination. If they fail to do so, they will be denied a desired credential.

The students' most intelligent strategy, given the circumstances, is to learn to memorize efficiently. They have little need for critical thinking skills, since they are expected to simply reproduce (or, if the test is multiple choice, often just recognize) the information that has been dispensed in the lecture. There is little need for understanding or constructing coherent perspectives. Furthermore, there is little call for them to develop active higher-order communication skills in a large lecture theatre where all the communication is moving in one direction.

One of the principal causes of the typical procedure in higher education sketched above is a fixation among educators, and those who influence them, on information. The popular literature has characterized our times as an information society. In the past, information did not represent a major distraction for education. However, with the spectacular proliferation of information in recent decades individuals and organizations seem to have become fixated on the challenge of accessing and assessing information. As a result, critics of education have demanded that the educational system focus on teaching individuals how to access information more efficiently.

But teaching students how to acquire and retain information is hardly a sensible goal for education, particularly higher education. Information, in and of itself, is fragmented and meaningless. Information has meaning and value only when interconnections are made among facts, ideas and experience — that is, only when knowledge is constructed from information. Knowledge represents order, coherence, and the possibility of productive action within the chaos of an information explosion. It is knowledge that has meaning and value for an increasingly complex society — information is merely raw material.

In contrast, the transactional perspective on learning, which we will present in this book, is designed to help learners to construct knowledge, not just acquire information. Certainly the transactional perspective is more complex but is also more honest with regard to the realities and challenges of a worthwhile teaching and learning experience.

With regard to approach, we agree with Marton and Booth (cited in Dart & Boulton-Lewis, 1998) that learning proceeds from the whole to the parts. In education, it is normally the responsibility of the teacher to provide a framework that requires the student to interpret and differentiate to increase understanding of the whole and its parts. In this it is much closer to the declared goals of higher education institutions, if not their current practice. Discussion of the transactional perspective will indicate clearly why the typical higher education process sketched above is largely misguided, given the declared goals of educational institutions, and will point to some alternative procedures for this and similar contexts.

Systemic factors. A number of other factors contribute to the incongruence between ideal educational outcomes and actual practice in higher education. Constraints such as inflated class sizes, competing and conflicting demands on instructional time, and increased demands for "accountability" in the educational process, have had the effect of creating a set of expectations that are incompatible with meaningful and worthwhile educational outcomes, and, in fact, with the needs of society in general. Such systemic constraints have the effect of creating a false hierarchy of expectations that are often hidden behind stated educational goals. The remedies for these systemic problems lie beyond the classroom, and to some extent beyond the scope of this book. However, we believe that keeping in mind the factors that comprise the ideal learning situation, as outlined above, will assist educators and educational administrators in making decisions that will address these systemic problems as well.

The Role of the Educator

The growing proliferation of information along with the compounding need to make sense of expanding knowledge bases have rendered simple information dissemination approaches to teaching and learning obsolete. We live in an increasingly interdependent and changing society where individuals must learn to work collaboratively and think critically and creatively. As a result, we are experiencing a transformation in the ways in which "quality" educational experiences are conceptualized. The emerging view is that meaningful and worthwhile knowledge is constructed by individuals and confirmed in a critical community of learners. Notwithstanding the desire of some to return to predictable and simpler times, it is becoming increasingly apparent that acquiring the ability to think critically and becoming a self-directed and continuous learner is an imperative. However, how one facilitates the development of these qualities in learners is far less apparent.

The complexity of the teaching-learning transaction is too often approached in a technical rule-governed manner that does not consider contextual and systemic constraints. It is not possible to understand the educational experience through a fragmented approach. Simply adopting the latest teaching technique or learning activity will not assure quality learning outcomes. An educational experience is a dynamic interaction of relationships among intentions, activities and learning outcomes. A teacher's values and subject matter expertise, as well as the learning activities she/he selects, are important factors in shaping the learner's educational experiences; however, they must be evaluated within a systemic perspective of the intended and valued learning outcomes.

The level of congruence between intended outcomes and demonstrated practices is far more important in understanding the nature of the teaching-learning transaction than is the application of specific teaching techniques. Congruence in this transaction will largely determine whether students approach learning by uncritically assimilating teacher conveyed information or, more appropriately, by assuming responsibility for constructing meaningful and worthwhile knowledge.

The transactional approach to teaching and learning advocated here recognizes both individual and societal perspectives, and assumes that one cannot be considered apart from the other. It also recognizes the inseparability of process and content. The individual perspective focuses on why and how individuals learn, and relies on concepts such as assuming responsibility, relevance and personal meaning. The societal perspective focuses on the content and context of learning, and relies on concepts such as reciprocal confirmation of knowledge and the control of learning environments. Societal and individual needs and values must be considered concurrently when considering learning in an educational context. Stated another way, individual learning in an educational context is socially situated.

The dynamics of an educational transaction where societal and individual perspectives are recognized allow for the critical analysis of traditional knowledge and the creation of new knowledge. A complex and rapidly evolving society must be open to critical inquiry and knowledge transformation. Meaningful and worthwhile knowledge cannot be prescribed and assimilated without critical awareness. This awareness can be effectively enhanced within a critical community of learners. By facilitating and modelling critical thinking and inquiry, students can be encouraged to assume increasing responsibility for their learning. The critical thinking/inquiry approach can provide an increasing metacognitive awareness of the learning process where students learn how to learn and are motivated to continue their learning. Collaboration and sharing not only increases depth of understanding but also awareness of learning approaches and strategies.

Concomitant with a shift in the conceptualization of learning (from student assimilation of information conveyed by the teacher to the student assuming responsibility for constructing knowledge) has been a shift in how the process of teaching is conceptualized. This shift is a product of an increased appreciation of the uncertainty of knowledge, need for individuals to be more responsible and self-directed (i.e. the adoption of a constructivist view of learning), and access to communications technology (i.e. learning networks). In a knowledge society, the role of the teacher changes from "information dispenser to that of orchestrator of tasks that enable mindful knowledge construction" (Shavelson, 1992, pp. 33–34). The teacher's function becomes one of facilitating the development of reflective thinking through the creation of a setting where students have the opportunity to assert personal control over learning tasks and to assume increasing responsibility for their learning.

The goal of this book is to provide a coherent and systemic perspective on the teaching-learning transaction. While the emphasis of this book is on the transactional nature of teaching and learning, it is not intended to diminish the importance of content and content expertise of the teacher. The challenge is how we, as teachers and content experts, present subject matter that can be meaningfully assimilated and accommodated into the knowledge structures of the students. This necessitates that teachers develop and continually deepen a new area of pedagogical (andragogical) expertise associated with a worthwhile educational experience. It explicitly focuses on the reciprocal and complementary relationship between individual cognition and collective discourse. This perspective integrates the educational processes of critical thinking and discourse (i.e. critical inquiry) as well as self-directed learning in the development of meaningful learning and worthwhile knowledge. By encouraging instructors to adopt a transactional perspective, the hope is that the gap between rhetoric and practice will be reduced, and the unity of teaching and learning realized.

Assumptions

The core of this transactional perspective of an educational experience is shaped by three assumptions. First, it is assumed that the ultimate outcome of effective education is the preparation of learners for acquiring knowledge, as contrasted with acquiring information. Second, there are two general outcomes that may result from an educational experience: personal meaning, which makes sense to the individual; and public knowledge, which has collective understanding, validity and worth. Third, learning in an educational context must be understood as constructing personal meaning and public knowledge; that is, we cannot realistically examine one in isolation from the other.

Given these assumptions, this examination of teaching and learning will focus on the critical transactional processes of constructing and integrating personal meaning and public knowledge. While this is generally true for all educational practice, it is particularly relevant in adult and higher education.

The focus here on the theory and practice of adult and higher education results from the congruence and synergy of core concepts in each of the fields. The merging of these concepts is gaining attention and beginning to shape practice. Given the common goals of continuous and lifelong learning and the facilitation of critical thinking and self-directed learning, there is a great opportunity for each field to inform the other. Interestingly, adult education has had a tradition of largely serving the informal learning needs of adults while higher education's focus has been formal learning experiences of young adults. With the growing interest in adult and continuing education programs among graduates of higher education, there is a need to provide conceptual clarity and coherence that can inform practice in these particular fields. However, these concepts also have considerable relevance in most other fields of education.

Several core processes are associated with balancing the development of personal meaning and public knowledge. In an educational context this centres around the teacher and student (see Figure 1.1). From a foundational perspective (i.e. what counts as knowledge), individual constructivism needs to be balanced by critical social collaboration. In setting a context for learning (i.e. who does what) two themes emerge — personal responsibility for learning balanced by the need for social control of public or disciplinary standards. Finally, with regard to educational processes and roles (i.e. how to implement), individuals must be able to think critically and strategically in approaching learning as well as be self-directed in implementing and sustaining collaborative learning tasks. Each of these core concepts is outlined below.

Constructivism and Collaboration

Learning in an educational sense involves the complementary activities of individual construction of meaning and social enculturation. Meaning and knowledge are constructed and reconstructed from a complex mosaic of social experiences, and it is this process of personal construction that ensures continuous development. The view that integrates personal reconstruction of experience and social collaboration we label "collaborative constructivism".

The seeds of what we call collaborative constructivism may be traced to Dewey (1916), who argued that meaningful and educationally worthwhile knowledge is a process of continuous and collaborative reconstruction of experience. For learning to be meaningful, tasks must relate to experiences and, therefore, have relevance to the student. Educational experiences must be authentic and not contrived if they are to have relevance and meaningfulness. Meaning is the personal discovery of connections amongst information and facts. Meaningful learning is the construction of these relationships or ideas through critical thought. The means by which further cognitive growth is facilitated is largely determined through an understanding of the nature and quality of the student's current state of knowledge. Students can best meaningfully construct knowledge when they are able to confront new information from the perspective and awareness of their existing knowledge base.

Meaningful and worthwhile learning outcomes are facilitated in a collaborative environment where individual students are recognized and supported, a variety of perspectives are presented and examined, and misconceptions are diagnosed. Students do not assimilate information and construct knowledge exactly as presented by teachers or textbooks. While learning is influenced by previous experience and knowledge, as well as social interaction, meaning is ultimately constructed by the individual. While it may be primarily the student's responsibility to integrate new information into previous knowledge structures in a coherent and consistent manner, in an educational context, it is the teacher's responsibility to precipitate and facilitate learning that has purpose and is focused on essential concepts and worthwhile goals. This demands that the teacher have the necessary content expertise to identify and structure the key concepts. Through collaboration and sustained communication the student moves beyond the construction of personal meaning to being exposed to new and different perspectives and the confirmation of knowledge through consensus building.

Collaboration and open communication are the central processes of an educational transaction in which ideas may become material for critical discourse and the construction of knowledge. Authentic communication and collaboration depend upon mutual respect and personal responsibility. In such an environment, education becomes an uncertain journey where teachers and students together explore new perspectives and paths of understanding. A critical distinction between information dissemination and knowledge creation is the degree to which ambiguity is tolerated. Approaches designed to disseminate information maintain strict control of content and outcome and are, therefore, very predictable (and usually comfortable) for teachers. Approaches designed to foster critical inquiry and meaningful knowledge construction require treatment of content in depth and less teacher control over specific learning activities.

Teachers' roles must be congruent with the aim of constructing worthwhile and meaningful knowledge. The teacher's responsibility is to create the setting where, in collaboration, students may define, explore, reflect upon, and verify his/her understanding of the curriculum. In this way, students may gain an appreciation of existing knowledge while possibly discovering new insights and perspectives which not only contribute to the understanding of the individual student but also to the continued development of societal knowledge.

Formal educational settings provide special contexts for learning. While learning in an educational context is intentional and formally organized, it must also be relevant to the needs of the student. Learning in educational settings must build upon and encourage the natural curiosity and intrinsic motivation of the student to examine new ideas and perspectives. This is best achieved when learning occurs as a mutually respectful and supportive transaction; such a climate is important for facilitating the construction of meaningful and worthwhile knowledge. Furthermore, the processes of collaboration and authentic communication are consistent with the assumptions that knowledge is uncertain (i.e., tentative) and that it cannot be transmitted in whole.

A transactional framework for adult and higher education (all education for that matter), implies that knowledge must be seen as a system of tentative constructions. The purpose of these constructions is to provide order and coherence to our experiences. However, to imply that knowledge is held by the teacher, independent of the student, has the potential to seriously distort the educational process. Such a view encourages simplistic and dangerous views of knowledge. Where ideology and unwarranted certainty prevail, the result is prescriptive and authoritative instruction. Such systems assume that knowledge can be packaged by the teacher and assimilated in whole by the dutiful and unquestioning student. Ultimately, teaching is reduced to distilled or oversimplified knowledge presentations that risk distortion by implying that knowledge is external and unambiguous.

In contrast to such simplistic views, students need to be confronted with the complexities of knowledge. They need to become aware of how meaning and knowledge is constructed. This goes beyond constructing meaning, it includes understanding the metacognitive process (i.e. the how) of constructing meaning and confirming knowledge as well as providing the opportunities and developing the confidence to be self-directed. Finally, students need to remain open to the worthwhileness of existing knowledge as well as to possible limitations or fallacies. In this manner, uncertainty with regard to what we think we know opens our minds to new possibilities.

Responsibility and Control

A transactional analysis of the educational context provides a means for examining two fundamental questions in education. The first question is, "Who is responsible for learning?" The second question is related to the first: "Who controls the nature and content of learning activities?" In the transactional perspective of teaching and learning, the onus of responsibility is in the personal world of the student and the issue of control is in the shared world of experience. This implies that learners must accept responsibility for their personal learning outcomes and that educators must ensure that these learning outcomes are situated within the domain of shared knowledge. Thus, taking responsibility determines the individual's context for learning and is related to personal learning goals. Sharing control maintains the integrity of the field of inquiry or discipline, and is related to collectively-determined standards in the discipline. Critical discourse is the interactive process that maintains a dynamic balance between individual needs and social standards.

The key factors in assuming responsibility are the provision of options and the capacity for choice. It is extremely difficult to accept responsibility for learning outcomes when one neither has options nor the opportunity to exercise choice regarding intended outcomes and the path to realizing these outcomes. However, the need for student choice must be balanced by a recognition of the demands of the discipline of inquiry. Thus, exercising responsibility and control in an educational transaction is a collaborative undertaking. Approaches that do not emphasize collaboration, including both teacher-centred or student-centred approaches, carry serious risks of distortion. Prescriptive teacher-centred approaches inevitably result in reduced meaning for students, and student-centred approaches are often inefficient and fail to recognize the importance of confirmed and validated knowledge. In a collaborative constructivist view of the educational process, teachers and students each have responsibilities for learning and both share control of the transaction.

Issues of control are resolved using collaborative processes within the educational context. In a collaborative relationship, control issues are open to negotiation. Control and responsibility are reciprocally related and commensurate with contextual constraints and student ability. As students' knowledge and abilities develop, they can assume increased responsibility and control. Responsibility and control together will encourage students to assume ownership of their learning and education.

Education may be a collaborative activity but, ultimately, learning is the responsibility of the individual. However, the degree to which authentic and relevant educational choices are provided serves to constrain or enhance the range of individual responsibility and depth of understanding. This somewhat paradoxical situation is at the basis of an understanding of the teaching-learning transaction. The interplay between activity and reflection constitute the social and psychological components of an educational transaction. Dewey (1969a) considered the co-ordination of the social and psychological factors to be the ultimate challenge for the educator. Thus, a major dilemma for educators is determining how to facilitate a transaction that encourages learners to assume responsibility for achieving potentially worthwhile learning outcomes.

Critical Thinking and Self-Directed Learning

Education, at its most fundamental level, is a transaction between teacher and student regarding subject matter of common interest. This transaction is not confined to a mere transfer of society's (or the teacher's) knowledge and values — as important as it may be. Knowledge-based educational outcomes are achieved when students actively assume responsibility for reconstructing their experiences and translating them into meaningful knowledge structures. The aim of education is to collaboratively develop the thinking and learning abilities of students in the pursuit of worthwhile and meaningful knowledge. To achieve such outcomes, students must be encouraged to think critically and to be self-directed in their continuous search for personal meaning and public knowledge.

If knowledge is viewed as a system of tentative constructions, then it must be developed through critical reflection and have a variety of authentic experiences as its foundation. This active engagement of the learner leaves little room for approaches that rely on passive acquisition of information. Students must have the opportunity and ability to critically make learning decisions with regard to constructing meaning and confirming knowledge.

Critical thinking is essential to meaningful learning and the construction of worthwhile knowledge. Critical thinking is praxic reflection regarding thought and practice; that is, the learner iterates between the personal and public worlds. Moreover, the learner approaches the task of learning with a degree of scepticism and the use of reason to justify knowledge. Critical thinking integrates the reflective and rational activities of the learning process with the shared activities of the educational experience. However, as we shall see, there is considerable complementarity and synergy between the cognitive and applied (mechanism) theories, respectively, of critical thinking and self-directed learning. The genesis of the critical thinking perspective is from the inside looking out, while the self-directed learning perspective is from the outside looking in. Another way to think of this is that critical thinking is concerned first with content, while self-directed learning is first concerned with context — at least historically. In this book, these concepts include both the internal and external worlds and we are challenged to rectify these two perspectives into an integrated and coherent whole.

Self-direction encourages the monitoring and management of individual and shared learning experiences and the enhancement of both extrinsic and intrinsic motivation. Self-directed learning recognizes both extrinsic (commitment to an external goal, praise, etc.) and intrinsic (personal interest) motivation. Self-directed learning is predicated upon actively and responsibly involving students in setting goals and maintaining effort during the learning experience. Self-monitoring focuses on the metacognitive strategies of learning how to learn. Self-management focuses on the external control of, and persistence in, learning tasks.

With respect to the teacher's role, the first challenge of self-direction is to ensure a climate of disciplined inquiry — a climate where control is shared and misconceptions are diagnosed. It is the responsibility of the teacher to ensure that control is collaboratively balanced and understanding is reciprocally confirmed. The nature of this transaction is based upon the interdependence of mutual respect and critical discourse. These are the essential elements of self-directed learning in an educational context.

Quality learning outcomes are possible when learners engage in critical thinking and self-directed learning activities. Most students need guidance to learn how to assess their own learning needs and how to take action to ensure these needs are met through appropriate learning activities. Sustained motivation (that is, the volition to persist in executing goal-directed learning activities) is the most important result of these interdependent processes. Together critical thinking and self-direction are key transactional processes.

Conclusion

Dissatisfaction with the educational system has historically resulted in swings from teacher-centred to learner-centred approaches. However, as a result of significant socio-economic changes and the need for critical and creative thinking abilities in the workplace, the processes of higher education have been called into question. This has resulted in a broad and sustained debate regarding approaches to teaching and learning. While there is a perennial cry to move "back to the basics", there is a growing consensus that we need to redefine the basics. Furthermore, we need to re-examine how students acquire these "basic" skills and abilities. In a knowledge society, the basics are increasingly being defined in terms of higher-order cognitive abilities such as critical thinking and the disposition for self-directed learning.

Facilitating responsible self-directed learning is a collaborative process. On the one hand, in an educational setting the teacher has legitimate epistemological authority balanced by responsibility for student development. On the other hand, students possess considerable cognitive independence, which should be developed by facilitating critical inquiry, concurrent with the responsibility to construct meaning and judge worthwhile knowledge. Thus, personal meaning-making and reciprocal confirmation are iterative phases of an interdependent teaching-learning transaction.

There is no one correct approach to teaching and learning. There is, however, increasing agreement that the ultimate goal of education is to have students learn to learn so they may continue learning throughout their lifetime. This necessitates the provision of opportunities for students to make learning decisions and, thereby, develop responsible approaches to the construction of meaningful and worthwhile knowledge. Regardless of their stage of development or the level of content under examination, students must regularly experience control over their learning if they are to become critical and self-directed (i.e. continuous) learners. Quality educational outcomes require environments where students have choice and are supported in their endeavour to assume responsibility for their learning. Assuming responsibility for constructing meaningful knowledge ensures that the learning experience have some relevance and value beyond the classroom.

It is important that teachers become aware of their beliefs and assumptions regarding the educational process. In addition to content expertise, teachers act according to their implicit or explicit assumptions and beliefs regarding knowledge and the way in which students learn. These inevitably influence approaches to teaching and guide practice. To act with awareness teachers must reflectively articulate and defend a rational and coherent framework of what counts as personal and public knowledge. They must also reconcile this with their approaches to directing the teaching-learning transaction. The purpose of this book is to assist educators in doing this.

In the chapters that follow we will be exploring the teaching-learning transaction in greater detail. Each of the concepts, themes, and processes that were introduced in this chapter will be discussed, and applications to teaching practice identified. We begin with a discussion of the foundational concepts and their genesis.

2

Foundations

Education is a relatively new field of study. For the coherent development of a relatively new field of study, it is necessary to systematically consider foundational ideas and theories. Furthermore, it is important that an educational framework explicitly explore its connections to relevant theoretical and philosophical foundations. While the following is not a philosophical discourse intended to reveal and resolve inherent contradictions in each of the theoretical frameworks discussed, it does identify the foundational ideas and concepts that we have used to construct a framework of the teaching-learning transaction in adult and higher education. It also brings into the open our values and assumptions as to what we consider worthwhile learning.

It should be stated at the outset that the educational framework constructed throughout this book is based largely upon the philosophical perspective of John Dewey. At the same time, the constituent concepts of this book have evolved from a variety of sources — three of which we focus upon in this chapter.

The discussion of foundational concepts begins with the democratic and problem centred educational ideals espoused by John Dewey. Next come the ideas of Carl Rogers and the unconditional trust he placed in students, and the freedom he would grant them. Rogers is included, not for his philosophical contribution, but because of his influence on the key concepts and practices in the field of adult education. Finally, we study the influence of Jurgen Habermas and the application of his ideas regarding communication and knowledge to the educational context. The relevance and coherence of Habermas' ideas constitute a theoretical framework that cannot be ignored in adult and higher education. Each of the perspectives provides crucial ideas and theories for the development of the educational framework presented here.

John Dewey

When it comes to educational philosophy, the pre-eminent scholar of the twentieth century is John Dewey. Nobody has had more influence in shaping modern educational thought and practice than Dewey. Dewey leaves a legacy of an astonishing wealth of insights regarding the nature of education. His works have as much relevance to education today as when they were first published during the early part of the twentieth century. Dewey's ideas are applicable to all levels of educational practice. They were founded upon the principle of "continuity" of learning which suggests that education must be cumulative and prepare the individual for continued learning throughout life. In particular, he explored "the relationships of the social and the individual and of knowledge and action" (Dewey & Childs, 1989) and emphasized the role of experience, collaboration and reflective thinking. His ideas are found in the works of many current educational theorists and are coincident with the assumptions and themes of this book.

John Dewey was a proponent of pragmatism and progressive thought with regard to education. Pragmatism is a distinctive American philosophy that "accepts the methods of science for understanding the human person and solving human problems" (Elias & Merriam, 1980, pp. 47, 48). It emphasizes the centrality of human experience in constructing knowledge. Truth is derived from human experience and, therefore, can never be absolute. Pragmatism is the underlying philosophy of progressive education. According to Dewey, progressive education was to integrate individual and societal needs. The school was to be the setting where students learned first hand the ideals and values of democracy. The progressive education of Dewey was originally a reaction to the authoritarian approach of traditional education. His student-centred ideas, however, were distorted and attracted much criticism. With the publication in 1938 of *Experience and Education*, Dewey responded to the extremes of student-centred education as well as those of teacher-centred education. He advocated a crucial role for teachers while maintaining a concern for student needs and interests.

A central theme that guided Dewey's philosophy, and which helps explain his general perspective on educational matters, is his rejection of dualism in all forms. For Dewey there was no distinction between the individual and society, since the two are one during any experience. He states that "Social cannot be opposed in fact or in idea to individual. Society is individuals-in-their-relations" (Dewey & Childs, 1981). His argument is that individual development is dependent upon community life. Therefore, education is a process of social interaction for the purpose of serving individual development. Conversely, a democratic society is dependent upon educated individuals. It is only in conceptual abstractions that a duality between the individual and society can exist.

Similarly, Dewey rejects the gulf between knowledge (thought) and action. He suggests that knowledge is not simply accumulated information without reference to application. Thought apart from action cannot yield valid knowledge. Dewey and Childs (1981) state, the "execution of the procedure which is suggested [by thought] effects consequences which enable the validity of the idea to be judged and which bring about its further development" (p. 92). By way of thought or reflection information is converted into authentic (meaningful) knowledge. From an educational perspective, when action is divorced from thought, teaching becomes information "transmission by a kind of scholastic pipeline into the minds of pupils whose business is to absorb what is transmitted" (Dewcy & Childs, 1981, pp. 88–89).

From Dewey's perspective, the reflective (individual) and collaborative (social) aspects of the educative experience are organically related. Consistent with the previous discussion, he believed "that the educational process has two sides — one psychological and one sociological; and that neither can be subordinated to the other or neglected without evil results following" (Dewey, 1959, p. 20). The implication for Dewey was that the teacher and student share a collaborative and reciprocal relationship in the learning process. Learning through coercion or external pressure, therefore, "cannot truly be called educative". If learning is to be continuous and not haphazard then the psychological structure of the student must be considered; but such considerations must be interpreted and translated within the sociological context. In short, educators cannot subordinate the goals and interests of the individual to preconceived social values and norms, nor can educators become so student-centred that there is little consideration of social values and norms.

Dewey (1938) emphasizes that "progressive education" should not translate into an extreme form of student-centredness, simply as a reaction to the excesses of authoritarianism in traditional forms of education. He argues strongly against the aimlessness and dangerous permissiveness of student-centredness (Dworkin, 1959). Without a selection of means to reach an intended and worthwhile aim "an activity ceases to be educative because it is blind" (Dewey, 1938, p. 84). Educators cannot evade their responsibility in establishing aims and activities through appropriate planning. However, educational aims provide general direction and should not strait-jacket the means. The means must include opportunities for the participants to spontaneously alter or direct objectives.

With regard to educational planning, Dewey (1938) states that the "educator is responsible for a knowledge of individuals and for a knowledge of subject matter that will enable activities to be selected which lend themselves to social organization, an organization in which all individuals have an opportunity to contribute something, and in which the activities in which all participate are the chief carrier of control" (p. 56). The point that Dewey is making is that control exists in the activity itself and is, therefore, shared by teacher and students. Learning in an educational situation is collaborative and exists within the communicative process. The leadership and control of the teacher will be established through collaboration and consideration of the educational aim, the characteristics of the student, and the general context of the process.

Issues of freedom and responsibility are balanced through the process of collaboratively establishing educational aims or purposes. Dewey (1938) states that "there is no defect in traditional education greater than its failure to secure the active co-operation of the pupil in construction of the purposes involved in his studying" (p. 67). Only through collaboration or a sharing of control is there the encouragement for the student to assume responsibility for significant learning. That is, students are likely to go beyond passive observation and act upon the subject matter if teachers act co-operatively with students.

According to Dewey (1938), the educator must start with an appreciation of students' current state of knowledge and ability. He suggests that it is the duty of the educator to determine "that environment which will interact with the existing capacities and needs of those taught to create a worth-while experience" (Dewey, 1938, p. 45). This can only be accomplished through sustained communication and a recognition of, and respect for, students' previous experiences. From such an understanding the educator can set the conditions for further growth experiences.

Communication is the basis upon which we share meaning and through "free intercourse and communication" we make provision for participation of all its members in a democratic society (Dewey, 1916). Communication also provides the means for commitment, responsibility, and orderly social change. Dewey's fundamental "belief that democratic social arrangements provide a better quality of human experience" was, of course, applied to the classroom. The educator must be faithful to co-operation and persuasion involving true two-way communication. Dewey (1938) recognizes the challenge of working out appropriate social relationships and methods and notes that these judgements and decisions are much more difficult in progressive education than is the case in traditional education.

Dewey argues that educationally worthwhile knowledge is the result of reflecting upon experience. He summarizes the idea of education as the "continuous reconstruction of experience" (Dewey, 1916, p. 80). However, the "belief that all genuine education comes about through experience does not mean that all experiences are genuinely or equally educative" (Dewey, 1938, p. 25). What counts as an educative experience is described by Dewey in terms of two intercepting principles — continuity and interaction.

The continuity principle is an attempt to determine worthwhile educational experiences. It recognizes the need to build upon students' previous knowledge and experiences in the process of "continuous reconstruction". Dewey (1902) suggests that the educational process is a "continuous reconstruction," moving from present experience out into that represented by the organized bodies of knowledge (p. 11). But, equally important, it must promote future educational growth and ensure the "quality of subsequent experiences" (Dewey, 1938, p. 35). That is, it is meaningful and arouses curiosity, strengthens initiative, and forms an attitude of interest and purpose. The quality of an experience is judged on whether it provides the foundation for new meaningful and worthwhile learning experiences. The essential role of the teacher is to judge the direction of an experience to ensure its continuity.

Dewey's second principle for identifying a meaningful and worthwhile (i.e. quality) educational learning experience is interaction. Interaction concerns the subjective world of the individual as well as the "total social set-up" or shared world. While the principle of continuity placed considerable emphasis on the cognitive aspect of experience, the principle of interaction "assigns equal rights to both factors in experience — objective and internal conditions" (Dewey, 1938, p. 42). Here ideas play the key role in the interface between the individual and social worlds. Ideas help individuals illuminate the external world and at the same time are shaped by worldly experiences (Prawat, 1999). It is this process that is mirrored in the ideal teaching-learning transaction. Continuity might be interpreted as being essentially about long-term capabilities related to learning how to learn, whereas interaction is concerned with generating ideas and managing the immediate educational transaction.

One of the primary concerns of the educator with regard to interaction is to arouse curiosity, desire and purpose through a full appreciation of student needs. It is the duty of the educator to determine "that environment which will interact with the existing capacities and needs of those taught to create a worthwhile experience" (Dewey, 1938, p. 45). Clearly the principles of continuity and interaction are inseparable. Dewey states that "continuity and interaction in their active union with each other provide the measure of the educative significance and value of an experience" (pp. 44, 45).

More specifically, Dewey (1916) believes that thinking is the method of an educational experience. He states that "No experience having a meaning is possible without some element of thought" (p. 145). Learning that is to have meaning educationally necessitates that the student assume the responsibility to reflect upon the subject matter. Thinking is the process of creating meaning through the process of actively making connections. Individuals do not acquire meaning as "theoretical spectators". Thinking may involve imaginary action and is, therefore, itself an experience.

Thinking is the acceptance of responsibility for consequences of actions and, in turn, actions test thinking. Dewey did not believe that students should only passively listen and observe the teacher. If students are to engage in significant learning which will lead to further growth experiences, then that experience will consist of alternating phases of reflection and active inquiry. Consistent with Dewey's rejection of dualism, thinking and acting are inseparable. Dewey (1916) states that the "nature of experience can be understood only by noting that it includes an active and a passive element peculiarly combined" (p. 139). This process of combining reflection and action is a method of inquiry for solving problems and constructing knowledge. Systematically connected ideas and meaningful learning are the outcomes of the process of inquiry.

Dewey referred to this method of constructing meaning and understanding as reflective thinking. Reflective thinking was the generalization from the method of scientific inquiry. The phases of reflective thought are suggestion — an "inhibition of direct action"; intellectualization — diagnosing and defining the problem; guiding idea — the occurrence of a hypothesis; reasoning — exploration of an idea; and testing — verification by overt action (Dewey, 1933). Dewey goes on to say that while all are indispensable traits of reflective thinking, in "practice, two of them may telescope, some of them may be passed over hurriedly, and the burden of reaching a conclusion may fall mainly on a single phase" (p. 116).

However, knowledge of reflective thinking was recognized by Dewey (1933) as providing "no guarantee for ability to think well" (p. 29). There must also be an attitude or disposition to employ reflective thinking. It is suggested that these attitudes are open-mindedness, whole-heartedness, and responsibility. Open-mindedness "includes an active desire to listen to more sides than one; to give heed to facts from whatever source they come; to give full attention to alternative possibilities; to recognize the possibility of error even in the beliefs that are held dearest to us" (Dewey, 1933, p. 30). Whole-heartedness reflects an intrinsic interest and enthusiasm and not an obligatory, perfunctory attention to the thinking process. Responsibility is the essence and integrity of good thinking. It is "to ask for the meaning of what they learn, in the sense of what difference it makes to the rest of their beliefs and to their actions" (Dewey, 1933, p. 32). Responsibility, as a quest to make sense of new ideas in terms of past experiences and future actions, goes beyond open-mindedness and whole-heartedness.

In summing-up, it is important to emphasize that reflective thinking is not a mechanical process but requires continuous judgement on the part of the in-dividual. Judgement is discernment and insight and is an integral part of all the phases of reflection and action. If education is not to be simply a process of amassing unconnected bits of information, then a process of analysis and synthesis requiring judgement is required. The antecedent of judgement is the uncertainty of complex situations. If concepts in education are not to be presented as fixed and certain, then doubt will exist and judgement will be required. In addition, if education is to consider students' previous experiences, then teachers are going to have to use judgement in presenting subject matter.

Dewey (1933) asks the question, "How shall we treat subject matter that is supplied by textbook and teacher so that it shall rank as material of reflective inquiry, not as ready-made intellectual pablum to be accepted and swallowed just as if it were something bought at a shop?" (p. 257). Just as reflective thinking requires a series of judgements on the part of students so too does the above question on the part of teachers. Dewey acknowledges the difficulty and challenge facing teachers if education is to be an experience of reflective inquiry. While the new road is "more strenuous and difficult" for teachers, he provides the caveat that "Nothing has brought pedagogical theory into greater disrepute than the belief that it is identified with handing out to teachers recipes and models to be followed in teaching" (Dewey, 1916, p. 170). Teachers must accept the challenge to reflect upon their practices and be prepared to make judgements that reflect the realities of their context.

With the rejection of dualistic thinking the challenge for educators is to avoid simplistic solutions and approaches to the educational transaction. Difficult judgements are required if teachers are to avoid the disrepute of a recipe approach to teaching. These judgements will always centre around balancing student interests and social norms. While Dewey was considered somewhat radical in his time, the reality today is that his views must be considered moderate and balanced. This should not be surprising considering his abhorrence of dualistic views of the world and his insistence on the need to integrate intellectual abstractions in practice. This rejection of dualistic thinking led Dewey to a transactional view of teaching and learning.

For Dewey, education should mirror a democratic society and through the growth of individuals serve a larger socializing function. The challenge is to balance individual and social concerns in order to design worthwhile educational ex-periences that prepare students for the future — not the past. Knowledge is regarded "not as fixed possession but as an agency and instrumentality for opening new fields which make new demands" (Dewey, 1938, p. 75). Thus, there is a need for continuity of learning — for learning how to learn. Dewey (1916) suggests that "the result of the educative process is capacity for further education" (p. 68). This ensures growth and diversity. It is through individual freedom to grow that diversity is encouraged and social change assured. Dewey (1916) states that a "progressive society counts individual variations as precious since it finds in them the means of its own growth" (p. 305).

Implications for adult and higher education. The legacy of John Dewey is enormous. His thought has much relevance today not only for childhood education but perhaps even more so for adult and higher education. Dewey did not believe that education should cease upon the end of formal schooling. Education is not merely preparation for adulthood. Consistent with his principle of continuity, Dewey (1916) believes that "education means the enterprise of supplying the conditions which insure growth, or adequacy of life, irrespective of age" (p. 51).

Elias and Merriam (1980) suggest that some of the basic principles of adult education originated in progressive thought and that, in many ways, adult education has remained faithful to the principles that inspired its beginnings. The translation of progressive thought to adult education was due to the work of Eduard Lindeman. Lindeman is credited with articulating and implementing "a vision of adult education which still constitutes the conceptual underpinnings of the field" (Brookfield, 1987b, p. 120). This vision was inspired by the progressive-pragmatic ideas of John Dewey (Stewart, 1987).

Lindeman's *The Meaning of Adult Education* (1926) is significant to adult education because it provided the foundation and set the course for the field's growth. The connection to Dewey's progressive thought is reflected in Lindeman's four assumptions regarding adult education. They are: that adult "education is life — not a mere preparation for an unknown kind of future living" (p. 4); that its purpose is "to put meaning into the whole of life" (p.5); that "the approach to adult education will be via the route of *situations*, not subjects" (p. 6); and "the resource of highest value in adult education is the *learner's experience*" (p. 6). Each assumption is clearly consistent with Dewey's educational philosophy, although Lindeman argued convincingly for its applicability to adult education.

Lindeman's congruence with the progressive-pragmatic philosophy of Dewey is also evident when he describes adult education as elevating "living itself to the level of an experiment," where its "chief purpose is to discover the meaning of experience" (cited in Brookfield, 1987b, p. 122). Lindeman believes that the adult education process should be co-operative and non-authoritarian. For this reason he places much emphasis on a democratic teaching-learning transaction and the discussion method. Organized discussion, according to Lindeman, goes beyond the "mere exchange of opinion and prejudice" and represents, in one sense, to adult education "what scientific method is to science" (cited in Stewart, 1987, p. 161).

Before leaving this section on Dewey it is important to highlight the themes that are integral to subsequent discussions. Dewey's ideas are essentially about experience and reflective thought with regard to having students collaboratively generate ideas and reconstruct experience, thereby confirming meaning for themselves. The collaborative nature of education is reflected in Dewey's (1938) belief that "social control resides in the very nature of the work done as a social enterprise in which all individuals have an opportunity to contribute and to which all feel a responsibility" (p. 56). In this statement we see the close connection of control and responsibility in meaningful and worthwhile learning. The themes of responsibility and control are embedded in Dewey's principles of continuity (responsibility for constructing and confirming experiences) and interaction (collaborative generation of ideas and control of the transaction). That is, the purposeful construction of meaning through the reciprocal reconstruction of experience.

Carl Rogers

Carl Rogers' views of education evolved from his philosophy and practice as a psychotherapist. He revolutionized psychotherapy with his existential and humanistic views. Existentially he believed that humans are free to choose and are personally responsible for their actions. This existential view is phenomenological in that personal growth is structured by the individual's perception of reality. Rogers reflects a humanistic emphasis by focusing upon personal dignity and demonstrating trust in the individual to grow responsibly. Humanism also represented a rational approach to self-fulfilment, which provides a connection to cognitivism. Rogers labels his views of psychotherapy as being client-centred and essentially non-directive. Similarly, his views of education were learner-centred and largely non-directive.

Similar to Dewey, Rogers believes that education starts with experiential knowledge that has the potential to change individuals. In fact, there is a close relationship between pragmatism and humanism in that both believe that relevant learning builds upon each individual's world of experience. Wittrock (1991) describes Rogers' model of experiential learning as having the characteristics of involving the whole person (cognitively and affectively), being self-initiated, being pervasive (behaviourally and attitudinally), being self-evaluated, and creating meaning. The aim of learning is to discover meaning through experience — not simply assimilate information.

The aim of education is the development of individuals who are open to change and have learned how to learn. Rogers (1969) states:

> The only man who is educated is the man who has learned how to learn; the man who has learned how to adapt and change; the man who has realized that no knowledge is secure, that only the process of seeking knowledge gives a basis for security. (p. 104)

Dewey would not have disagreed with this statement. Both Dewey and Rogers see the futility of assimilating irrelevant, disjointed and dated information.

The aim of learning how to learn clearly has inherent value and appeal. The challenge, however, is how to design the educational process to best facilitate such growth. Rogers (1969) begins by stating that teaching, as instruction, is "a relatively unimportant and vastly overvalued activity" (p. 103). According to Rogers, such a view of teaching implies that knowledge is static and only the teacher knows what needs to be and shall be learned. He advocated a radical break with traditional education wherein teaching is replaced by a process of facilitation.

For Rogers (1969) the aim of education is the "facilitation of change and learning" (p. 104). Facilitation involves transforming a group into a community of learners where the aim is, to "free curiosity; to permit individuals to go charging off in new directions dictated by their own interests; to unleash the sense of inquiry; to open everything to questioning and exploration; to recognize that everything is in process of change" (p. 105). To achieve this aim is to create the conditions which encourage self-initiated and significant experiential learning. The question is whether this learning is educational.

Rogers (1969) believes that the attitudinal qualities that facilitate self-directed and significant learning "exist in the personal relationship between the facilitator and the learner" (p. 106). The attitudinal qualities are realness, prizing, and empathic understanding. Realness or genuineness is the most basic of the facilitation qualities. While this quality is not always easy to achieve, when "the facilitator is a real person, being what he is, entering into a relationship with the learner without presenting a front or facade, he is much more likely to be effective" (p. 106). Those who are successful in facilitating learning accept and care for learners and prize their feelings and opinions. Empathic understanding further establishes a climate for self-directed learning. It means having "a sensitive awareness of the way the process of education and learning seems to the student" (p. 111) and not evaluating or judging.

He goes on to describe three assumptions underlying these attitudinal qualities of the facilitator. First is an inherent trust in the capacity of learners to grow. Facilitation must be based upon "the hypothesis that students who are in real contact with problems which are relevant to them wish to learn, want to grow, seek to discover, endeavour to master, desire to create, move toward self-discipline" (Rogers, 1969, p. 114). Second, the qualities of a facilitator of learning previously outlined are developed by taking risks and being willing to accept the uncertainty of exploring unexpected paths of learning. Finally, it is important to accept that facilitators cannot always maintain the attitudinal qualities described. For this reason when a facilitator does not feel accepting or empathic it is more constructive to be honest about one's feelings.

Beyond creating a climate, Rogers believes that, if learning is to be self-initiated, then the students must be confronted by problems and issues that are real and relevant to them. In addition, he suggests that one of the most effective means for facilitating constructive learning is the "intensive group experience". However, in a revealing passage Rogers rejects imposing freedom upon students. He states that "when a group is offered the freedom to learn on their own responsibility, there should also be provision for those who do not wish or desire this freedom and prefer to be instructed and guided" (Rogers, 1969, p. 134). Again, we see that the freedom of the individual is paramount.

Much emphasis is placed upon providing freedom for creative learning. Rogers is often very categorical with statements such as there is no place for lessons, assigned readings, and the facilitator "does not evaluate and criticize unless a student wishes his judgement on a product" (Rogers, 1969, p. 144). It is not clear, however, how students can learn how to learn within a climate of what appears to be excessive freedom. Surely developing learning capabilities demands the discipline of a variety of learning experiences. Should not teachers model critical learning behaviours if change is a goal of education? Is there no place for challenging entrenched views of students with constructive criticism? Is it not possible to develop a trusting relationship and still capitalize on the knowledge and experience of the teacher? Is facilitation and self-direction simply providing freedom to students to learn what and how they wish? These issues will be addressed in subsequent chapters.

Implications for adult and higher education. Rogers' contribution was to focus upon the psychological climate of learning to encourage students to assume responsibility for constructing meaning. Existential and humanistic assumptions place great emphasis on the existence of choice and the acceptance of personal responsibility for one's actions. For this to happen Rogers believes that learning must be relevant and must consider the current knowledge and experiences of the students. He also gives considerable attention to the attitudinal qualities of the facilitator. These qualities were seen as necessary for developing a trusting relationship and freeing the individual for creative learning. While these may be defensible positions, there is a difficulty with Rogers' perspective in that he focuses almost exclusively on the human interpersonal aspects of the educational transaction. Moreover, he believes in educating the whole person, but little discussion is provided with regard to the cognitive or intellectual aspects of learning. In Dewey's (1933) terms, what measures are "taken to make sure that the activities terminate in that which makes them educationally worthwhile ... namely, the achievement of a fairly definite intellectualization of the experience" (p. 154). Even in terms of creativity the basic suggestion is to simply show trust and provide freedom to discover and learn. Little consideration is given to the larger social context and social change.

The field of adult education, through the writing of Malcolm Knowles (1970), adopted the perspective of student-centredness and self-direction. The concept of self-direction will be critically explored and developed more thoroughly in Chapter 5. However, it will be shown that during the 1970's and 1980's the field of adult education attempted to distinguish itself from childhood education based largely upon Knowles' argument that adults are problem-oriented and are self-directed learners. Considerable emphasis was also placed on the freedom of individuals to learn what and how they wished. Facilitation in adult education placed great emphasis on climate setting established through mutually respectful and trusting relationships.

Rogers' perspective on learning in education is a clear break with traditional education. Notwithstanding the contributions that he has made in terms of concepts such as self-directedness and learning to learn, as well as stressing the importance of a community of learners and teacher qualities, his excessive and nearly exclusive focus on the individual raises serious questions with regard to the unity theme of this book. Rogers' focus on individual freedom certainly distinguishes him from Dewey and Habermas (to be discussed next) — both of whom take a holistic view of the individual and society.

Jurgen Habermas

Jurgen Habermas has explored the relationship and integration of knowledge, interests, and ideology that shape learning. His thoughts are grounded in critical theory which, in contrast to positive and interpretative social sciences that describe the world as it is, "tries to understand why the social world is the way it is and, more importantly, through a process of critique, strives to know how it should be" (Ewert, 1991, p. 346). Critique is used to increase awareness of ideological knowledge distortions. Critical theory emphasizes individual emancipation in which, "on the basis of his or her enlightenment, he or she takes freeing action that changes the social system to permit the realization of his or her unique human potential" (Ewert, 1991, p. 346). Habermas, however, should not be viewed within a traditional Marxist critical theory which is largely concerned with economics. He has developed a comprehensive and consensus building critical social psychological theory which goes beyond the preoccupation of critical theory with critique and confrontation. As a result of his concern for both the subjective and inter-subjective (i.e. social participation), he has been called a critical constructivist (Loving, 1997).

The focus of Habermas' work is the development of a theory of knowledge and means of knowing. His theory of rationality is less concerned with accepted knowledge than with how individuals construct and validate knowledge. Rational processes are not separate from human discourse and, therefore, all theory must be justified through argumentation. The goal is to transcend the positivist and interpretivist paradigms by relegating them "to their respective spheres of influence and thus deflating any claims for the superiority of one or the other methodology" (Lakomsky, 1991, p. 317). Habermas comprehensively addresses issues that go to the source of social organization and how we conceptualize experiences. The theme of knowledge development and education as a social process was discussed previously. It is, therefore, not difficult to see why many educators have attempted to apply Habermas' theories to education, although Habermas himself does not ground his theory in an educational context.

Knowledge constitutive interests. The two central doctrines of Habermas' theory — knowledge constitutive interests and communicative competence — address the source and method of knowledge development. The three areas of knowledge constitutive interests are the technical, practical, and emancipatory. Each involves different methods of systematic inquiry corresponding to the natural/positivistic, interpretive and critical sciences. The social context in which each influences is, respectively, work/environment, interaction/language, and personal/power. Knowledge constitutive or cognitive interests are:

> ...the means through which we organize our daily experience. In effect, our perception and knowledge of reality is organized in a structured manner by our interests. Our discrete cognitive interests in controlling nature, social harmony, and individual growth each respond to a different problem in human experience but also lead to different forms of knowledge and knowing. (Ewert, 1991, p. 347)

Habermas' theory of cognitive interests is developed from the belief that no one source or methodology is appropriate or adequate to account for all forms of human knowledge.

Technical interests concern the control and prediction of events in the external environment. The problem of technical rationality, for Habermas, was not what it offers instrumentally but its extension as the only form of reason. The instrumental rationality of technical interests demonstrates a prescriptive goal-directed ideology where the application of technical expertise/rules under controlled conditions will produce an observable and measurable product. Unfortunately, such a prescriptive means-end approach to education often reduces learning to assimilating meaningless information that can be measured by standardized tests. Education ceases to be a human generative process but, instead, becomes an industrialized process for transmitting societal values and beliefs. Change and critical analysis are not considered valued goals and education becomes ideological in that only one politically correct set of social values and knowledge framework is considered.

In contrast, the practical interest provides knowledge through understanding the context and norms of a particular environment. Grundy (1987) states that the "practical interest is grounded in the fundamental need of the human species to live in and as part of the world, not to be, as it were, in competition with the environment for survival" (p. 13). It is concerned with understanding communication and social action, and is practical in the sense of being useful in developing understanding and guiding everyday social actions. Practical interest is intersubjective in that its concern is "in understanding the environment through interaction based upon a consensual interpretation of meaning" (Grundy, 1987, p. 14). From this perspective, education is seen as social activity, not a prescribed end state, and meaning is constructed through the complex interactions among teacher and students. Consistent with practical interest, Ewert (1991) suggests that education is a fluid "practice that is guided by complex, sometimes competing intentions, that are modified in the light of circumstances" (p. 352). For this reason, the inherent control that the educational process affords is at the discretion of the professional judgement of educators. If content and process are prescribed in a flexible manner, then the need for collaborative decision making will be present; and, thus, the experience and judgement of an open-minded teacher is a necessity.

Habermas' third area of human interest — emancipation — is the knowledge gained from reflection and is derivative of the technical and practical. Habermas initially relied on the critical reflective procedures of psychoanalysis to bring to conscious awareness distortions which prevent true understanding of self and action. It is the most fundamental interest in that it is an interest in knowledge for the sake of knowledge — a unity of knowledge and interest (Habermas, 1971). Self-reflection represents autonomy from the outside world in order to become critically aware of personal and social constraints on thought and action. Mezirow (1981) states that insights "gained through critical self-awareness are emancipatory in the sense that at least one can recognize the correct reasons for his or her problems" (p. 5). Emancipation, however, is concerned with both awareness and empowerment. Emancipation assumes the ability of individuals to be autonomous and responsible. That is, individuals who are both autonomous and responsible (well intentioned) reflect upon and appreciate the reasons that initiate action. The emancipatory cognitive interest is defined by Grundy (1987) as "a fundamental interest in emancipation and empowerment to engage in autonomous action arising out of authentic, critical insights into the social construction of human society" (p. 19).

To become emancipated through education is problematic. The difficulty according to Habermas is that consensus arrived at through interaction, that is practical knowledge, may not be valid knowledge. Consensus itself does not determine valid knowledge. While emancipation is about self-reflection and self-knowledge, this does not deny the role of a teacher or the group as long as the autonomy of the student is respected. That is, education is a respectful reciprocal collaboration where the student is ultimately free and responsible for constructing meaning. Critical reflection is informed by experience. Collaboration or discourse with a teacher and among fellow students for the purpose of critiquing ideology may be helpful to stimulate critical reflection. Mezirow (1991) states that the "intent of education for emancipatory action…would be seen by Habermas as the providing of the learner with an accurate, in-depth understanding of his or her historical situation" (p. 6). Emancipatory education integrates objective and subjective worlds through discourse and reflection.

Communicative competence. The centrepiece of Habermas' critical theory is the concept of communicative competence where meaning emerges inter-subjectively or interactively. It provides a relationship between knowledge interests and the means of achieving rational or valid consensus. It is a pragmatic theory of rationality rooted in the practical problems of everyday living. Habermas' challenge was to provide standards of rationality and the potential for emancipation through an analysis of ordinary speech and discourse. His argument is that life free from unnecessary domination is anticipated in acts of communication. Carr and Kemmis (1986) state that his "theory of communicative competence is an ethical theory of self-realization which transposes the source of human ideals onto language and discourse" (p. 141). That is, emancipatory knowledge embodying autonomy and responsibility is embedded in democratic and reciprocal communication processes.

Fundamental to any speech situation is the distinction between the shared world and the private world. The speech act assumes comprehensibility and "situates the sentence in relation to external reality ('the' world of objects and events about which one can make true or false statements), inner reality (the speaker's 'own' world of intentional experiences that can be expressed truthfully or untruthfully) and normative reality of society ('our' social life-world of shared values and norms, roles and rules ... and that themselves are either 'right' — legitimate, justifiable — or 'wrong')" (McCarthy, 1978, p. 280). The members of a communication community have the ability to distinguish between the shared (external, social) world and the private (internal) world. Roderick (1986) states that "Competent speakers have the ability to relate these different 'worlds'. They are able to take different attitudes to these 'worlds' and to evaluate the different validity claims raised within these attitudes" (p. 110). Communicative competence is a unifying theory linking knowledge and action as well as socialization and ideology (McCarthy, 1978).

The concept of communicative rationality arises in the context of being able to differentiate and co-ordinate the shared and private worlds or dimensions of communicative action (including nonviable action). Habermas (1984) states that the concept of communicative rationality "carries with it connotations based ultimately on the central experience of the unconstrained, unifying, consensus bringing force of argumentative speech, in which different participants overcome their merely subjective views and, owing to the mutuality of rationally motivated conviction, assure themselves of both the unity of the objective world and the intersubjectivity of their lifeworld" (p. 10). An argument is the process of criticizing validity claims based upon reason systematically connected to the problematic expression (Habermas, 1984). Individuals manifest their rationality when challenged by resorting to argumentation. Understanding is reached inter-subjectively through argumentation or critical discourse. Mezirow (1985) suggests that "it is a consensus among participants in a discourse that determines validity, and ideally, consensus validity is based upon the cogency of arguments alone" (p. 143). Therefore, communicative competence is dependent upon rational argument for purposes of intersubjective understanding and where reason, rather than authority, tradition or coercion, predominates.

In the critical social theory of Habermas, discourse or critical discussion holds a pre-eminent position. It presupposes an expectation that rational agreement or consensus can be reached through argumentation. On the other hand, when speech is not oriented to understanding, "strategic" forms of communication emphasizing deception, conflict and competition take over. A key distinction is made by Habermas between routine speech, where consensus is achieved and understanding is not problematic, and critical discourse, where "validity claims about the rightness, truthfulness, or sincerity of a speech act, tacitly presumed in conversation, can be raised and responded to" (Ewert, 1991, p. 359). Such validity claims become explicit when communication is problematic and disagreement results. With critique the supposition of reasonable and well intentioned (i.e. responsible) communicative action is lost.

There are, however, a number of other conditions or assumptions that must be made if we are to have confidence in such consensual validation. The ideal speech situation, which is anticipated by all speech, "requires a democratic form of public discussion which allows for an uncoerced flow of ideas and arguments and for participants to be free from threat of domination, manipulation or control" (Carr & Kemmis, 1986, p. 142). Habermas' argument is that free and open communication, that is, emancipation and the pursuit of rational autonomy, is promised by all speech situations. In Habermas' (1973) words:

> Discourses help test the truth claims of opinions (and norms) which the speakers no longer take for granted. In discourse, the 'force' of the argument is the only permissible compulsion, whereas cooperative search for truth is the only permissible motive. (p. 168)

Thus, the primary interest is in reaching agreement or consensus through speech.

Implications for adult and higher education. Habermas' critical social science is a combination of theory and practice which transforms consciousness and social action. To begin to understand its implications for education it is important to re-emphasize some crucial issues. First, it is different from traditional critical theory. Ewert (1991) explains that "Critical theory as critique only states the problem, usually from a particular ideological perspective [and] ... does not concern itself with practical solutions that would deal with the multiple factors impinging on educational practice" (p. 375). Second, the critical social theory of Habermas incorporates a political determination for rational consensus or agreement. In addition, it is an inclusive theory in which there are three knowledge constitutive interests (technical, practical and emancipatory) and corresponding methods of validating knowledge (positive, interpretive and critical). Methodologies are therefore judged appropriate to the interests or problem at hand. The implication is that understanding within each knowledge domain may require varying educational approaches. In short, it is a theory tolerant of diversity and disdainful of the certainty of ideology.

While Habermas' theory is not a finished product and is not explicit with regard to educational practice, its aim of enlightenment and emancipation offers much in articulating educational theory and practice. After a comprehensive review of articles concerned with Habermas' theory and education, Ewert (1991) concludes that he has influenced thinking about pedagogical, administrative and social theory in education and will have an increasing impact on educational thought and practice. One reason given for this influence is its consistency with critical thinking (see Chapter 4).

Young (1990) has attempted to construct a critical theory of education consistent with the work of Habermas. He begins by making it clear how traditional teaching and learning is different from critical teaching and learning. Young suggests that the educational dilemma is that the teacher, on behalf of society, attempts to teach a prescribed curriculum which is supposedly in the student's best interest. This inevitably leads to an indoctrinatory style of teaching and learning not based upon discourse and understanding. The structure and process is controlled by the teacher. The student's first concern is what the teacher wants which results in a belief that knowledge "is a commodity which you come to possess,…and it is possible to assess and certify possession of it" (Young, 1990, p. 96). The following statement reveals the risk of traditional education in transmitting societal knowledge and values in a prescribed manner:

> When education becomes an instrument of a collective purpose without at the same time being an expression of individual interest it loses its capacity for rationality, since rational social participa- tion must rest on the communicative autonomy of the participants rather than upon some pre-decided and believed-to-be incon- trovertible foundational knowledge. (Young, 1990, p. 87)

A critical teaching and learning approach, according to Young (1990), is one where students are given opportunities to develop their critical capacities that enable them to continue to learn. It is a constructivist and co-operative approach to learning where understanding is reached through discourse and agreement. Critical discussion necessitates a rational autonomy but as a member of a democratic social community. Critical teaching should "assist students to make an effective job of reconstructing the already problematic parts of their life-world through com- municative, problem-solving learning" (Young, 1990, p. 71). Perhaps the most revealing statement by Young (1990) regarding his critical theory of education is that it "bears a strong resemblance to Dewey's problem solving method of pedagogy" (p. 119). Critical teaching and learning consistent with Habermas is a process of rational dialogue where ideas are exposed to free critical judgement and oriented to inter-subjective understanding.

Habermas has also had a significant influence on thought in the field of adult education. Mezirow (1981) presents the theory of Habermas "as a theory positing three generic domains of adult learning, each with its own interpretive categories, ways of assessing knowledge claims, methods of inquiry and, by implication, each with its own distinctive learning modes and needs" (p. 3). He believes that emancipatory action, or in his terms perspective transformation, "may be the most distinguishing characteristic of adult learning" and "the foundation for formulating a comprehensive theory of adult education" (Mezirow, 1981, pp. 11,16). Consistent with emancipatory self-reflection, Mezirow (1981) commits adult education to self-directed learning as a central goal and method. This is an important concept that will be discussed further in Chapter 5.

With the emphasis on self-reflection and autonomy for emancipatory and self-directed learning in adult education, the question arises as to the role of the teacher. Mezirow (1990) states emphatically that adult educators do not simply act as passive facilitators of learning. He suggests the adult "educator sets democratic norms to govern critical discourse and fosters participation in dialogue…as an empathic provocateur, gently creating dilemmas by encouraging learners to face up to contradictions between what they believe and what they do" (Mezirow, 1990, p. 366). Addressing such contradictions and their practical consequences raises serious ethical dilemmas for educators.

The critical social science of Habermas is a collaborative social process that combines critical reflection and discourse with the deliberate intent to negotiate understanding and act to overcome contradictions and constraints. Educators are concerned with helping students understand contradictions, alternatives and consequences of practical action. While educators may challenge and explore assumptions and meaning, it is done collaboratively and openly without prescribing exclusively, in an authoritarian manner, the educator's personal beliefs or particular courses of action. The educator's views along with the student's views must be open to critical reflection and discourse. Ultimately, however, the individual must be allowed to self-reflect and construct meaning. It may be ideological and beyond the educational domain for educators to become leaders of social action. The inherently democratic communicative process of a critical education theory, if respected, will guide ethical educational practice; however, ethical educational practice still comes down to the professional judgement of educators reflecting upon the circumstances of particular educational settings.

Habermas rejects the authoritarianism and manipulation of both the traditional right and radical left. Educationally, there must be protection against indoctrination through a democratic and open transaction. Too often both the political right and left pretend to know what is in the student's best interest. Young (1990) argues that too many "critical educators have brought the whole of the life-world under a general rhetoric of criticism, causing an unspecified and free-floating fear to permeate even the most innocent of aspects of daily life" (p. 70). Both traditional and critical theory do not explicitly advocate sufficiently free and open discourse and reflection where the rationally autonomous individual is responsible for constructing meaning. Consistent with Habermas and a critical theory of education, Young (1990) states that the main function of critical educators "should be to assist students to make an effective job of reconstructing the already problematic parts of their life-world through communicative, problem-solving learning. In conjunction with this, some limited degree of gentle reconstitution of connected, but yet questioned, aspects of the life-world may be necessary" (p. 71).

In summary, Carr and Kemmis (1986) suggest that critical social science "is not only a theory about knowledge, but also about how knowledge relates to practice" (p. 149). They state that:

> ...its epistemology is constructivist, seeing knowledge as developing by a process of active construction and reconstruction of theory and practice by those involved; that it involves a theory of symmetrical communication (a process of rational discussion which actively seeks to overcome coercion on the one hand and self-deception on the other), and that it involves a theory of political action based on free commitment to social action and consensus about what needs to be and should be done. (pp. 148-149)

It is for these reasons that an educational theory based upon critical social science offers much for an open and democratic society.

Constructivist and collaborative orientations are foundational principles of a critical theory of education. A critical educational theory treats means and goals in a collaborative and open manner. It resists ideologically focusing on any one form of knowledge or method as the definitive approach to learning in an educational context. A critical theory of education is committed to enhancing the democratic process in the classroom and a strengthening of the social whole through greater individual responsibility and control. It is the teacher's enormous responsibility and judgement to travel down the middle road with their students between coercion and self-deception. A critical educational theory is a comprehensive and balanced attempt to integrate individual and social concerns in the teaching and learning transaction.

Discussion

Reflection upon the previous concepts reveals several themes. The purpose here is not to document the differences among the foundational thinkers discussed above, although we have noted how Rogers differs from Dewey and Habermas by his focusing on the individual without considering legitimate societal influences. On the other hand, the differences between Dewey and Habermas are more qualitative and, therefore, more difficult to articulate briefly. However, it could be said that Habermas' liberation from hegemony and the emancipation ideal would likely contrast somewhat with Dewey's reflection upon experience and democratic ideal.

The immediate goal is to identify the commonalities that can be built upon in developing a teaching-learning framework appropriate for adult and higher education. While the theories discussed above reflect concerns particular to the times during which they were constructed, it is interesting to note how similar some of their central themes are. It is anticipated that identifying commonalties among these theories will assist us in recognizing essential values and truths regarding the nature of education and the teaching-learning transaction.

The core themes identified are change, experience, reflection, collaboration and constructivism. The assumption of change precedes and shapes each of the themes. It is safe to say that each of the previous theories in its own way is a reaction to static curricula and authoritarian educational processes. Each of the theoretical frameworks outlined views knowledge as, at best, tentative, and dependent upon changing personal and social realities. Ensuring a dynamic evolution of socially validated knowledge requires the adoption of an experience and reflection based educational process. Through a rejection of existing authoritarian values, Dewey advocates a reconstruction of knowledge based upon experience. Education is both a process of maintaining cultural continuity and directing the course of change. Rogers' view of change is directed largely to facilitating individual freedom and self-awareness. He believes the educated individual is one who had learned how to change. Habermas believes that change is necessary if individuals are to be emancipated from ideological knowledge distortions. Considerable emphasis is placed upon informed action to change power relationships in order to release the individual's full potential.

Each of the three theoretical perspectives accepts that knowledge is influenced by experience in the sense that relevant learning is oriented to everyday concerns. As noted previously, experience is clearly a key component of Dewey's philosophy. Knowledge is constructed from experimenting with the environment in a social context. This is not unlike Habermas' technical and practical knowledge domains. Rogers, on the other hand, recognizes the influence of social interaction but, as a "humanist", emphasizes the need to create one's own sense of reality and self-concept. The most comprehensive and explicit treatment of experience is provided by Habermas through his identifying of three knowledge constitutive domains and the methodology used to validate each form of knowledge. Experience in the technical domain has to do with manipulating natural objects; while communicative action constitutes experience in the practical and emancipatory knowledge domains.

Without question the most obvious commonality among the three perspectives is the place for personal reflection in the process of constructing knowledge. Dewey places reflective thinking at the centre of his method for reconstructing experience. Reflective thinking is intended to resolve problems and anticipate the consequences of possible action. The fundamental goal for Rogers is the development of the self-concept through self-directed learning. Rogers' concept of student centredness emphasizes the individual reflecting upon his or her reality and upon what constitutes knowledge. Habermas, of course, explicitly states that self-reflective knowledge is the most authentic form of knowledge since it is the reliable way to become aware of personal and social constraints. For each of these theorists, reflection provides the means to construct personal meaning through attaining a state of cognitive autonomy or independence.

However, construction of meaning through reflection is only one phase of the educational process. Although the process of constructing meaning occurs in the private world of the individual, constructing meaning is triggered and validated in the shared world. This brings us to the issue of collaboration in the educational process. Collaboration speaks to the nature and quality of the relationship between teacher and student. The existence of a truly collaborative educational experience goes to the heart of what an educational experience ought to be. It provides for change through experience and reflection as well as modelling a consensual rationality. The strongest argument for a collaborative relationship is that it provides the climate for students to take responsibility for their learning. But it also implicitly rejects the teacher as indisputable authority and recognizes that all knowledge is humanly constructed and thus uncertain.

Dewey argues strongly that education is more effective in a collaborative democratic environment. Learning is both a personal and social process where the opportunities for growth are enhanced through co-operation and collaboration. Again, consistent with his rejection of dualistic notions, Dewey believes the individual gains intellectual autonomy through collaborative action. Even with Rogers' primary concern for individuals defining themselves, he recognizes that the person is influenced by experiences in a changing natural and social world. From an educational perspective, he advocates that the teacher and student enter into a personal relationship where each maintains their identities. Teachers must be genuine, trusting and willing to take risks while collaboratively discovering or creating new ideas. Habermas, of course, does not speak directly to the teacher-student relationship; however, his entire theory is based upon an ideal speech situation where problems of understanding can be raised openly in critical discourse with the expectation of consensual agreement. Rational argument, not authority or tradition, predominates and requires a democratic form of discourse.

As noted previously, collaboration provides the climate and encouragement to assume the responsibility to construct personal meaning. Constructivism is the process where the individual must ultimately assume responsibility to construct meaning based upon experience. To assume responsibility for constructing meaning necessitates having the control and being willing to risk making decisions. Education, therefore, must create the climate where students are given the control to responsibly construct their own knowledge and opportunities for communicative action.

Responsibility and control. The themes identified in the previous discussion are important core concepts. However, they are also representative of two fundamental perspectives on the educational transaction — those of the personal (individual) and shared (social) worlds. More specifically, it is suggested that the themes of reflection and constructivism are largely private issues and, therefore, relate more to the personal world. On the other hand, experience and collaboration are largely social issues and, therefore, relate primarily to the shared world. These two perspectives and their corresponding theories are encompassed by the two core issues of this book — responsibility and control. It is argued that responsibility and control represent fundamental educational issues that are crucial to understanding the teaching-learning transaction.

In one form or the other, responsibility and control have been the focus of much educational debate. While the previous theoretical frameworks place greater emphasis on personal or shared issues, each recognizes and attempts to provide an integrative view of how knowledge is created. It is the assumption here that responsibility does not exist without personal control; and control is meaningless or oppressive without the accountability of responsibility. The challenge is to integrate issues of responsibility and control in a coherent view of the educational process.

Generally speaking, responsibility represents the authenticity of dealing with reality in an open and truthful manner. The use here of the term responsibility is in reference to cognitive processes. That is, responsibility is being personally accountable for the consequences of cognitive decisions in the exploration and construction of meaning arising from experience. It has also been used frequently to refer to taking responsibility for the decisions and consequences of one's social actions. While both originate from within and have important implications for education, it is the responsibility for meaningful learning that is the primary focus here.

The term "control" also has different uses. Given the variety of connotations and uses for the term control, as well as its emotional overtones, it is important to clarify its meaning. Control is reflective of the shared world, and correspondingly it is concerned with shared (co-operative) action. It is contrasted with the concept of power, which is seen as dominance over others. Control is realized interdependently through sustained two-way communication. On the other hand, power is exerted unilaterally, creating a potential situation of conflict and oppression. From the perspective of control, consensus is negotiated, which secures the agency of others for the good of all participants. This sense of "control" was used by Dewey in balancing competing concerns when managing the educational setting. Guteck (1988) states that for Dewey, "Control came from the cooperative context of shared activity" (p. 103).

Conclusion

The discussion in this chapter has identified and analysed many of the essential foundational assumptions, values and beliefs of education. It is through these principles that educators begin to understand the nature of the educational process. Although each person must eventually examine and construct their own set of principles, it is immensely valuable to build upon and incorporate the ideas of leading theorists who have spent years reflecting upon the essence of education, knowledge and learning. Having such an understanding cannot help but facilitate a critical examination of one's assumptions regarding the educational process as well as broaden and confirm one's values and beliefs.

The perspectives and ideas presented in this chapter have been selected on the basis of their congruence and relevance to constructivist views of education. What has emerged are two key themes consistent with a collaborative constructivist view of education. The themes are responsibility and control. In turn, it is the themes of responsibility and control that will assist in developing a transactional approach to teaching and learning.

While a coherent philosophy can be pragmatic and serve educators in their professional practice, such a philosophy must also be parsimonious, while embodying the essence of the educational experience. The challenge is to explore the pragmatic implications of the previously identified themes. We begin by exploring the learning process more explicitly. The themes are revisited from the perspective of selected theories of learning.

3

Learning Perspectives

The obvious purpose of an educational experience is learning. However, learning in an educational context should have specific outcome expectations and standards. That is, the learning must not only be meaningful to the individual, but also of value and worth from a societal perspective. An understanding of this dual requirement provides an important framework for those designing educational experiences. The risk is that if an educator operates without such an understanding, she or he may be promoting the wrong kinds of learning outcomes.

It is equally important that educators understand not only the goals of the learning process, but also the learning process itself. An understanding of how people learn can provide the educator with the means to adapt to changing educational conditions and ensure the achievement of intended and worthwhile outcomes.

The challenge is to provide order to a complex process that is largely inaccessible to direct study. This challenge has been addressed by several significant theories of learning. We will review the major developments in learning theory that have occurred during this century. Our exploration begins with a clarification of the nature of learning in an educational context, and continues with a discussion of what constitutes knowledge.

Learning and Knowledge

The nature of learning and knowledge cannot be taken for granted. The understanding of learning shapes how we approach the educational transaction and what learning outcomes are valued. Thomas (1991) advises that because "the meaning of words change over time, so it is desirable to subject them to fresh examination at frequent intervals" (p. 15). He goes on to say that in English the "word learning can be a verb as well as a noun; that is, it can be used to represent a process or action as well as an outcome" (p. 16). This distinction is important since in an educational context process and outcome are integrally related.

Learning in an educational sense is a special type of learning. It is obvious that much learning occurs both incidentally and intentionally as a result of living. Generally, this type of learning is defined as a change or potential change of behaviour as a result of experience. While such a definition is not inconsistent with learning in an educational context, it does not reflect what makes educational learning special. If we are to understand the educational process, then we must have some appreciation of the learning outcomes associated with an educational endeavour. Judgements have to be made about the outcomes and methods of learning that are educationally valid. Learning in an educational sense must be purposeful and that purpose (worthwhile aim) should be established with the awareness and participation of the learner. The aim should seek truth and knowledge that will lead to continuous growth. Notwithstanding the inadequacy of any definition of learning, the following definition is suggested as being consistent with learning in adult and higher education:

> The construction, reconstruction, negotiation and exchange of personally significant, relevant and viable meaning. (Thomas & Harri-Augstein, 1985, p. xxiv)

Learning that is purposeful and provides for appropriate negotiation and exchange stands the best chance of leading to meaningful and worthwhile knowledge outcomes. The construction of personal meaning is validated or becomes viable knowledge through the process of critical discourse. By integrating personal and societal values and knowledge, understanding can be achieved. Salomon (1992) argues that the concept of learning in education has changed. He states that the "changed conceptions of learning lead us to believe that learning is a constructive socially and knowledge-based process whose quality greatly depends on the extent to which it is mindfully and intentionally carried out" (p. 46). Such a view of learning, emphasizing the intentional construction, negotiation and exchange of meaning, is central to a collaborative constructivist view of the teaching-learning transaction.

A distinction has been made between incidental learning in the natural societal setting and intentional, planned learning in an educational context; however, things are not quite so simple. Although our focus here is upon intentional and planned learning in a formal educational context, it must be noted that purposeful and planned learning may occur in a natural societal setting. Notwithstanding the lack of formal recognition, this latter form of learning may also be considered educational. Often this would be associated with an individual who has learned how to learn and has an emancipation interest. Furthermore, learning in an educational context has been described in terms such as rote versus meaning-ful or declarative (what) versus procedural (how). Such categorizations have proven useful but may also give the false impression of sharp and mutually exclusive boundaries. Rote learning may well have a useful place in constructing knowledge.

As an example, in making the distinction between rote and meaningful learning, Ausubel, Novak and Hanesian (1978) state that:

> One involves the short-term acquisition of single, somewhat contrived concepts, the solution of artificial problems, or the learning of arbitrary associations ... The other consists of the long term acquisition and retention of the complex network of interre-lated ideas characterising an organised body of knowledge that learners must incorporate into their cognitive structures. (p. 12)

This kind of sharp distinction can be misleading in appearing to suggest that rote learning of basic content does not play an important role in constructing meaningful knowledge and solving important and persistent problems. Declarative knowledge may be inert but it may also play a key conceptual role in understanding a phenomenon or solving a problem significant to the individual. Expertise and deep understanding are as much about cognitive procedures as about content structure.

Bereiter (1992) argues that the common-sense view of knowledge comes in two varieties — knowledge about something (declarative) and knowledge about how to do something (procedural). He suggests, however, that such a view is not adequate for education. In general, it does not provide for an understanding of a constructivist or deep approach to learning. More specifically, it does not explain the progressive and developmental nature of knowledge construction on an educational or scientific level. Bereiter (1992) argues for "problem-centred knowledge" which acts as an organizing point for knowledge construction at a high level.

Bereiter (1992) also suggests that education is, and should be, concerned with higher-level concepts. Unfortunately, higher-level concepts lack the concrete reference and inherent interest of basic-level concepts. To overcome this inherent limitation with teaching and learning higher-level concepts, Bereiter (1992) argues for problem-centred knowledge that "depends on problems that persist or recur so that they become organising points for knowledge" (p. 346). Persistent problems are problems or issues of explanation and understanding — not instrumental or educationally contrived problems. Persistent problems of explanation and understanding are most likely to generate conceptual learning and awareness of our world. Students who take an active and intentional approach to learning are "characterized by a highly elaborated structure of persisting problems of understanding" (Bereiter, 1992, p. 349).

An active and intentional approach must also consider the contextual application of knowledge; that is, a "conditional" understanding with regard to when and why this knowledge is relevant and useful to resolve dilemmas or problems. Declarative and procedural knowledge must at a minimum include conditional knowledge (Marzano et al., cited in Dart & Boulton-Lewis, 1998).

Problems of understanding and explanation are knowledge problems. Content provides the building blocks to construct knowledge that has meaning and usefulness to solve persistent and significant problems. The processes that count most are not content-free processes but, instead, are those "processes by which knowledge problems are tackled in a progressive manner that leads to the building up of effective problem-centred [concept-centred] knowledge" (Bereiter, 1992, p. 351).

A similar position is taken by Prawat (1993) when he argues that educators should reconsider their commitment to practical problem solving which over-emphasizes the instrumental nature of learning. Describing what he calls an "idea-based social constructivism", Prawat (1993) states that educators should focus "instead on the teaching of important ideas developed within the disciplines"

(p. 5). Consistent with our view here, Prawat (1993) argues for embedding general skills such as critical thinking within the regular curriculum (see Chapter 4). He states:

> The ideal curriculum, from this perspective, is one that strikes a balance between "truth" (the acquisition of basic subject matter knowledge) and "competencies" (the acquisition of inquiry and problem-solving skills)...Instead of viewing curriculum as a "fixed agenda," it urges teachers to think of curriculum as matrix or network of big ideas. (p. 13)

In this way teachers work collaboratively with students to make connections and solve problems of understanding.

More recently, Prawat (1998) discusses the importance of big ideas in precipitating interest and sustaining effort in learning. John Dewey proposed this idea-based approach to achieve "true motivation" and unify content and learner. In this regard, Prawat (1998) states:

> The image of the ideal learner in Dewey's scheme is attractive — the student who is hooked on a big idea and eager to elaborate on anticipations which that idea gives rise to in his or her own learning community and then to test those anticipations against real world objects and events. (p. 219)

This process goes to the heart of critical thinking, higher-order learning, and collaborative constructivist approaches to teaching and learning which will be discussed in subsequent chapters and picked up more specifically in Chapter 6.

In higher-order learning the challenge is one of understanding ideas and concepts of the discipline or subject. Both Bereiter and Prawat focus on problems of explanation or understanding. Although Bereiter (1992) uses the phrase "problem-centred knowledge" his focus, like Prawat, is on concepts. Knowledge of the textbook can be made meaningful if it is "seen as a relevant to some persisting problem of understanding or getting along in the world" (Bereiter, 1992, p. 348). In other words, through the dissonance of a problem situation students actively attempt to make sense of their situation. To reiterate, the "problem for education is to involve students in problems of explanation and to help them move towards deeper levels" (Bereiter, 1992, p. 353) of understanding. Explanation is the educational means of moving from personal meaning to shared understanding and eventually public knowledge.

From a social constructionist perspective, Gergen (1985) states that knowledge is a social artefact. Knowledge is the product "of historically situated interchanges among people ... [T]he process of understanding is not automatically driven by the forces of nature, but is the result of an active, cooperative enterprise of persons in relationship" (Gergen, 1985, p. 267). This would seem particularly true for the educational enterprise; however, the caution is that the individual cognitive perspective must not be lost.

For constructivists who emphasize the individual cognitive perspective, knowledge refers to conceptual structures that individuals construct to create meaning when previous understanding is inadequate to explain current experience. Meaning is not imposed from the outside but is embedded in the cognitive reconstruction of the individual's experience. Unlike positivism with its objective view of reality, the "basic concern of constructivism is with how people make sense of the perplexing variety and constantly changing texture of their experience" (Candy, 1989, p. 98).

Constructing meaning is embedded in a social-historical context. The previous description of constructivist knowledge reflects the important role of social interaction by noting the tradition of thought and language. Glasersfeld (1989) suggests that in "connection with the concept of viability, be it 'utilitarian' or 'epistemic', social interaction plays an important role" (p. 129) in constructing meaning. In other words, the viability of meaning both externally (utilitarian) and internally (epistemic) is dependent upon social interaction mediated through language and culture. While the construction of meaning is a personal respon-sibility, it is embedded in social experience and establishing its viability is a social process.

These constructivist assumptions are implicitly or explicitly embedded in various cognitive and socially situated theories of learning. Moreover, they are not inconsistent with the philosophical positions of Dewey, Rogers and Habermas discussed in the previous chapter. The implication is that knowledge is constructed by the individual but precipitated and influenced through social interaction and collaboration. This shifting from experience to reflective thought and back demonstrates the complementarity of social and cognitive views of construc-tivism.

Constructivist views of learning in an educational context are being adopted ever more frequently by educators in higher education. The primary reason is the inherent recognition of both cognitive and social processes as well as the concern for contextual flexibility in maintaining the appropriate balance between these two main processes. Constructing meaning may be a personal responsibility but it is embedded in a dynamic sociocultural context with its particular control contingencies.

The conception of learning and knowledge creation suggested here is labelled "collaborative constructivism". Collaborative constructivism moves beyond the objective (empiricist) versus subjective (rationalist) dichotomy with regard to how knowledge originates. Personal meaning and knowledge is seen to be a derivative of social interchange and negotiated understanding. Cognitive and social action are complementary elements of a differentiated whole — they are not antithetical.

The meaning of learning and knowledge discussed previously are crucial to understanding the educational transaction described in this book. To further our understanding of knowledge acquisition in an educational context we turn to an examination of existing theories of learning.

Contrasting Learning Perspectives

Just as there are various types of learning there are also various theories of learning. To further complicate the situation, these theories often overlap, which makes classification difficult and sometimes misleading. However, based upon a rough chronological development of learning theories, three general perspectives are identified. The first is the behaviourist tradition with its exclusive focus on reinforcement of behaviours through the arrangement of environmental contingencies. The second perspective constitutes the cognitive learning theories with their focus on mental processing. The third perspective attempts a more systemic approach in considering the interaction of the environment and the individual in understanding the learning process. It is this third perspective that has particular relevance to the teaching-learning transaction discussed in this book. However, to set the stage, the contrasting perspectives of behaviourism and cognitivism are first discussed. In the next section we shall address learning theories which take an integrative (holistic) perspective.

The behaviourism that evolved at the beginning of the twentieth century was both a rejection of the mysticism and mentalism of classical theories of learning and an embracing of the objectivity and prediction of science. It is not concerned with how knowledge is constructed but only with prediction and control of behaviour. The assumption is that cognitive processes could not be validated, therefore, only observable variables associated with learning new behaviours are relevant. It was thus fitting that the study of animals in the laboratory would became the source of behavioural principles.

The essence of behaviourism is a preoccupation with behaviour and the belief that the environment controls and shapes behaviour. It is interesting to note that behaviouristic assumptions continue to dominate educational practice. It manifests itself in the need to prescribe observable learning outcomes and to control the behaviour of students. This traditional teacher-centred approach is reflected in the setting of behavioural objectives as well as a reliance on programmed and pre-packaged curricula. Most importantly, shaping student behaviour encourages the use of assessment practices that measure reproduction of prescribed content. Because it is difficult to measure outcomes such as understanding, behavioural approaches to education reinforce passive assimilation of prescribed course content. The teacher has full responsibility and control for designing and orchestrating the learning experience.

In contrast to the environmental focus of behaviourists is the concern for personal insight and information processing of the cognitive learning theorists. Cognitivists rejected the reductionism of behaviourism for not being able to explain higher cognitive processes. Cognitivism has its roots in Gestalt psychology. Gestaltists are concerned with how individuals solve problems and emphasize the cognitive process of insight. Insight "is defined as the sudden perception of relationships among elements of a problem situation" (Lefrancois, 1972, p. 189). It was therefore concerned with the perception of wholes. The emphasis had shifted from what happened to learners from the outside to how learners interpret experience and solve problems. In short, the learner becomes an active processor of information and solves problems by making cognitive connections.

Ausubel, Novak and Hanesian (1978) present a cognitive view of learning where new material is related "to relevant aspects of existing cognitive structure, ascertaining how the resulting new meaning can be reconciled with established knowledge, and recoding it in more familiar and idiosyncratic language" (p. 62). This represents a shift from practical problem solving to meaning construction. Ausubel, Novak and Hanesian (1978) differentiate between rote and meaningful learning with the latter subdivided between reception and discovery learning. However, the extrapolation of rote learning from the laboratory to the classroom has had its problems. Education based upon rote learning is reproductive assimilation resulting in a collection of arbitrary facts which are difficult to retain and if they are, because they are disjoint, they may not be useful in guiding future experiences. In addition, such learning is based upon extrinsic motivation which may reduce intrinsic motivation and continued learning.

On the other hand, meaningful learning is connected to previous knowledge and is coherent and plausible. Meaningful learning necessitates that new material have relevant anchoring ideas. To provide this anchor, Ausubel, Novak and Hanesian (1978) propose using advance organizers to bridge the gap between existing and new knowledge. An advance organizer is an introductory framework or general set of ideas. While discovery (problem solving) learning has its place in education, particularly for older learners, it is not practicable for assimilating large amounts of subject matter. The question arises, however, as to how much structure and content can be advanced (prescribed) if the learner is to retain the responsibility for constructing meaning. This emphasis on cognitive structure led to the work on schema theory which is integral to the information processing orientation.

A relatively recent trend in cognitive learning theory has been termed the information processing or cognitive science approach. This approach uses the computer to analogize the information processing capabilities of humans. Using the computer analogy, cognitive psychology "is about how people take in information, how they recode and remember it, how they make decisions, how they transform their internal knowledge states, and how they translate these states into behavioral outputs" (Lachman, Lachman & Butterfield, 1979, p. 99). Shuell (1986) suggests that cognitive psychology has influenced learning theory in the following ways:

(a) the view of learning as an active, constructive process;
(b) the presence of higher-level processes in learning;
(c) the cumulative nature of learning and the corresponding role played by prior knowledge;
(d) concern for the way knowledge is presented and organized in memory; and
(e) concern for analyzing learning tasks and performance in terms of the cognitive processes that are involved. (p. 415)

All of these concepts have important implications for learning in an educational context.

The limitation of the information processing view of learning is its almost exclusive focus on the mind and its cognitive structures or schemata. While a schema theory of learning is an active and developmental process, it does not adequately consider the influence of the learning context or application to other contexts. The mind of the individual is paramount and the environment is only a source of information. From an educational perspective this creates serious problems with regard to the context of the teaching-learning transaction. Such a technical information processing model does not adequately consider the full psycho-social context of an educational transaction. The cognitive model is described by Streibel (1991) as being "a rational reconstruction of minimally situated actions", whereas human learning is experiential and the "interpretations of lived experiences by the participants determine the meanings of actions in the 'life-world' of situated actions" (p. 121). That is, there is a reduction of the complex phenomenological and social world of the learner. Thus, both behaviourist and cognitivist views of learning are reductionistic in their views of learning.

The main problem with an information processing model of learning is that from an educational perspective the teacher may be reduced to disseminating information or deterministically structuring input for a prescribed output. Little emphasis is placed upon cultural context and its influence on the interaction between teacher and learner or among students. The result is an extreme form of learner-centredness but without consideration of self-concept, beliefs, interests, and intentions. Bruner (1990) suggests that the originating impulse of the cognitive revolution became technicalized and shifted from "mind and meaning to computers and information" (pp. 4–6). In essence, this represented a shift from a concern for constructing meaning to a focus on memory structures and schemata for efficient recall of information. This created the opportunity for an integrative approach and a focus on cognitive processes that were socially situated.

Integrative Learning Perspectives

Bruner (1990) argues that it "is man's participation in culture and the realisation of his mental powers through culture that make it impossible to construct a human psychology on the basis of the individual alone" (p. 12). Social and cultural conditions have a profound effect upon cognitive processes. Saljo (1991) suggests that culture "allows us to perceive the world as meaningful and coherent and at the same time it operates as a constraint on our understandings and activities" (p. 180). Conversely, constructing valid meaning connects individuals to culture. Bruner (1990) states that our "culturally adapted way of life depends upon shared meanings and shared concepts and depends as well upon shared modes of discourse for negotiating differences in meaning and interpretation" (p. 13). It would seem that learning "is neither wholly subjective nor fully encompassed in social interaction, and it is not constituted separately from the social world (with its own structures and meanings) of which it is a part" (Lave, 1991, p. 64).

Social cognition. While Dewey certainly argues against dualistic thinking and the separation of the individual and society, some choose to emphasize the social component of cognition. Vygotsky is one who focuses on the social context in developing a socio-culturally situated theory of cognition. Vygotsky's fundamental hypothesis is that higher mental functions are socially and culturally formed. Conceptual development evolves from interaction with others. This human interaction is mediated by language and other semiotic devices which also make possible reflection upon and analysis of experience and cognitive reconstruction at a higher order. Thus, as a result of this social and individual dialectic, "Vygotsky visualized a form of internal dialogue where the mature thinker plays all the roles, the function of such inner dialogues being that of planning, guiding, and monitoring thought and action" (Brown & Palincsar, 1989, p. 408). Cognitive development results from the integration and transformation of social interactions or experiences.

From an educational perspective, Vygotsky emphasizes the social origins of knowledge and the importance of building upon current knowledge and developmental states. This led Vygotsky to develop the concept of a "zone of proximal development". This is the place where cognitive development occurs and is defined in terms of the actual level of development and the potential that could be achieved through the collaboration of more capable others. The zone of proximal development is an interactive system that recognizes and builds upon different perspectives and levels of understanding. This zone is widened with the support of teachers or a collaborative community of learners. The zone of proximal development emphasizes the teaching-learning transaction and the socio-cultural context.

Another theory of social cognition is provided by Bandura. This represents an integration of behaviourism and cognitivism. The essence of Bandura's (1977) social learning theory is to approach "the explanation of human behavior in terms of a continuous reciprocal interaction between cognitive, behavioral, and environmental determinants" (p. vii). Thus, behaviour can influence the environment and the environment can influence behaviour. Such experiences shape thoughts which in turn may influence behaviour. Out of this reciprocal interactionism evolves self-regulatory processes.

Self-regulation may result from direct learning experiences or through symbolic and vicarious processes. Bandura (1977) suggests that the capacity of humans to use symbols provides a means for reflective thought, to intentionally guide future action and to deal with the environment. A very important aspect of this theory is the ability to learn vicariously through observation and modelling. Bandura (1977) states that the "capacity to learn by observation enables people to acquire large, integrated patterns of behavior without having to form them gradually by tedious trial and error" (p. 12). For reasons of efficiency and safety, most cultural patterns are acquired through the indispensable benefit of models and the imitation of behaviour. However, learning that has been acquired verbally or vicariously must be confirmed or validated periodically through the effects of action; that is, either through direct experience or by comparison to the judgement of others through discourse.

Individuals enhance and maintain their actions through control of self-prescribed standards. That is, "motivational effects do not derive from the goals themselves, but rather from the fact that people respond evaluatively to their own behavior" (Bandura, 1977, p. 161). Motivation derives from self-regulation/direction and perceived self-efficacy. Individuals with perceived high self-efficacy, or belief in one's proficiency, are generally highly motivated and accomplish more. This "is because people with high perceived self-efficacy tend to have more control over the events in their environment" (Hergenhahn, 1988, p. 332). Thus, control is very important for learners to be self-directed and feel capable of taking responsibility for constructing and confirming meaning.

Developmental cognition. Piaget was the first to outline a developmental cognitive theory. He was concerned with cognitive characteristics and knowledge that arise when adapting to the environment as well as when reflecting upon these experiences. Tennant (1988) states that Piaget believed "that the growth of knowledge is based upon the interplay ... between the person acting on and 'constructing' the world and the world acting on the person" (p. 75). It must be stated explicitly that while Piaget focuses on internal cognitive processes, he does not believe that cognitive development is in-born or purely maturational. His position is that both individual development and environment are inherently bound together; however, Piaget did not comment on larger sociocultural influences. Consistent with this view, it is interesting to note that "Piaget provided speculation that individual development is facilitated by cooperation between peers in resolving cognitive conflicts provided by their differing perspectives" (Rogoff, 1990, p. 34). This process of publicly sharing differing perspectives for cognitive development and validation is a very important principle that could have been more fully developed by Piaget.

Cognitive structures (knowledge) and formal operational thought were explained by Piaget using the concepts of schema, assimilation and accommodation. The term schema was used to describe a cognitive or knowledge structure (meaningful connection of information) representing a general potential of how an individual might respond to a situation. To explain how schemata are constructed, Piaget used the terms assimilation and accommodation. If an existing schema is satisfactory for interacting with and understanding the environment, then these experiences will be assimilated into the existing schema. However, when the schema is not adequate a disequilibrium will result and an attempt will be made to accommodate the schema which is congruent with the new situation. As a result, cognitive structures are modified or new schemata are formed and cognitive development progresses.

Piaget's work was a turning point in understanding that learning develops through stages and is influenced by experience (Phillips & Soltis, 1985). While his interest was in child development culminating in abstract thought in adolescence, it also laid a foundation for understanding learning and cognitive development in adulthood. Tennant (1988) suggests that Piaget's most pertinent legacies with regard to adult learning are an emphasis on qualitative developmental stages, the active role of individuals in constructing knowledge, and a conception of mature thought. His legacy has precipitated research on adult cognitive development in terms of "whether, and how, formal operational thought is generalized, extended, and maintained" (Tennant, 1988, p. 79).

A wide range of research has explored and proposed new structures or patterns of thinking that goes beyond Piaget's culminating stage of abstract thought. This research considers cognitive development in adulthood (Merriam & Caffarella, 1991). Perry (1970) studied the cognitive development of college students and has proposed a developmental model with important implications for higher education. While his model of cognitive development is structural, he suggests a continuous dynamic when he states that "Perhaps development is all transitions and 'stages' only resting points along the way" (Perry, 1981, p. 78).

Perry (1970) conducted extensive interviews with college students regarding the fundamental nature of knowledge. He proposed four basic positions of intellectual development and several other transition points. The positions are: dualism where authorities have the answers and things are right or wrong; multiplicity (complex dualism) where ambiguity is acknowledged, and while authorities can legitimately differ as to what is the truth, there is still a trust in authority; relativism where ambiguity is the fact of life and knowledge is interpreted and justified within a generalized context; and, commitment in relativism where active reasoning is necessitated and the individual is responsible for making sense of life but remains open to new perspectives and values.

Perhaps most interestingly from an educational perspective is the finding that most students enter college at the late dualistic stage where education is seen as primarily accumulating information. In other words, while they may be maturationally capable of operating at Piaget's formal operational stage, they have not assumed the responsibility of creating meaning based upon their own experience. These students are still waiting to be told what is to count as knowledge and truth. This has enormous implications educationally that will be explored subsequently.

Another developmental model influenced by the work of Perry is proposed by King and Kitchener (1994). Their reflective judgement model is based upon Dewey's educational goal of developing reflective thinking. Like Dewey, they suggest that reflective thinking is initiated with the awareness of a problem and an uncertainty about the solution. Reflective thinking includes knowledge and reasoning skill as well as an assumption of knowledge (epistemic) uncertainty. Reflective judgements are derived from the reflective thinking process. King and Kitchener (1994) state:

> Reflective judgements are based on the evaluation and integration of existing data and theory into a solution about the problem at hand, a solution that can be rationally defended as most plausible or reasonable, taking into account the sets of conditions under which the problem is being solved. (p. 8)

The reflective judgement model describes a developmental process concerning individuals' assumptions about what constitutes knowledge and how they evaluate, explain and defend their beliefs on controversial issues and ill-structured problems. Each stage in the seven stage model "includes assumptions about what can be known and how certain one can be about knowing; it also includes assumptions about the role of evidence, authority, and interpretation in the formation of solutions to problems" (Kitchener & King, 1990, pp. 160–161). The developmental progression moves from knowledge certainty in the early stages; to recognizing elements of uncertainty in the middle stages; and finally, to the belief that knowledge is contextual and actively constructed.

The first stage, usually found in young children, is characterized by the assumption that knowledge is absolute and does not need to be justified. Stage two reflects an ultimate truth that is held by authority figures (this is similar to Perry's dualism). The third stage recognizes that truth may be inaccessible (evidence is incomplete) but truth and certainty do exist. This is typical of first year college students. In stage four the uncertainty of knowing is acknowledged and ill-structured problems are afforded legitimacy. During the fifth stage individuals believe knowledge is contextual and is dependent upon interpretation (typical of graduate students). The sixth stage goes beyond contextual relativism where individuals argue that evaluation may compare evidence and opinion across contexts which provides a basis for making judgements (advanced graduate students). Stage seven represents a belief that knowledge can be constructed through critical inquiry and "can be evaluated as having greater 'truth value' or being more 'warranted' than others" (Kitchener & King, 1990, p. 165). In addition, their data reveal that the majority of college students do not go beyond stage four before age 24. Finally, the authors believe that appropriate educational experiences (that is challenging assumptions) will promote reflective thinking growth.

While developmental theories do not exclude environmental influences, they tend to focus on cognitive changes. That is, these theories may not explicitly describe socio-cultural influences but they do recognize that cognitive development is dependent upon adequate learning experiences. It is also important to emphasize that at the higher cognitive levels are a contextual relativism and a concomitant responsibility for learners to construct meaning for themselves. The challenge seems to be to understand the influence of the socio-cultural environment on cognitive development.

Before leaving the discussion of cognitive development it should be noted that, while there is evidence of developmental stages, there is little to suggest that the stages are immutable or rigidly hierarchical. Individuals may move to advanced stages in one context, or content area, and then revert to earlier stages in another. In addition, it is not clear whether these stages are a result of environmental or biological influences. It is likely that a combination of maturational and contextual factors influence progression through the stages. In this regard, it would be expected that an appropriate and stimulating educational environment would significantly influence the cognitive development of the students.

Socially shared cognition. Current cognitive learning theory has begun to take a more fully integrative and systemic view of the learner in a sociocultural context. Previously described theories acknowledged environmental influences but continued to describe learning largely from a cognitive perspective. An integrative perspective views knowledge more systemically as a reconstruction of experience. Cognition is integral to social processes and social processes are integral to cognition. The cognitive and the sociocultural dynamics are beginning to be perceived as one. Cognition cannot be accounted for solely by logic, reasoning, and information processing independent of context. The individual's experience and interpretation of the specific contingencies of the situation will determine how meaning is constructed. Resnick (1989) outlines three interrelated aspects of current cognitive learning theory:

> First, learning is a process of knowledge construction, not of knowledge recording or absorption. Second, learning is knowledge-dependent; people use current knowledge to construct new knowledge. Third, learning is highly tuned to the situation in which it takes place. (p. 1)

The first aspect of current cognitive learning theory emphasizes that information is not simply imprinted but is interpreted. Students are not just assimilators of discrete blocks of information but builders of knowledge structures. The second aspect of recognizing and building upon current knowledge has profound implications for education. Resnick (1989) cites evidence that thinking and learning are very much dependent upon knowledge schemata. Resnick and Klopfer (1989) suggest that modern cognitive theory has a central place for knowledge. They state:

> A fundamental principle of cognition, then, is that learning requires knowledge, Yet, cognitive research also shows that knowledge cannot be given directly to students. Before knowledge becomes truly generative — knowledge that can be used to interpret new situations, to solve problems, to think and reason, and to learn — students must elaborate and question what they are told, examine the new information in relation to other information, and build new knowledge structures. (p. 5)

Resnick and Klopfer go on to explain that subject-matter content and thinking-skill processes must be joined early in education if depth in either is possible.

The third aspect of current cognitive learning theory emphasizes that learning is socially situated. Again, Resnick (1987) cites evidence to suggest that the most successful programs teaching higher-order cognitive skills are co-operatively based. While there are several reasons for this, including occasions for modelling, Resnick and Klopfer (1989) suggest that "most important of all, the social setting may let students know that all the elements of critical thought — interpretation, questioning, trying possibilities, demanding rational justifications — are socially valued"

(p. 9). Therefore, modern cognitive learning theory argues strongly for discourse in the construction of knowledge.

A conversational and self-organized learning theory is provided by Thomas and Harri-Augstein (1985). They suggest that learning must be personally significant and meaning incorporated into personal experience if it is to be useful and increase the capacity for future learning (learn how to learn). This view is based upon the assumption that no one can know themselves or reach their potential unaided. Conversation is a creative encounter where the outcome can not be predicted entirely. Participants in conversation "harmonise or synchronise so that the passing of control back and forth between them achieves an enterprise that neither could have created separately" (Thomas & Harri-Augstein, 1985, p. 92). Control is also manifested in terms of negotiating needs and self-assessment of meaning. The authors state that "self-assessment is the vehicle of all self-organisation and control" (p. 193). It will be seen subsequently that assessment has a very powerful effect on a student's approach to learning.

It is the position of Thomas and Harri-Augstein (1985) "that the process of learning is necessarily conversational" (p. 237). The five levels of conversation identified are designated factual or ritualistic, instructional or informational, explanatory, constructional, and creative. The first three levels by themselves can only lead to impersonal and alienated learning. For learning to be personally significant (personal learning) individuals must incorporate it into their understanding by reflecting upon their experience. Constructive and creative conversational/content levels represent personal and self-organized learning and "are the construction, reconstruction and negotiation and exchange of personally relevant and viable meaning" (p. 262). The constructive level operates within existing content frameworks and effects the quantity of personal learning. The creative level of conversation engenders a change in assumptions and has an impact on the quality of personal learning.

In a teaching-learning conversation the way of sharing meaning is through understanding. Thomas and Harri-Augstein (1985) define understanding as not being the same as agreement, "but it does imply that one person can enter into the personal meaning system of another" (p. 245). This suggests that meaning is a personal reconstruction while understanding is an appreciation of another's perspective. Understanding can be extended to the group where areas of agreement and disagreement can be identified and through negotiation extend and validate shared meaning. If teaching/learning is to be concerned with understanding, then it must always be a conversational process where all participants possess control. As Thomas and Harri-Augstein (1985) state:

> … Only by accepting and recognising that teaching/learning is a conversational process can personal meanings of teachers and learners be mapped one on to the other. First the experiential and behavioral evidence of learning must be pooled and then the purposes of the learner and the purposes of the teacher must be clarified, shared and negotiated. (p. 309)

Bereiter (1992) states that "the teaching of high-level concepts inevitably involves a considerable amount of discourse" (p. 352). While declarative or content knowledge is necessary for discourse, it must go beyond this if teaching is to facilitate the development of high-level concepts. Classroom discourse must focus upon problems of explanation and understanding. Bereiter (1992) believes that classroom discussion should be aimed at solving problems of explanation. The position here is that explanation caries the individual beyond personal meaning and isolation. It is the educational context and the teacher's responsibility to encourage and facilitate expression and interaction so that learning moves from meaning to understanding and knowledge creation. Conversation or discourse is seen to be essential to a meaningful and worthwhile educational experience and is integral to the teaching-learning model described in Chapter 5.

Spiro et al. (1988) provide a theoretical framework for a "new constructivist" perspective of advanced knowledge acquisition emphasizing context when constructing meaning in ill-structured subject domains. They argue that "the aims and means of advanced knowledge acquisition are different from those of introductory learning" (p. 375). Introductory learning is characterized by content exposure for purposes of recognition and recall while advanced knowledge acquisition necessitates a deeper understanding and application to diverse contexts. In reacting to reductive tendencies and oversimplification of conceptual development, Spiro et al. (1988) suggest several themes to master complexity and knowledge transferability. The authors conclude:

> Central to the cultivation of cognitive flexibility are approaches to learning, instruction, and knowledge representation that: (a) allow an important role for multiple representations; (b) view learning as the multidirectional and multiperspectival 'criss-crossing' of cases and concepts that make up complex domains' 'landscapes' (with resulting interconnectedness along multiple dimensions); and (c) foster the ability to assemble diverse knowledge sources to adaptively fit the needs of a particular knowledge application situation (rather than the search for a precompiled schema that fits the situation). (p. 383)

Deep and surface cognition. Another area of research that has significantly influenced thinking about learning in higher education is associated with the quality of learning outcomes and approaches to learning that shape such outcomes. The early movers of this research were Marton (Marton & Saljo, 1976), Entwistle (Entwistle & Ramsden, 1983), and Biggs (1987) along with their respective colleagues. We shall focus first on Marton and his Gothenburg University group. Marton (1992) explored human understanding of phenomena and the student's learning experience. He suggests that understanding represents an experiential relationship among individuals and phenomena; further, changes in "understanding constitute the most important form of human learning" (p. 253). Understanding involves the abstraction of meaning and is contrasted with rote learning. This concern for understanding evolved from Perry's work that reflects developmental approaches to learning which culminate in construction of meaning (Saljo, 1979). Saljo (1979) states that the "background of this interest is that the level of processing that a person adopts in relation to a learning material can be thought of as having a close relationship to his conception of learning" (p. 7).

In a seminal study of different levels of information processing (reading and understanding academic articles) with Swedish university students, Marton and Saljo (1976) examined processes and strategies of learning and qualitative differences in outcome. A basic assumption of this research is that to understand learning, particularly in an educational context, "a description of what the students learn is preferable to the description of how much they learn" (Marton & Saljo, 1976, p. 4). The results revealed two clearly distinguishable levels of information processing which were labelled deep and surface.

In surface level processing the student has a reproductive and unreflective conception of learning and, as such, is directed to a rote learning strategy. On the other hand, deep level processing is directed toward comprehension of the intentional content or the significance/meaning of the material. With deep level processing there is an intention to organize content by relating new and previous knowledge as well as relating evidence and argument (Ramsden, 1988a). By taking a deep level approach there is a better chance of both understanding and recalling specific information. Recognizing different levels or quality of cognitive outcomes has important implications for approaches to learning and how educators might influence these approaches.

The next phase of the research was to explore the relationship between the learner's conception of the learning task and the quality of the outcome. In reviewing the literature, Marton and Saljo (1976) concluded that learning is affected by the type of test anticipated. Students interpret and anticipate intended requirements and narrow the task accordingly. Their study attempted to induce alternative levels of processing and outcome through the nature of questioning. They found that the demand characteristics had considerable effect on the level of processing. That is, learning depends upon the type of evaluation anticipated. Marton and Saljo (1976) state that while "many students are apparently capable of using 'deep' or 'surface' strategies, it may be that the current demands of the examination system at school level are interpreted by them as requiring mainly the recall of factual information to the detriment of a deeper level of understanding" (p. 125).

The purpose of the research program of Entwistle and his colleagues (Entwistle & Ramsden, 1983) at the University of Lancaster was to extend the work of Marton. They used both qualitative and quantitative research approaches to obtain "firmer" evidence of the existence of approaches to learning and their stability in students. Their qualitative research results "confirmed the remarkable explanatory power of the qualitative methods" (p. 177) of the Gothenburg investigations and "confirmed the importance of the fundamental difference between deep and surface approaches" (p. 194). Using quantitative methodology, an approaches to studying inventory was developed and administered to 2208 undergraduate students in the disciplines of art, social science, applied science, and pure science. Extensive analyses "confirmed the importance of the meaning [deep] and reproducing [surface] orientations in all the academic disciplines" (p. 193).

In addition, it is suggested that the learner's intention or motivation in the deep approach is internal, while in the surface approach it is external in the sense of satisfying external demands. Finally, it is argued that specific aspects of a learning environment also affect approaches to learning and quality of outcome (Entwistle, 1991). Contextual effects were perceived interest and relevance, teacher attitude and enthusiasm, and forms of assessment.

Biggs (1987) operationalizes approaches to learning as a composite of deep, surface and achieving process factors. Each of these approaches is composed of students' motives and strategies for learning. Corresponding motives are to gain understanding (intrinsic interest), meet minimal requirements (instrumental interest), obtain highest grades (ego interest). Corresponding strategies are to read widely and integrate new information (meaning), focus on bare essentials and memorize (rote learning), and schedule time and follow-up on all suggested readings. Approaches to learning reflect a complex relationship between personal and situational factors that lead to differing approaches to learning and the quality of the learning outcome.

It should be noted that Biggs (1987) begins with the person and places considerable emphasis on the "fairly consistent orientations" displayed by students; but he does state that, within limitations students will "deliberately choose those approaches to learning that are most likely to bring about the sort of outcome that is desired" (p. 75). Therefore, situation constraints still have the potential to influence learning approaches and outcomes. Related to the issue of styles versus approaches/orientations, Schmeck (1988) states that the "teacher has little control over the student's style but has a lot of control over the situation, and by structuring the situation, the teacher can influence the student's perceptions and thus their motives and approaches to learning" (pp. 344–345).

Some researchers have addressed approaches to learning primarily from a situation and outcome perspective. Ramsden's (1988b) special concern is with the educational environment. He identifies three related contextual domains influencing students' approaches to learning in higher education. They are teaching or method of transmission, assessment, and the curriculum or content of what is learned. Furthermore, "context influences student learning indirectly through students' perceptions of the requirements of learning tasks. Perceptions of tasks describe a relation between the student's experience and the three domains" (Ramsden, 1988b, p. 160). While there is a clear recognition of student entering characteristics, these are seen as indirect. As such, the immediate situation is of primary importance in influencing the approach to learning.

Ramsden (1988b) argues that the educational import of his model "is that in so far as contextual variables are in the control of instructors, it is possible to structure the environment of learning in such a way that adaptive responses are congruent with instructors' aims" (p. 161). The evidence would appear to strongly support the contention that educators, through their efforts in structuring the learning environment and setting learning outcomes, can have significant effects on the quality of learning.

Educators must consider how approaches to learning influence the nature and quality of the outcomes. Conversely, deciding on intended outcomes should shape the process or approach students take to learning. Marton (1988) states that "what is learned (the outcome or the result) and how it is learned (the act or the process) are two inseparable aspects of learning" (p. 53). Process and outcome are of a relational character and together they represent what a learning event is for the learner. Educators need to recognize this relationship and be sure intentions are congruent with learning tasks and activities. If we think of learning as a change of understanding or qualitative change in conceptions, "there is very little learning taking place in the educational system" (Marton, 1988, p. 73). Unfortunately, "students may acquire huge bodies of knowledge (cluster of facts) without appropriating the conceptualizations on which those bodies of knowledge are based" (Marton, 1988, pp. 74–75).

The issue of fragmented facts and coherent frameworks goes to the core of this book. Meaningful learning is concerned with assimilating and accommodating ideas and broad conceptualizations, which provide the means to order facts and information. The crucial point from an educator's perspective is that meaningful learning largely proceeds from the whole to the parts. This is explained by Marton and Booth (1997; cited in Entwistle, 1998).

> In our view, learning proceeds, as a rule, from an undifferentiated and poorly integrated understanding of the whole to an increased differentiation and integration of the whole and its parts. Thus, learning does not proceed as much from parts to wholes, as from whole to parts, and from wholes to wholes. (p. 95)

If educators would understand this and start with an organizing framework, students would not only learn better and faster but with considerably less anxiety.

Teachers must accept that their judgements and decisions do make a difference in how students approach learning and the type of outcomes achieved. It is also true that teachers in adult and higher education must consciously decide what are the desired and worthwhile learning outcomes that they wish to facilitate. If the role of education is to encourage deep and meaningful learning, as many would argue, then educational processes and outcomes must be commensurate with these aims. That would mean balancing assessment for understanding and recall, providing appropriate choice of content and method, assigning an appropriate workload, negotiating relevant and clear goals, and adopting teaching methods that balance interactive and presentational approaches.

It has been argued that quality of learning defined in terms of deep or meaningful learning is dependent upon the student's approach (orientation) to the learning task. In turn, educators influence this approach to learning through their expectations, activities and particularly their assessment procedures. Entering college students do not generally know how to approach learning in a meaningful manner. The problem is that they do not have the study skills and the students themselves feel this is the area of greatest need (Chipman & Segal, 1985). Chipman and Segal (1985) suggest that there is good reason to improve students as learners since even "good students have a limited repertoire of such skills" (p. 2). They go on to state that while development of higher cognitive skills has always been a very important goal for educators "explicit instruction in these skills is rare and that students' mastery of them is frequently inadequate" (p. 5).

The debatable issue is whether this is best done within the context of specific courses or as a separate area of study. The position here is that study skills and metacognitive strategies should be taught within the context of specific courses. This issue will be discussed more fully in the context of facilitating critical thinking in the next chapter.

Learning Style

At this point, it is important to distinguish approaches to learning from learning style. The paradigm of approaches to learning emphasizes the relationship among intention, process and outcome. Schmeck (1988a) suggests that an approach to a learning task "is the result of a relation between person and environment, neither of which is observable without the other" (p. 10). On the other hand, learning or cognitive style refers only to the person. It is defined as "the stable, traitlike consistency in one's approach to attending, perceiving, and thinking" (Schmeck, 1988a, p. 8). Parenthetically, Schmeck (1988b) argues that "all cognitive styles can be encompassed by one broad, inclusive dimension of individual difference, labelled 'global versus analytic'" (p. 327). However, what is required for a deep or meaningful approach to learning is an absence of a rigid style; or the development of a versatile style (Pask, 1988). For example, students should be able to think globally and analytically. Reliance on one or the other will not be conducive to a deep approach necessary to achieve understanding.

There is considerable confusion regarding what is meant by learning style. Learning style is often confused with learning strategy or orientation. Confusion surrounds whether it is an expressed preference or a habitual behaviour (Curry, 1990). In addition to the lack of clarity surrounding terminology, there is considerable diversity and little commonality with regard to learning style constructs and instruments. Numerous constructs exist and instruments purport to measure student's preferences for being taught, cognitive processing tendencies, and personality descriptors. Not surprisingly, validity issues are also a prevalent concern. In a recent review of learning style instruments, Curry (1990) concludes that "many important claims about the nature of learning styles, the validity of diagnostic instruments and the effects of their use to improve instruction have not been systematically evaluated in practice" (p. 17).

Learning and cognitive style concepts have been popular in educational psychology. Cognitive style constructs focus on individual differences and "assume that individuals can be described by certain psychological characteristics, traits, or styles that influence the way they perceive, organize, and react to different environmental stimuli" (Pintrich, 1990, p. 828). However, a distinction must be made between learning styles which are relatively stable personality traits and learning strategies (approaches) as discussed in the previous section. Pintrich (1990) notes that the traditional personality approach to cognitive styles has been justly criticized on a variety of grounds. Cognitive styles are applied across situations in a consistent and unreflective manner. Cognitive strategies, on the other hand, stress information processing styles and are "assumed to be a function of student choice and control, as well as of the nature of task demands" (Pintrich, 1990, p. 829).

The belief in learning styles is based partly upon the premise of learner centredness and student control over learning methods. In other words, if methods are adapted to individual learning style this will lead to engagement in learning and increased motivation. The implicit assumption is that educational methods should be adjusted to meet learning styles. The difficulty here is that outcome is contingent upon process and, conversely, process determines the quality of the outcome (Ramsden, 1992). Learning styles do not always match curriculum demands. To go to the core of the matter the question is whether teachers should attempt to adjust the curriculum to meet each student's learning style or assist students to adapt their learning strategies to the demands of the curriculum. In practice, effective teaching does a little of each, but the ultimate goal is to expand student strategies and approaches to learning; not limit them by allowing students to learn only in the way that matches their preferred learning style and interests. Such an unreflective approach does little to develop metacognitive strategies or efficiently address the specific demands of subject content.

Learning styles represent a relatively consistent personal preference or predisposition to information processing and learning. The student, however, is not well served if they do not acquire an understanding of the subject content or have not acquired the cognitive strategies required of the subject content. The integrity of the educational process and the demands of the curriculum must not be sacrificed in the name of individualization. It is the responsibility of the teacher to help the student recognize the limitation of their preferred learning style and expand their cognitive strategies in order to be successful in a variety of learning settings. In other words, the goal is to learn how to learn through awareness and adoption of a variety of cognitive strategies. The student's learning style may not be appropriate for the particular curriculum goals. This may well necessitate the adoption of a learning strategy or approach not preferred by the student, but will be far more meaningful and educationally worthwhile.

A danger of focusing on learning styles is to rely on one strategy which may be fine for acquiring information in a stable environment; but what about complex environments that necessitate judgement and decisions? Plans give way to strategies in action as a result of unanticipated conditions. Adoption of one strategy, regardless of content, is not congruent with intelligent reactions to complex situations. Intelligent action does not always follow prescribed or fixed sequences; therefore, various learning strategies will be required. It is argued that intellectual development results from responding to complex environments that require assessment, judgement, decisions and strategies that are capable of addressing new contingencies.

With regard to learning style, Dixon (1985) states that "Preference does not imply that these ways are the only or perhaps even the best ways for the individual to learn a given subject matter" (p. 16). The teacher's responsibility is not necessarily to accommodate to individual student learning style but to recognize them as a possible starting point and only a preferred method of learning. The best use of learning style information by the teacher is to provide insight to students regarding their learning preferences. That is, students should become aware of their preferred learning style, but for the purpose of acquiring new and appropriate strategies. Even here, a better instrument would be to use an approach to learning questionnaire (Biggs, 1987) which considers both personal and situation influences.

Increased control and responsibility for learning is dependent upon increased metacognitive awareness and ability. However, metacognitive awareness and ability (know how to learn) comes about by monitoring student comprehension and understanding. Educators must attend to curriculum needs and outcomes to achieve quality learning and develop successful learning strategies. Understanding thinking problems are contextually based and entering learning styles are not likely to assist this process — even if valid and appropriate measures were available. Acceding to preferred learning styles accomplishes little in the long term.

To depend upon one style of information processing is naïve and dangerous. Such an approach does not consider content nor worthwhile outcomes. Despite the intuitive appeal and the enthusiasm for addressing learning styles, the educational implications remain unclear and the promise unrealized (Currey, 1990; Joughin, 1992). There is no evidence that relying on preferred learning style promotes the development of worthwhile and meaningful learning — which is the central issue. From an educational perspective it is the development of worthwhile and meaningful learning that is the goal. Learning style, at best, is a starting point for increased metacognitive awareness and the encouragement of students to assume greater responsibility for constructing meaningful knowledge structures. At worst, acquiescence to student's learning style will not provide the checks and balances of responsible teaching and the confirmation of acquiring meaningful and worthwhile knowledge.

Conclusion

A distinction was made in the previous discussions between reproductive (surface) and meaningful (deep) learning. In isolation, there are questions as to the educational viability and quality of reproductive forms of learning. These unexamined and nonreflective learning experiences are limited in encouraging transformative and continuous learning. When reproductive learning is not part of the process of constructing meaningful concepts, then, at best, it is largely forgotten and, at worst, it is ideological. Reproductive learning, by itself, narrows the focus of vision and excludes everything except that which is immediately relevant to a particular task. What is learned is not likely to be relevant or meaningful and when individual interests are removed from the classroom, the chances are that the information will be quickly forgotten. To avoid such outcomes, educators must provide organizing concepts and opportunities for students to assimilate and accommodate new information with existing knowledge structures and, thereby, (re)construct new knowledge.

Educating for meaning must be seen as a comprehensive experience. That is, a theoretical framework of learning must be adopted or developed that encompasses the cognitive processes of constructing meaning as well as the sociological process of sharing and negotiating meaning for the purposes of justification. Recognizing the socio-cultural context in justifying knowledge also assists the individual in constructing knowledge in the first place. As Resnick (1991) states with regard to thinking and social functioning, we "seem to be in the midst of multiple efforts to merge the social and cognitive, treating them as essential aspects of one another rather than as dimly sketched background or context for a dominantly cognitive or dominantly social science" (p. 3).

The approach to learning defended here is consistent with Dewey's (1916) rejection of the psychological and sociological dichotomy and his view that education is a "continuous reconstruction of experience" (p. 80). That is, the educator must recognize previous experience and knowledge and then facilitate their reconstruction through the integration of continuously changing subjective and objective realities. It is a much more complex view of learning than the individual, cognitive centred perspective or the collective, social centred view. While this perspective is far more challenging, the understanding of the teaching-learning transaction it provides is richer, it better reflects the challenges of the educational process, and identifies higher quality learning outcomes. In this collaborative constructivist approach, perspectives on learning in education account for a process of critical reflection as well as a need for social discourse and self-direction in constructing personal meaning and consensual knowledge. It is also clear as to what counts as knowledge — that is, how knowledge originates and how it is sanctioned.

Given the complexity of the educational transaction, no single theory of learning can fully inform the teaching-learning process. A theory is generally thought of as a predictive system with particular assumptions, concepts and explanatory capabilities. It may be more useful for educational purposes to construct a framework of learning. A framework is "a general pool of constructs for understanding a domain, but it is not tightly enough organized to constitute a predictive theory" (Anderson, 1983, p. 12). A framework of learning must be systematic, coherent and comprehensive development of thought; but it does not have to be fully absent of internal inconsistencies and contradictions. A theoretical framework that is highly consistent and predictive gives a false sense of certainty and denies the complex reality of the educational process. Even if it were desirable, in education it is impossible to control all the variables in order to predict higher-order learning outcomes with certainty.

Buchmann and Floden (1992) state that concepts central to teaching and learning "have multiple aspects no single perspective can contain" (p. 9). They advise educators to distinguish coherence from consistency. Learning is about constructing coherence while consistency leads to singleness of conception, narrowness and rigidity. On the other hand, they suggest that learning theories, though not coincident, do have points of contact. A framework of learning must be based upon a balance of form and flexibility; it must be coherent but is never comprehensive or complete. Coherence suggests an intelligent pragmatism where different and sometimes apparently contradictory perspectives are adopted with awareness and reason. Learning theories should not be chosen at random or for convenience. Neither should we expect a working framework be so paradigmatically pure as to be inflexible and, therefore, practically of little value.

Adult and higher education must ensure the continued cognitive development of its students. Modern socially-situated cognitive learning theories provide the most realistic and promising framework to guide the facilitation of meaningful learning in an adult and higher education context. Worthwhile and meaningful learning builds upon facts and information through the critical thinking process. Modern cognitive learning theory provides a perspective that is thinking and meaning centred, but insists on a central place for socially valued knowledge and instruction (Resnick & Klopfer, 1989). Thinking is the process by which meaning and knowledge is constructed. This process must start with existing knowledge but, through a recursive process of critical reflection and discourse, personal meaning and worthwhile knowledge is constructed. It is this process (i.e. critical thinking) to which we now turn our attention.

4

Critical Thinking

Interest in critical thinking goes back to at least the time of Socrates. The essential elements of critical thinking can, in fact, be derived from Socrates (Furedy & Furedy, 1985, p. 52). These essential elements consist of a method of questioning and initiating dialogue for the purpose of rationally examining the basis of knowledge. This method eventually evolved — and narrowed — into what we now refer to as the method of scientific inquiry. This, in turn, was re-generalized by Dewey into what we now call reflective (i.e. critical) thinking. This rich heritage is reflected in our educational system to the extent that critical thinking and critical discourse have come to be regarded as the hallmarks of higher education.

Critical Thinking and Education

It was early in the twentieth century that Dewey laid the foundation for the modern critical thinking movement in education. However, interest in this movement waned as behaviouristic learning theories began to dominate. Even with the growing acceptance of cognitive approaches to learning in the 1960s, and notwithstanding the rhetoric describing higher-order thinking as an educational goal, the actual facilitation of critical thinking in educational settings has only recently gained momentum. Halpern (1984) notes that "Despite what may seem to many to be an obvious need in higher education, it is only in recent years that educators have been concerned with designing educational programs to improve thinking and decision making" (p. 2). Although much still needs to be done to understand and facilitate the development of critical thinking, at least almost everyone now agrees that it is an important if not a central aim of higher education.

Dewey (1933) uses the term reflective thinking in a manner consistent with what we now term critical thinking. He examines the values of reflective thinking and discusses why reflective thinking must be an educational aim. In essence, Dewey argues that reflective thinking gives increased control and enriches meaning. For Dewey, control is of practical value because it allows us to consciously plan and ward off the unfavourable, or modify natural things to better serve our needs. Reflective thinking deepens the meaning of our experiences, leading to "continual growth of meaning in human life" (Dewey, 1933, p. 21). While the cumulative effect of these values leads to a truly human and rational life, for "anything approaching their adequate realization, thought needs careful and attentive educational direction" (Dewey, 1933, p. 22).

From a societal perspective, education is not only concerned with documenting and maintaining knowledge (one of Dewey's values) but also with generating knowledge. As a consequence, education is necessary for developing an under-standing and appreciation of the value and importance of existing knowledge while ensuring the continuous development of society through the generation of new knowledge. Critical thinking is required for both concerns; knowledge is acquired as well as generated through critical thinking. Therefore, there is an intimate and important connection between critical thinking and education. McPeck (1981) argues that not only would it "be a good thing if our educational institutions could get students to be critical thinkers, but also that, in so far as the purpose of schools is to educate, this task logically cannot be accomplished without critical thinking" (p. 34). In other words, critical thinking is the means to meaningful and worthwhile learning.

Siegel (1988) also attempts to justify critical thinking as an educational ideal. Before outlining his reasons he states:

> If we accept critical thinking as a fundamental ideal, we ex-plicitly acknowledge the desirability of the attainment by students of self-sufficiency and autonomy. The critical thinker must be autonomous — that is, free to act and judge independently of external constraint, on the basis of her [or his] own reasoned appraisal of the matter at hand. (p. 54)

Siegel then describes respect for persons, self-sufficiency, initiation in rational traditions, and requirements for democratic living as "four putative reasons for regarding critical thinking as a fundamental educational ideal" (p. 61). The focus is clearly on the individual and the necessary respect and responsibility afforded students in order for them to acquire the ability to think critically and function rationally in society.

A reflective paradigm of critical educational practice goes beyond an individual focus. Lipman (1991) argues that education "should primarily aim at the produc-tion of persons who can reason well, have good judgement, and are disposed to think in new ways" (p. 92). While the primary objective of the reflective paradigm is the intellectual autonomy of the learners — which is to think for themselves, in "reality, the reflective model is thoroughly social and communal" (Lipman, 1991, p. 19). From an educational perspective, learning outcomes are a result of "participation in a teacher-guided community of inquiry" (Lipman, 1991, p. 14). Accordingly, education is seen here as a complex process where individuals are encouraged to be intellectually autonomous, but understanding is shaped and confirmed through a collaborative learning process. This important juxtaposition of autonomous (private) and communal (shared) worlds will be addressed in the discussion of the critical thinking/learning cycle described later in this chapter.

Critical thinking is integral to the educational enterprise. The fundamental assumption is that meaningful and worthwhile learning is realized through a process of critical thinking where students have the necessary control to assume responsibility for their learning. The challenge is to explore and describe the concept of critical thinking in an educational context.

Critical Thinking Analysed

Just as all learning is not alike, neither is all thinking alike. While there may be some general consensus as to the nature of critical thinking, it is far too complex a topic to conceptualize in a simplistic manner. Not surprisingly, there is no clear agreement as to its precise meaning. According to McPeck (1981), the source of the "confusion stems from approaching the concept as though it were a self-evident slogan whose precise ingredients were considered to be clear and self-justifying" (p. 2). He goes on to say that whatever "critical thinking may be precisely, it is quite clear that it is thinking of some sort" (p. 3). In this regard, McPeck distinguishes between voluntary (directed) and involuntary (just happens) thinking. It is, of course, voluntary, purposeful thinking that is of interest here.

The fact that thinking is a complex internal process is what makes it so difficult to understand. However, for our purposes two issues need to be highlighted. The first is that thinking is considered a "purposeful mental activity over which we exercise some control" (Ruggiero, 1984, p. 2). That is, thinking must be directed. Moreover, it is possible and necessary to take control of our thoughts in critical thinking. Ultimately, each individual is responsible for constructing personal meaning. Secondly, since thinking is purposeful it is goal directed, that is, there is a search for the resolution of a dilemma or a solution to a problem. Thinking may be a separation from the external world but it begins and ends with the external world. Gordon (1988) reflects this in the following description of thinking:

> When one thinks as a thinker, the person detaches herself or himself from the world of appearances, enters the realm of inner dialogue, ideas, or pure concepts, as various philosophers have called this realm, and hopes to return to the world of appearances with a broader understanding and a more perceptive vision. (p. 52)

Dewey (1933) also considers the relationship of the external and internal world. He defines thinking as "that operation in which present facts suggest other facts (or truths) in such a way as to induce belief in what is suggested on the ground of real relation in the things themselves" (p. 12). Dewey believes that the purpose of thinking is to make connections based upon objective experience in order to induce broader truths. Thinking can thus be seen as a purposeful detachment from the external world to freely search for connecting facts, explore ideas, and contemplate values; however, the relevance and credibility of the meaning derived must be grounded in experience.

In Dewey's (1967) terms, thinking is associated with imagination and is defined "as knowledge of universal elements; that is, of ideas as such, or relations" (p. 177).

Conceptualizing these relations gives meaning to perception and experience. Dewey (1967) states that "perception grows through the medium of conception; conception grows through its synthetic reference to perceptions" (p. 184). It is through the reciprocal relationship between the perception of particular facts and the conceptualization of general ideas that meaning exists for the individual. It is erroneous to assume "that thought has a nature of its own independent of facts or subject-matter…" (Dewey, 1969b). Conception and fact are but two ways of looking at the same thing (Dewey, 1967). Constructing meaning is both a universalizing and particularizing activity. The breadth of meaning is enhanced through the integration of ideas while depth grows through the synthesis of more facts consistent with the concept. Ideas and facts are mutually constitutive, in that, ideas illuminate facts, and facts shape ideas (Prawat, 1998).

Next, we turn to what the adjective "critical" adds to the concept of thinking. At the outset it should be stated that it does not necessarily represent a negative kind of thinking. At the core of critical thinking is making a decision and having to choose between options based upon reason (Mezirow, 1998). Notwithstanding the need for scepticism and critical examination, critical thinking is a constructive and holistic conception. Dewey (1933) suggests that if an individual were not critical then thinking would not be reflective. The implication is that without a state of doubt or scepticism there would be no need to inquire further into the situation and reflect upon the problem.

The critical element is reflected in a sense of open questioning, but it is not perceived to be pernicious. Peters (1972) states that the individual who is accustomed to reason "is one who has taken a critic into his own consciousness, … is prepared to discuss things, [and] to look at a situation impartially" (p. 212). It would appear that the development of criticism is an essential aspect of reason. Furthermore, Peters suggests that reason transcends the particular, is opposed to arbitrariness, and accounts for the facts. Thus, reason must play an essential role in critical thinking and is the means for expressing doubt and critiquing ideas.

Knowledge is the result of thinking but not just any kind of thinking. Paul (1990) emphasizes that "Knowledge exists, properly speaking, only in minds that have comprehended and justified it through thought. And when we say think we mean think critically" (p. 46). The adjective "critical" clearly qualifies thinking in an important way. While we have distinguished between directed (purposeful) and non-directed thinking, Paul (1990) goes further in distinguishing between strong and weak sense critical thinking. Paul (1990) defines critical thinking as:

> …disciplined, self-directed thinking which exemplifies the perfec-
> tions of thinking appropriate to a particular mode or domain
> of thinking. It comes in two forms. If disciplined to serve the
> interests of a particular group, to the exclusion of other relevant
> persons and groups, it is sophistic or weak sense critical thinking.
> If disciplined to take into account the interests of diverse persons
> or groups, it is fairminded or strong sense critical thinking.
> (p. 51)

At the outset, it is important to emphasize in this definition that all critical thinking reflects an intellectual autonomy noted earlier. However, in addition to being disciplined and responsible, weak sense critical thinking is egocentric and motivated by vested interests. It violates the standards of "fair-minded truth" and objective reason. Weak sense critical thinking is dominant in the everyday world where individuals are striving for success, power, and advantage.

Strong sense critical thinking exhibits traits of mind such as humility, courage, perseverance, integrity and faith in reason. According to Paul, these traits are applicable to all domains of knowledge. At the same time, learning to think in particular disciplines is shaped "by standards inseparable from values presupposed in each discipline. Every discipline is to some extent unique, but also overlaps with other disciplines" (Paul, 1990, p. 50). While Paul appears to be arguing for critical thinking as constituting both general and epistemologically specific skills, he states emphatically that the goal and model of critical thinking is the "disciplined generalist". That is, students should be encouraged to cut across disciplines and develop general critical thinking skills, thus avoiding "atomistic" and weak sense critical thinking. This is a very important issue in terms of how educators might foster critical thinking and, therefore, will be addressed more fully in a subsequent section.

Similarly, Siegel's (1988) conception of critical thinking reflects both general and specific skills. Siegel suggests that a critical thinker is appropriately moved by reasons and possesses a critical attitude or spirit. The central component is the reasons conception which states that "a critical thinker must be able to assess reasons and their ability to warrant beliefs, claims and actions properly. This means that the critical thinker must have a good understanding of, and ability to utilize, principles governing the assessment of reasons" (Siegel, 1988, p. 34). Siegel goes on to say that such principles are both subject-specific and subject-neutral. Subject-neutral principles are general principles which apply to a variety of contexts and are typically regarded as "logical".

However, it is not sufficient for critical thinkers to simply be able to assess reasons, they must also value good reasoning and be disposed to engage in reason assessment. As Siegel (1988) states:

> One who has the critical attitude has a certain character as well as certain skills: a character which is inclined to seek, and to base judgement and action upon, reasons; which rejects partiality and arbitrariness; which is committed to the objective evaluation of relevant evidence; and which values such aspects of critical thinking as intellectual honesty, justice to evidence, sympathetic and impartial consideration of interests, objectivity, and impartiality. (p. 39)

The critical disposition or attitude represents a host of "rational passions". This conception of critical thinking "is as much a conception of a certain sort of person as it is a conception of a certain set of activities and skills" (Siegel, 1988, p. 41). Dewey (1933) also argues for the integration of attitudes and thinking ability/skills. He states that thinking ability "alone will not suffice; there must be the desire, the will, to employ them" (p. 30). Dewey identifies the attitudes of openness, passion, and responsibility to search for meaning as necessary for reflective thinking.

It has also been suggested that we must have a disposition of caring if we are to be critical thinkers. Thayer-Bacon (1993) proposes a model of critical thinking that stresses constructive thinking that includes caring as an essential element. She states that caring is "being receptive to what another has to say, and open to hearing the other's voice more completely and fairly. Caring about another... requires respecting the other as a separate, autonomous being, worthy of caring" (p. 325).

Collaboration is an essential aspect of critical thinking. Therefore, in a critical/constructive conception of thinking "it is important to encourage collaboration as well as debate; to emphasize connection as well as separation; and to cross the barrier between self and other, bridging private and shared experience" (Thayer-Bacon, 1993, p. 339). Recognition of these reciprocal relationships among caring, collaboration and critical thinking is essential to the development of a critical community of learners.

McPeck (1990a) refers to critical thinking as "a certain combination of what we might think of as a willingness, or disposition (call it an 'attitude', if you like), together with the appropriate knowledge and skills, to engage in an activity or problem with reflective scepticism" (p. 42). Reflective scepticism is not pernicious but a healthy questioning which comes into play when we suspect something is amiss. While both Siegel and McPeck suggest that there must be both an ability and willingness to be a critical thinker, this is where the similarity ends.

Much debate in critical thinking circles was precipitated by McPeck (1981) when he argued for an epistemological approach to critical thinking. Contrary to Paul and Seigel, McPeck (1981) categorically states that "there is no universal skill nor curriculum subject that is properly called critical thinking" (p. 18). In this respect, he appears to take a non-dualist perspective that does not separate process and content nor thought and fact. Critical thinking as a process is not an end in and of itself separate from content. Facilitating critical thinking is neither learner centred nor content centred.

McPeck (1990a) does not believe there is a set of supervening skills (generalized reasoning skills) and, therefore, critical thinking is primarily domain-specific and context-dependent. He states, "I wish to redirect attention away from generic processes of reasoning, be these logical skills or general strategies, and to have you consider the proposition that the content of various subjects and/or problems determines (i.e. creates) the appropriate process of reasoning, and not vice versa" (McPeck, 1990a, p. 35). Learning how to think is dependent upon considering what to think. As McPeck repeatedly emphasizes, thinking has to be about something. Thus, critical thinking is largely a matter of knowledge and should be taught as an integral process in acquiring curriculum content. In other words, the educational implication of this epistemological approach to critical thinking is that it '"cannot be profitably taught' in isolation from specific subjects because 'critical thinking is not a general skill'" (McPeck, 1990a, p. 95).

The educational implications of this perspective for fostering critical thinking are enormous. In short, critical thinking differs according to subject and is dependent upon an understanding of that subject; that is, "it requires knowledge of the epistemic foundations of the field" (McPeck, 1981, 155). Knowledge itself is dependent upon good reasons and not unreflected obedience to authority. Conversely, reasoning and justification is dependent upon an understanding of the specific content and internal logic of the subject. Critical thinking is, therefore, central to knowledge development and challenges reliance on unjustified information. This perspective rejects those programs which attempt to teach critical thinking from a formal or informal logic (philosophical) perspective. It may help students to reason philosophically but there is minimum transfer to other subjects and contexts. Being able to think and talk in the language of various disciplines provides the best possibility for transfer of critical thinking skills. Parenthetically, this perspective has important implications with regard to notions of allowing students to rely on their preferred style of learning. This was discussed in Chapter 3.

There is little disagreement as to the ultimate goals and purposes of critical thinking in education. The question is which is the most direct and efficacious method for facilitating critical thinking. The strongest argument for an epistemic approach to critical thinking is from a practical teaching-learning perspective. McPeck (1990a) suggests that an epistemological approach allows teachers to remain on familiar turf since they do not have to learn new subject matter such as informal logic and other general thinking skills. Notwithstanding the theoretical arguments, it would seem that a disciplinary approach would be more direct and efficacious. The teaching of thinking should occur concurrently with the teaching of content.

That is not to say, however, that there is no place for general thinking skills courses or that attitudes or dispositions are not generalizable. The argument here is that a disciplinary based approach offers greater transfer to other domains and from an educational perspective is more practical and efficacious. Curriculum does not have to be redesigned or constructed. Although informal and formal logic courses are not unhelpful in developing general canons for thought and intellectual virtues, there is a danger that educators will rely on these courses to address the pressing need to develop critical thinkers. Teachers of all subjects must assume the responsibility to facilitate critical thinking in a sustained manner. The fundamental argument is that through the study of a variety of disciplines and specific content, critical thinking can best address subject relevant problems.

Part of the vagueness and confusion surrounding critical thinking is understanding its relationship to other types of thinking such as problem solving and creative thinking. We need to ask ourselves whether critical thinking is similar to problem solving; or whether critical thinking is complementary to creative thinking. The following section explores these relationships.

Problem Solving and Creative Thinking

Critical thinking and problem solving are often seen as being similar due to their emphasis on rational processes. In previous discussions we have seen that critical thinking often is initiated when a problem is perceived. Kurfiss (1988) suggests that "a major difference between the two is that critical thinking involves reasoning about open-ended or 'ill-structured' problems, while problem solving is usually considered narrower in scope" (p. 45). That is, critical thinking may be concerned with complex issues and less with the instrumental goal of finding and executing the solution to a particular problem. We believe that understanding problem solving will help us understand critical thinking.

D'Angelo (1971) views problem solving as a part of but only "contingently necessary" for critical thinking. He states:

> It would be inaccurate to define critical thinking in terms of problem solving. Critical thinking consists of more skills than are used in the problem solving approach, and some of these steps include intuitive and creative elements that do not involve any evaluation or justification. (p. 19)

While McPeck (1981) does not believe that critical thinking encompasses all rational thought, he does suggest that formal and informal logic plays a minor role and that critical thinking might be broader than problem solving. In any event, we must recognize the complexity of critical thinking and not over simplify or isolate it. The challenge is to meaningfully integrate problem solving concepts with our understanding of critical thinking.

To be fair, there are those who see critical thinking from a narrower perspective. Those who view critical thinking from within the informal logic movement might see little difference between critical thinking and problem solving. Again, we see little consensus with regard to definitions. The same is true of creative thinking, although the challenge to define such a construct may be more difficult than defining problem solving.

The complexity of creativity is demonstrated by the fact there are "four significantly different approaches to the problem of creativity" (Mooney in Taylor, 1988, p. 100). Creativity may be approached from the perspective and defined in terms of the environment, a product, a process, or a person. Perhaps the most readily understandable view is from a product or person perspective. For example, White (1972) states that a "creative thinker is one whose thinking leads to a result which conforms to criteria of value in one domain or another. 'Creative' is a medal which we pin on public products" (pp. 135–136). In addition, creative individuals are those who have produced something of value. Innovative might also be another descriptor of creative thinking. Educationally, however, the concern is primarily with the process and the environments that will facilitate it.

From a process perspective, creativity would appear to be part of problem solving and critical thinking. Sternberg's (1988) research suggests that the higher order executive processes relevant to creativity are recognizing the existence of a problem, defining the problem, and formulating a problem solution. Similarly, Torrance (1988) describes the process of creativity as "sensing difficulties, problems, gaps in information, missing elements, something askew; making guesses and formulating hypotheses about these deficiencies; evaluating and testing these guesses and hypotheses; possibly revising and retesting them; and finally communicating the results" (p. 47). Both descriptions are clearly concerned with creative problem solving. This overlap of creativity and problem solving is also noted by Halpern (1984) when she states that "Many decisions are involved in solving a problem, and generating satisfactory solution paths often requires considerable creativity" (p. 162).

Creativity has also been described as not an ability but more of a thinking style in which the individual often redefines problems in their own terms rather than accepts others' definitions (Perkins, 1986). Therefore, creative and critical thinking cannot be clearly separated. Perkins (1986) states:

> ...if you're talking about really good critical thinking, you're talking about thinking that is insightful. It's not just nitpicking; it cuts to the heart of the matter — and that, rather plainly, is creative thinking. So from a philosophical point, one has to acknowledge that the two are hand-in-glove and it can't be any other way. (p. 15)

It is worthwhile noting at this point that in the previous statement creativity would appear to be associated with insight. Dewey (1933) discusses the possibility of an idea springing up automatically in terms of reflective thinking. Passmore (1972) suggests that critical thinking "conjoins imagination and criticism in a single form of thinking" (p. 423). This unitary approach to thinking is the perspective taken here. Moreover, it is consistent with Dewey's ideas. For Dewey, inquiry and reflective thought is an imaginative and creative process. Similarly, we see critical thinking as not being possible without insight, imagination and creativity. The challenge is to parsimoniously represent these overlapping concepts.

A Model of Critical Thinking

To reiterate, critical thinking is seen here as a broad and inclusive process of higher-order thinking. To this point, critical thinking has been associated with scepticism, creativity/insight, reason, judgement, and warranted action.

Much of the current work on critical thinking is consistent with Dewey's (1933) conception of practical inquiry and reflective thinking. Perhaps the relevance of Dewey's conception today is due to the fact that his reflective thinking cycle was based on the generalized scientific process, although Dewey rejected positivistic thought. Dewey sees reflective thinking as a form of inquiry that includes imagination, deliberation and action. The "complete act of reflective activity" includes a pre-reflective situation, five phases of reflective thought, and a post-reflective situation. In reference to the pre-reflective and post-reflective situations, Dewey (1933) states that "the two limits of every unit of thinking are a perplexed, troubled, or confused situation at the beginning and a cleared-up, unified, resolved situation at the close" (p. 106).

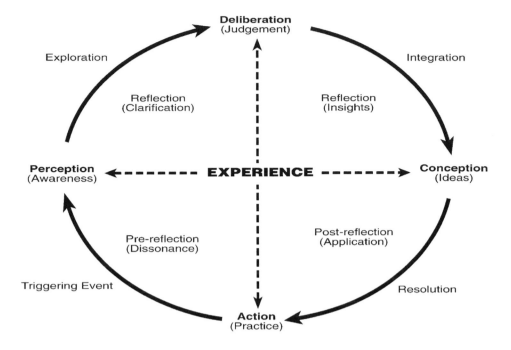

Figure 4.1: Practical inquiry.

Dewey describes a generalized and practical method of inquiry. For Dewey, consistent with his philosophy of pragmatism, inquiry is a practical and natural endeavour based upon experience. Inquiry emerges from practice, and inquiry shapes practice. Practical inquiry is based in the context of needs, desires, interests and conflict that requires resolution. It addresses the problems of every-day life. Practical inquiry is a process of searching and exploring, finding the means to reach desired end goals or conflict resolution. According to Dewey, the product is knowledge or belief and the will to act.

A generalized model of practical inquiry is represented in Figure 4.1. This model of practical inquiry reflects the essential components of the process most closely associated with the shared world. This model emphasizes the pre- and post-reflective phases of inquiry, which are firmly grounded in the external world of practice. Reflection and learning is precipitated and shaped by the context of practice. That is, reflection and practice are "mutually constitutive"; thought is not independent of fact.

Two dimensions or orientations define the practical inquiry model. The dimensions are integrally related concepts. The first axis represents the action-deliberation dimension. Action is the ultimate test of understanding and the stimulus for further understanding. Deliberation is the process of critical reflection aimed at making sense of external actions and practice. This dimension reflects the extremes of a unified and coherent view of the shared and individual worlds.

The second orientation is the perception-conception dimension. Perception is the initial recognition of a problem and the assimilation of associated facts, while conception is the authoring/generation of ideas that give meaning to perception. As a result of conceptual understanding, perception is further enhanced. Practical inquiry is dependent upon the integrity of this reciprocal relationship between perception and conception. Facts and ideas are but concrete and abstract ways of looking at the same problem. Perception and conception are processes of relating to experience. They are on the cusp and represent the unity of the shared and individual worlds. That is, the coming together of concrete and abstract experiences.

The axes and the natural cycle are analogous to the seasons of the year, where winter and summer are opposite ends of the spectrum and spring and fall are seemingly transition points. To stretch the analogy, the phases of practical inquiry could be seen as corresponding to the seasons of the year. That is, the quadrants — triggering event; exploration; integration; and, resolution — might, respectively, correspond to each of the seasons beginning with spring.

In any case, the dimensions together represent a coherent transactional view of inquiry. The perception-conception orientation takes hold of experience, while the action-deliberation orientation creates meaning from experience. In a sense, perception and conception mediate action and deliberation. As we shall see in a subsequent discussion of intuition and insight, perception and conception may be imperceptible transition points between action and deliberation.

The axes and quadrants also represent the natural cycle (logical phases) of the inquiry process. This cycle begins with experience and the perception of a need or desire; proceeds to deliberation (critical reflection) and the search for understanding; then to conception and the authoring of ideas and meaning; and, finally, to resolution through meaningful action. Practical inquiry is intended to "discover the meaning of experience".

Not inconsistent with the practical inquiry model is the expanded model of critical thinking (see Figure 4.2), which more fully explores the phases of reflective thought. Again, following Dewey's lead, we begin by reviewing his five phases of reflective thought:

1. suggestions, in which the mind leaps forward to a possible solution;
2. an intellectualization of the difficulty or perplexity that has been felt (directly experienced) into a problem to be solved, a question for which the answer must be sought;
3. the use of one suggestion after another as a leading idea, or hypothesis, to initiate and guide observation and other operations in collection of factual material;
4. the mental elaboration of the idea or supposition as an idea or proposition (reasoning, in the sense in which reasoning is a part, not the whole, of inference);
5. testing the hypothesis by overt or imaginative action. (Dewey, 1933, p. 107)

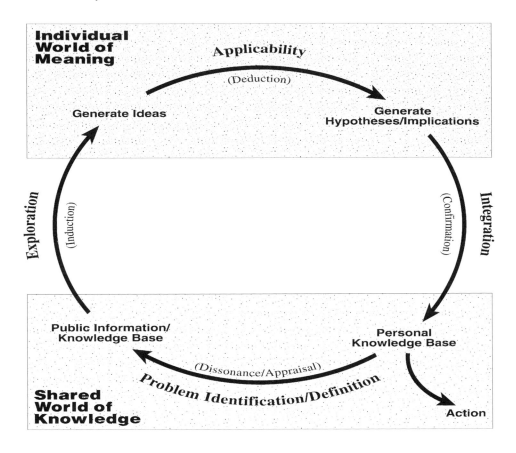

Figure 4.2: Critical thinking/learning cycle.

The previous cycle is not intended to be fixed. Dewey's view is that the phases do not necessarily follow in order, some may telescope, others may be passed over hurriedly, and a single phase may require a seemingly disproportionate amount of development. In short, no rules can be set with regard to order or importance of the phases of the reflective thinking process.

Brookfield (1987a) identifies a common pattern when identifying the phases of critical thinking. He states that many "different terms are used to describe these phases, but their essential components appear remarkably similar" (p. 25). Brookfield's (1987a) five phases are: a trigger event, an appraisal of the situation, an exploration to explain anomalies or discrepancies, a development of alternative perspectives, and an integration in ways of living. Brookfield's phases of critical thinking closely parallel those of Dewey's. Along with the work of Dewey, Brookfield's model has contributed to the conceptualization of the critical thinking process presented next.

The model of critical thinking presented here consists of five phases — problem identification, problem definition, exploration, applicability, and integration (see Figure 4.2). While the term problem is used here, it is interpreted to include broader issues; not just narrow or instrumental types of problems. As will be made clear when the phases of the critical thinking/learning cycle are described, it is crucial to explicitly recognize the personal and shared worlds. From an educational perspective, it is necessary to distinguish between reflective (personal) and collaborative (shared) activities. These activities cannot be separated in practice and, therefore, must be viewed within a larger whole. At the same time, reflection is primarily associated with the issue of personal responsibility while collaboration is more concerned with issues of control. Critical thinking is, in essence, the process of learning in a deep and meaningful manner.

The critical thinking cycle reflects a learning process that is consistent with education goals. The cycle describes the process of constructing meaning and confirming knowledge structures. Moreover, to think critically is to make judgements and decisions. This necessitates opportunities to exercise choice and assume responsibility for the construction of meaningful knowledge structures.

Problem identification. The initial phase of the cycle is the recognition of some confusion or perplexity as a result of a problem or issue arising out of an experience. Dewey refers to this phase as the pre-reflective situation. There is often a specific "triggering" event that precipitates critical reflection and learning. However, there must also be an underlying need or goal to trigger the critical thinking/learning process. These triggering events may be macro level life transitions (Aslanian & Brickell, 1980), relatively minor issues of curiosity, or a range of issues and problems typically found in educational settings. They may be positive as well as negative events or experiences. The last point is that each individual's existing knowledge and experience will determine what is, in fact, a triggering event. Therefore, not all students will be motivated to learn critically under the same circumstances.

Problem definition. Thinking becomes more directed and purposeful during the second phase. Appraisal and understanding of the exact nature of the problem is the focus here. One of the most important tasks may be to define or redefine the issue or problem. Dewey and Childs (1981) suggest that we begin with uncertainty and contingency in the context of which we define a problem or propose a definite question. Since it is the basis upon which learning and action proceeds, the problem must be understood as well as the situation will allow. The process of defining the problem or question may itself encompass subsequent stages of the critical thinking cycle.

The view of Schon (1983) is that we need to emphasize the problem setting and thus construct or re-frame problems from ill-defined and uncertain situations. This may require the questioning of basic assumptions which constrain thinking. However, as Dewey (1933) notes, "We take that to be true which we should like to have so, and ideas that go contrary to our hopes and wishes have difficulty in getting lodgement. We all jump to conclusions; we all fail to examine and test our ideals because of personal attitudes" (p. 28). It is very difficult, if not impossible, to criticize one's own thinking.

At this point the critical spirit must be present. It has been noted previously that, to avoid ideology, intellectual autonomy is necessary. This does not mean, however, that individuals avoid questioning and clarifying assumptions. Because questioning assumptions is exceedingly difficult for the individual, a critical community of learners is very helpful and often necessary. This problematic situation and the role of others is recognized by Brookfield (1987a) when he suggests that critical helpers are necessary to function as mirrors in helping us interpret and question our deeply held beliefs and assumptions. At this stage, the individual begins to critically assess the situation in order to understand the problem and be open to alternative explanations.

Exploration. This phase may alternate between the shared world and the personal world of reflection and contemplation. The search for possible explanations of the issue or problem is initiated by identifying appropriate knowledge and exploring for relevant ideas and their connections. The goal is to find alternative explanations and this is where the discovery and creative thinking process may be most prevalent. For this reason, scepticism and the critical attitude may be less prominent. Admittedly, there exists a somewhat contradictory balance of the creative and the critical faculties. However, there is an interplay between the critical attitude which tends to be more focused and the creative (expansive) thinking that seeks the holistic view.

A critical attitude, in conjunction with expansive thinking, is very important to ensure that we are engaging in strong sense critical thinking; that is, an open and fair-minded authoring/selection of ideas. This is the point where the selective gathering of evidence and authoring/selection of ideas to serve narrow interests can corrupt the thinking process. On the other hand, an authentic and expansive search for truth will precipitate and facilitate the creative thinking process.

Very often at this stage one will return to the original problem definition and redefine it as a result of ideas revealed. In some situations novel ideas or conceptualizations may reveal themselves as solutions or explanations to other problems or issues. This represents a creative judgement. Perkins (1986) argues that "Creative people tend to be less solution minded than non-creative people. They think hard not just about what the answer is to the problem they already have or that somebody gave them, but what the problem should be: how the problem might be formulated, how it might be reformulated" (p. 14).

Similarly, Lipman (1991) suggests that creative thinkers discover ideas and then look for unasked questions or applications. Creative thinking at this point may be seen as divergently seeking the solution to undefined problems. While a solution to an undefined problem may appear nonsensical, it is meant to suggest that thinking may be creatively sidetracked to the problem definition stage. However, another possibility during the exploration stage is that thinking will be compressed and an insight will suddenly reveal the sought after solution; that is, thinking will move directly to stage five. Insight is seen to be concerned with the original problem definition — a kind of convergent creativity. Insight and intuition will be discussed subsequently.

The identification of ideas is crucially important in critical thinking and problem solving. They are the source of meaning and understanding. In interpreting Dewey's approach to thinking and problem solving, Prawat (1997) states that, "An idea establishes the agenda for problem solving by creating expectations about what is likely to happen if one follows a certain course of action" (p. 20). Ideas are the foundation and guide for critical reflective action. Ideas organize and make sense of the contingent facts. Therefore, the search for relevant and efficacious ideas is a turning point in anticipating solutions or outcomes of particular actions.

Applicability. The result of the exploration phase is a conceptualization of the issue or problem. The applicability phase is clearly in the reflective and private world of the individual, although the individual may return repeatedly to the socially shared world. During this phase, ideas are explored through reason analysis and justification to assess their applicability. Considerable reliance may be placed upon logical reasoning during the early part of this phase and judgement during the latter part. In essence, individuals assess the acceptability or potential of an idea by considering the contingent situation through imaginative and judicious thought.

The applicability phase is extensive and central to critical thinking. At the beginning of this phase, reflection is an open (constructive) process where individuals tentatively make sense of the information that emerged during the exploratory phase. As critical thinking progresses, reflection becomes a process of deliberation. An assessment of the idea occurs by reflecting upon the worth of the idea. That is, judgements and decisions are made and thinking becomes more focused around an idea or hypothesis. Individuals begin to commit to a particular explanation and implications are considered. It is at the end of this phase and the transition into the integration and confirmation stage that a clear understanding and commitment to the idea and explanation emerges.

The process of reflection and deliberation is central to several prominent theories in adult and higher education. The cognitive development theory of Kitchener and King (1994) focuses on reflective judgement (justifying beliefs) and the changing of epistemic assumptions through reflective thinking. However, they emphasize that their reflective judgement model is not synonymous with critical thinking since critical thinking involves other forms of reasoning. It is also suggested that cognitive development models are longitudinal representations, while the critical thinking model presented here is more time and context specific.

Another theory that informs the reflective process associated with the applicability phase is Mezirow's transformation theory. This theory is concerned with constructing and transforming meaning through reflection. In particular, meaning perspectives are transformed through epistemic reflection, not unlike the reflective judgement model. Although considerable emphasis is placed on the reflective process, the phases of transformation closely parallel the critical thinking cycle (Mezirow, 1994).

At the applicability phase, although ideas are but hypotheses or conjecture, they are crucial for the individual to make sense of the world. Prawat (1999), referring to Dewey and Peirce, states that they argue that ideas "are instruments of knowledge that connect the old and the new, the known and the unknown, the antecedent and the consequent" (p. 60). The idea is the connection and transaction between the individual/private and the social/shared worlds. The systematic connection of ideas is the path to personal meaning and public knowledge. While the idea may have personal meaning, it must be acted upon either imaginatively or overtly before it can be confirmed. This explains Dewey's contention that knowing is doing (Prawat, 1997). Therefore, the active testing of ideas is crucial to the critical thinking process and is the focus of the next stage — integration.

Integration. The final phase in the critical thinking cycle represents a return to the socially shared world. The idea or hypothesis is tested during this phase. Ideas or hypotheses "prior to active test are intellectually significant only as guides and as plans of possible actions. The actions when undertaken produce consequences which test, expand, and modify the ideas previously tentatively entertained" (Dewey & Childs, 1981, p. 95). Confirming and adopting an idea is to integrate it into our meaning system. The confirmation of a problem solution or resolution of a dilemma will result in understanding. An unsatisfactory resolution should trigger a renewed search. While the cyclical process of critical thinking may begin anew, there is the possibility that the individual will proceed to the applicability phase if previously generated conceptualizations are promising.

The initial process of confirmation is sharing the idea or hypothesis within a critical community who provide insights and a conceptual test of the idea/hypothesis. This is helpful in refining understanding necessary to more deeply integrate the concepts into the individual's personal knowledge base. Notwithstanding the interaction with others, the initial confirmation process can be viewed as a cognitive process and imaginative (vicarious) test.

As the confirmation process develops, individuals become ready to act upon their understanding. Behaviour is changed and performance itself is tested. In scientific terms, the hypothesis is systematically and rigorously tested. This is Dewey's post-reflective situation and can be viewed as a temporary exit from the largely cognitive processes of the critical thinking cycle. However, this may be short lived. Individuals immediately begin to receive feedback from their performance and reflect in, or upon, their actions. This will then, most likely, initiate the critical thinking cycle anew with the identification of other problems.

Confirming and integrating concepts is crucial if the purpose of critical thinking is knowledge development. Jarvis (1988) contrasts knowledge with ideology and belief. Knowledge is considered meaningful and verifiable. On the other hand, information and belief must be treated critically if it is to be verified and become knowledge. Jarvis (1988) argues that without verification "it has to be recognised that as hypothesis, ideology, or belief they should not be accorded the status of knowledge" (p. 167). The confirmation phase may emphasize the collaborative aspects of critical thinking but it is important to emphasize the alternation of collaboration and reflection throughout the cycle. This movement from the private to the shared world is essential to the development of meaning and the confirmation of knowledge in the best sense of an educational experience.

Consistent with Habermas' theory described in Chapter 2, critical thinking is conceptualized here as representing an emancipatory form of education which integrates objective and subjective worlds through discourse and reflection. In essence there is a fusion of the personal and shared worlds while maintaining the integrity of each. Standards of rationality are provided through discourse in a critical community of learners. Paradoxically, autonomy and responsibility is embedded in the dialogue of a critical community. Therefore, critical thinking and learning is collaborative but recognizes and encourages the intellectual autonomy of the individual. Consistent with Habermas' emancipation interest, Dewey also believed that it was the individual who ultimately validates ideas (Prawat, 1999).

Dewey's view of the authorship of ideas is that they emerge in the socially shared context. However, potentially illuminating ideas need to be situated in a system of related ideas. It is at the integration stage that personal confirmation relies heavily on verbal discourse and negotiation (Prawat, 1999). In this regard, Lipman (1991) states that a "community of inquiry is a deliberative society engaged in higher-order thinking" (p. 209). He adds that deliberations are not merely conversations but logically disciplined dialogues which furthers the interests of both individual and community. A dialogue, in turn, is a collaborative inquiry where "disequilibrium is enforced in order to enforce forward movement" (Lipman, 1991, p. 232).

Seixas (1993) suggests that there is a remarkable congruence between the scholarly community and the educational community of inquiry, although he does address some serious limits to the analogy. He states that the 20th-century pragmatists abandoned the search for certainty and gave "the community of inquiry a central place in the advancement of knowledge" (Seixas, 1993, p. 308). By stimulating criticism and striving for consensus the community of inquiry yields knowledge that is as objective as possible. Knowledge is developed in the public forum of intense sustained critical analysis and discourse. In a somewhat similar manner, the constructivist position supports the concept of the classroom as a community of inquiry where knowledge is developed through sustained critical scrutiny. From this perspective, individual learning "is fundamentally a communal activity, carried on within a shared culture" (Seixas, 1993, p. 310).

Before we leave this discussion of the critical thinking/learning cycle, two points need to be re-emphasized. The first is the explicit recognition and placement of reflective and collaborative processes. Critical thinking moves iteratively between the shared (public) and the individual (personal) world. Secondly, the process is not fixed linearly and the phases may not always be distinguishable. Since all knowledge must be considered tentative the cycle never ends. The end of the cycle usually raises more questions, which mark the beginning of the next cycle. Uncertainty accompanies all knowledge, which is the catalyst for sustained critical thinking and continuous educational development. The fact that the phases of critical thinking may not be linear or distinguishable is the essence of the discussion with regard to intuition and insight.

Intuition and Insight

The question to be addressed next is whether there is a place for insight and intuition in rational thought. The concept of intuition goes back to ancient times. Noddings and Shore (1984) have described how Plato believed that intuition was a reliable source of knowledge and Aristotle regarded it as "an infallible source of truth" (p. 7). Although we no longer place the same faith in the infallibility of intuition, there is an important link between Aristotle and modern theorists. Aristotle placed the concept of intuition in the realm of intellectual inquiry. He pointed out that all reasoning ultimately depends upon induction or intuition if we are to avoid an endless regression of proofs. For Aristotle, experience and intuition is equated with induction; intuition is "the result of an inductive process" (Kal, 1988, p. 56). There is, invariably, an intuitive leap of understanding in the inductive process since there is never a one-to-one correspondence between ideas and facts. According to Noddings and Shore (1984), Aristotle's notion of intuition was fundamentally an intellectual process, a form of telescoped rationality. Aristotle himself used the term "intuitive reason".

Unfortunately, since Aristotle the concept of intuition began to take on a mystical quality that has persisted to modern times. This mystical view suggests that intuition provides insight without prior knowledge, purpose, or reason. Intuition is seen as a mysterious unconscious process. The mystical view of intuition is an epiphany-like experience associated with having visions and with the supernatural. The source of this mystical view seems to be the suddenness of the intuitive product and the lack of a satisfactory theory to explain its basis in experience and previous learning (Bastick, 1982). This mystical quality, however, is not the notion of intuition that will be explored here. Instead, our interest is with cognitive notions of intuition (but not excluding the affective domain) that are directed toward understanding and the construction of externally validated forms of knowledge.

Dewey places intuition and other qualitative elements, such as passion and imagination, at the core of his theory of inquiry. Feeling, reasoning and action represent an organic whole. Dewey (1930/1984) states:

> intuition is closely connected with the single qualitativeness underlying all the details of explicit reasoning. I may be relatively dumb and inarticulate and yet penetrating; unexpressed in dcfinitc ideas which form reasons and justifications and yet profoundly right. (p. 249)

Moreover, Dewey's view is that reflective thought is predicated upon a passion to resolve a problem or achieve a more desirable possibility.

Jim Garrison (1997) states that, according to Dewey, inquiry "is a creative artistic activity" (p. 24). He goes on to say that for Dewey, "Ideas emerge, or are brought forth, from an affective, intuitive background..." (p. 96). Intuition is the background of inquiry where vague, inexact ideas emerge that influence thought and reason. While intuition helps us grasp data for subsequent thought, Dewey believes that it is also "the product of practical deliberation" (Garrison, 1997, p. 33).

Intuition may reveal the close relationship of learning and emotions — thoughts and feelings. Bastick (1982) suggests that thought elements are related by their associated feelings and "intuition is dependent on our feelings at all stages from initial perception where feeling impressions of the information are created: through the intuitive processing where feelings may change, to the final intuition which has its accompanying feeling of certainty" (pp. 58–59). Thoughts have attendant feeling associations and the intuitive product may be dependent upon feelings; that is, the product is made conscious by an awareness of feelings. Bastick (1982) believes that "Intuitive processing manipulates feelings and only involves words through their connotative and affective associations" (p. 300).

Intuition is increasingly being recognized as a key element in discovery, problem solving, understanding and knowledge generation (Entwistle & Marton, 1994; Goldberg, 1983). Often it is seen as an unexpected vague sensation or feeling while at other times there is a clear perception or solution to a problem. Invariably, however, a need to understand and a concomitant focus of thought, direction, and purpose precede it. A general notion of intuition is having either a vague awareness or a clear perception of something without the use of discrete and easily identifiable rational steps. While it is a myth that intuitive insights occur without previous knowledge, they are very much associated with feelings and a sense of connectedness. Such myths that intuition occurs "out of the blue" without previous direction or focus of thought do little in furthering our understanding of intuition and its place in the thinking/learning process.

Another issue that needs to be explored in understanding intuition is the role of the unconscious or preconscious. Clearly there are intuitive leaps that come at unexpected moments away from attempts to consciously resolve an issue or dilemma. At the same time, we have to be careful not to attribute too extensive or lofty a role to the unconscious. First, as we have alluded to previously, intuition is invariably preceded by considerable intellectual effort and progress. Bastick's (1982) view is that obsessive and dedicated immersion in the subject over time integrates feelings and ideas into a global inclusion, resulting in the intuition.

Perkins (1981) suggests that intuitive (mental) leaps are more like hops and "are less mysterious and more explainable than they are usually taken to be" (p. 49). He also believes that the unconscious supports many mundane activities and is "where the action is". This is not to say that we can explain covert processes or that intuition is simply rapid logical thought processes. The intuitive process is still relatively unreachable and open to speculation.

However, in education we are particularly interested in the cognitive implications of intuition — i.e. intuition as a process directed toward idea generation and

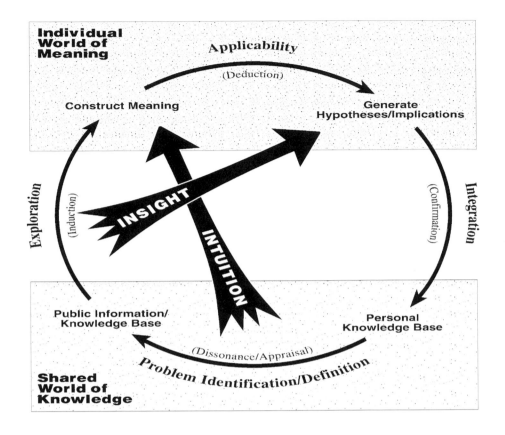

Figure 4.3: Intuition and critical thinking.

knowledge development. It should be predicated upon an individual having taken responsibility for his/her own learning and having been challenged to actively search for ideas and construct knowledge. To take it beyond the mystical, intuition is seen to result from a deep understanding of a subject area or problem situation. From such an understanding, abstract patterns become apparent and the individual is able to process larger "chunks" of information and bypass analytical steps. The ability to perceive large meaningful patterns (i.e. system of ideas, schema) is important for a cognitive view of intuition.

Entwistle and Marton (1994) support this in their analysis of how students construct and scientists intuit understanding. They studied the intentions and processes by which students develop understanding. Understanding was associated with a "tightly integrated 'bundle' of ideas and related information and experience" (p. 175) which the authors called a knowledge object. Parallels were noted with descriptions of scientific intuition. The description of intuition by Nobel laureates suggests that it is involved with conceiving "integrated wholes" (i.e. knowledge objects) which provide understanding. Entwistle and Marton (1994) conclude that the "parallels with the experiences of intuition do suggest that the phenomenon identified as students revise [study] for finals may represent a more general feature of mental life" (p. 176).

Intuition is an aspect of creative thinking. Bowers et al. (1990) define intuition in terms of the context of discovery as distinct from the context of justification. While human cognition is by its very nature intuitive, Bowers et al. suggest that it applies only to the context of discovery. They define "intuition as a preliminary perception of coherence (pattern, meaning, structure) that is at first not consciously represented, but which nevertheless guides thought and inquiry toward a hunch or hypothesis about the nature of the coherence in question" (p. 74). While the preliminary stage is largely unconscious the problem solving proceeds gradually "as previously encoded information is activated by clues to coherence" (p. 95). Interestingly, Bowers et al. (1990) view intuition as having two stages. The guiding stage involves an implicit perception of coherence that unconsciously guides thought. The integrative stage "involves integrating into consciousness a plausible representation of the coherence in question" (p. 74).

The intuitive process is different from conscious reasoning. It appears to work with complex and poorly structured problem situations. Intuition can "make unusual connections, imaginative associations that are not obvious and would not show up in a logical sequence. It is intuition that leaps across chasms of missing information, making sideways detours, and brings together unusual, even illogical combinations" (Goldberg, 1983, p. 36). Intuition is a non-rational or unconscious form of induction in that it suggests general propositions or constructs from divergent facts and information. In short, it provides hunches with a low prediction of success (Finke, 1992).

Intuition and insight in critical thinking. Previously it was suggested that intuition may consist of either a vague sensation or clear perception. These two forms of intuition are distinguished in terms of intuition and insight respectively. Distinguishing between intuition and insight recognizes intuitive hunches that are ill-formed and insights that are coherent conceptualizations. The essential difference is that intuition is temporally more closely associated with action (i.e. arises from experience) while insight is more associated with thought (i.e. arises from reflection). As a result, conscious reasoning follows intuition while conscious reasoning precedes insight.

In terms of the critical thinking/learning model, insight occurs during the exploration phase (see Figure 4.2). At this point, the person likely has an explicit understanding of the situation or problem and the relevant knowledge base. The insight is a clear perception of a solution or hypothesis without reliance on conscious reasoning. Insight is seen to follow the generation of "preinventive structures" or tentative conceptual representations. Insight is characterized by the individual being immersed in a well defined problem.

On the other hand, intuition is accompanied by a feeling, hunch or fuzzy vision that necessitates a move to more formal reasoning to better understand the issue. Intuition usually follows immediate experience and occurs at the problem recognition phase. Expert knowledge does not appear to explicitly play an important role. It has been suggested that intuition is more of a clever guess or hunch. Although some understanding of the problem or dilemma must have preceded the intuition, it occurs to a lesser degree without previous conscious exploration. That is, without a conscious and formal questioning of assumptions and initial search for conceptual representations or alternative paradigms.

Perkins (1981) argues that insight is more concerned with discovering the solution or point more readily while intuition has more to do with lack of reasons. He believes insight "depends on rapid reflexive processes of perception and understanding" (Perkins, 1981, p. 155). Tacit knowing or recognition appears to follow the route of insight (i.e. skipping the explicit conceptualization and applicability phase). Schon (1983, 1987) refers to this as knowing-in-action. It would appear that much of this tacit knowing is habitual knowledge that does not present a problem or require reflection. For this reason we would rule out knowing-in-action as an intuitive cognitive process.

It is suggested here that intuition plays a major role in what Schon (1983, 1987) refers to as reflection-in-action. Reflection-in-action occurs when in the midst of an activity there is a surprise and the usual patterns of knowing-in-action (i.e. habitual responses) fail us. In this situation we may immediately rethink our knowing-in-action by focusing "interactively on the outcomes of action, the action itself, and the intuitive knowing implicit in the action" (Schon, 1983, p. 56). There is an immediate conceptualization of the problem situation and confirming of it through imaginative or real action. Schon (1987) suggests that inappropriate assumptions may be intuitively discarded and compressed with restructuring (i.e. re-conceptualizing). Parenthetically, reflection-on-action could be considered to represent the complete critical thinking model. Knowing-in-action reflects formal structures and logical connections made explicit through previous reflection-on-action.

Intuition/insight and reason. If we are to understand intuition and insight as a cognitive process, then we will have to address the complementary relationship of intuition and reason and how they work together in a holistic view of thinking and learning. Dewey (1967) views intuition as the union of perception and reasoning. He rejects the notion that intuition opposes reasoning. Dewey (1967) states that intuition "is most properly confined to those acts of knowledge…in which we know ultimate wholes" (p. 206). It is "re-cognizing" knowledge and the recognition of coherent systemic meaning. There is a unity of the creative and the rational processes. It is the process of conceptualizing the systematic interconnectedness of ideas.

It is assumed here that the intuitive mode of perceiving is not a distinct alternative method of understanding complex problems or situations. Further, it is assumed that neither intuitive/insightful nor analytic approaches alone are sufficient for an understanding of thinking and learning. Salk (1983) states that "Intuition and reason play a powerful role in our lives and it is necessary, therefore, to understand each separately and together" (p. 79). Perkins (1981) believes that "reasoning is an important means to insight" (p. 71). We shall elaborate upon these statements within the context of the critical thinking model.

The critical thinking model used here has the advantage of providing the framework in which to discuss and explain the complementary nature of intuition and reason. Intuition and reason can be understood both separately and together as part of a holistic thinking/learning process. According to Goldberg (1983), rationality and intuition are symbiotic in nature in that when "we are thinking through a decision or problem, we tend to hop back and forth between conscientiously applied analysis and intuition" (p. 33). He suggests that at times rationality precedes intuition, while sometimes "intuition feeds and stimulates rational thought and evaluates its products" (Goldberg, 1983, p. 33). Similarly, Noddings and Shore (1984) recognize the complementary nature of intuition and reason when they state "we do not deny the importance and feasibility of verifying intuitions through reason or experience" (p. 26). These views are consistent with the two forms of intuition described here and the model that integrates intuition and reason.

Intuition has been generally described as a understanding or awareness without the sudden use of discrete rational steps and is very much associated with feelings. It comes to the fore when there is considerable uncertainty and complexity due to a novel or surprising situation. While intuition occurs spontaneously and it is not immediately apparent how it was arrived at, most often it is based upon a profound concern or knowledge of the issue or problem. To nurture intuition is not to be less rational — just the opposite. Intuition is either fertilized by rational and critical analysis or it is clarified by rational analysis; however, both must be confirmed through application and experience. Solutions to complex problems cannot be forced. The intuitive mind must be allowed to make connections and reveal insights, often in moments of distraction or quiet reflection. Intuition without reason is an illusion of truth and leaves us mired in mysticism. Rational thought without intuition lacks inspiration. It is like taking a trip back and forth on the same road; while it is very predictable we never discover new roads and vistas.

If the business of education is thinking and learning, then we must find models that help us understand intuition and its role in discovering and constructing meaning. This discussion has attempted to reduce the mystery of intuition. Its reality is defended by describing it within the context of the critical thinking/learning cycle. It is believed that separating intuitive and rational thought reduces our understanding of the learning process and consequently we are likely to devise unnatural and contrived educational situations that bear little resemblance to how people construct meaning and solve real problems. Stewart (1988) states that "intuitive thinking enables students to better comprehend complex relationships, to put things into better perspective, to generate new ideas, to perceive more ways to integrate facts, concepts and generalizations" (p. 176). When educators recognize the symbiotic relationship between intuition and reason, then students will be able to assume increased responsibility for learning and gain greater control of the educational transaction.

Developing Critical Thinkers

The assumption made here regarding the teaching of critical thinking is that it essentially precipitates and emerges from the process of constructing meaning and validating understanding. Therefore, critical thinking is primarily developed within the context of assimilating and accommodating a discipline's knowledge base. Critical thinking operations and strategies should be made explicit but the first priority will be to construct meaning. Furthermore, it should be noted that attitudes and dispositions for critical thinking will be acquired as a result of the construction of meaningful and relevant knowledge and the intrinsic motivation that such learning engenders. The critical spirit cannot be acquired vicariously, it must be developed through the experience of constructing meaningful knowledge.

Other approaches may attempt to teach generic thinking skills in stand-alone courses (formal and informal logic); or integrate subject matter and thinking skills and maintain a roughly equal balance between the two (Prawat, 1991). The difficulty with the former is that there is little evidence that general critical thinking abilities exist which are useful in specific contexts. In terms of the latter, it is difficult for students to concentrate on process skills (critical thinking) while trying to understand the content. In short, it may be virtually impossible to be absorbed in the critical analysis of subject matter and simultaneously consider the metacognitive processes one is using. The position here is that students learn critical thinking in the process of learning new subject matter in a deep and meaningfully manner.

McPeck (1990a) argues "that critical thinking is not a content-free 'general ability,' nor is it a set of 'specific skills'" (p. 27). Instead, he contends "that if we improve the quality of understanding through the disciplines...you will then get a concomitant improvement in critical thinking capacity" (p. 21). McPeck (1990b) admits there may be some general thinking skills, but their usefulness is inversely proportional to their generality. Glaser (1984) also argues "that abilities to think and reason [critical thinking] will be attained when these cognitive activities are taught not as subsequent add-ons to what we have learned, but rather are explicitly developed in the process of acquiring the knowledge and skills that we consider the objectives of education" (p. 93). Like McPeck, Glaser (1984) suggests that general thinking skills are weak because they do not assist in solving specific problems.

In a fashion similar to the two previous authors, Resnick (1987) suggests that it would be prudent to teach higher cognitive skills within traditional school disciplines. The advantages, according to Resnick (1987), are that it provides a natural knowledge base to practice higher order thinking skills. Moreover, the discipline itself provides criteria as to what constitutes good thinking, and a discipline approach "will ensure that something worthwhile will have been learned even if wide transfer proves unattainable" (p. 36). Such an approach would also have the added benefit of integrating process skills and outcome knowledge. That is, constructing meaningful and worthwhile knowledge is dependent upon a process of critically constructing meaning — the two cannot be separated. How students acquire knowledge is crucial to the quality and usefulness of the educational experience. To reiterate, if content determines reasoning processes, then specific critical thinking courses that focus exclusively on reasoning processes without the context of a discipline have to be considered suspect.

The teaching approach advocated here is that of a collaborator who encourages thoughtful analysis but also challenges thinking that may be fallacious. For this reason discipline based dialogue within a critical community of learners has been emphasized. For students to defend a position necessitates that they critically examine ideas and make judgements. McPeck (1990a) suggests that one of the more effective methods of getting students to examine ideas is to engage them in argument. He notes:

> Perhaps the most refreshing — indeed, the most liberating — thing about honest argument is that it requires taking the other person's reasons seriously, no matter how bizarre they might seem, and addressing them head-on. In argument, notice, people have to treat each other as equals. Thus, in the arena of argument even the teacher's traditional authority must give way to reasons. (McPeck, 1990a, p. 52)

Weinstein (1993) believes that there "are many suggestive commonalities between critical thinking and social theories of reasoning…[and it] comports nicely with recent and credible pedagogical approaches such as cooperative and collaborative learning" (p. 99). After examining various promising teaching programs, Resnick (1987) writes that many of these programs rely on social interaction for much of their teaching and practice. (One of these promising programs is that by Brown and Palincsar (1989), which will be discussed in Chapter 6.) Possible reasons for the success of interactive methods are suggested by Resnick (1987). The first is that the social setting provides opportunities for modelling effective thinking which makes explicit appropriate thinking strategies. Secondly, as noted previously, dialogue or "thinking aloud" allows fellow students or a teacher to critique and shape thinking. Thirdly, the social setting may motivate students and have them "come to think of themselves as capable of engaging in independent thinking and of exercising control over their learning processes" (p. 41). The resulting "disposition to critical thought is central to developing higher order cognitive abilities in students" (p. 41) and requires long-term cultivation.

The importance of modelling critical thinking and dialogue in facilitating its development demands further examination. In accordance with the previous discussion, Passmore (1972) concludes that the critical spirit "can be taught only by men [and women] who can themselves freely partake in critical discussion" (p. 241). The ability of the teacher to adopt the critical spirit may be the most important connection between critical thinking and its development educationally. The view of Siegel (1988) is that the critical manner "demands of a teacher a willingness to subject all beliefs and practices to scrutiny, and so to allow students the genuine opportunity to understand the role reasons play in the justification of thought and action" (p. 45). However, there may be a risk for teachers in modelling critical thinking. Modelling critical thinking requires the courage to freely explore and, therefore, be open to criticism and new perspectives.

A "prerequisite to teaching is being able to think well" (Nickerson, 1991, p. 6). Teachers who cannot think well will never be able to model critical thinking and teach by example. Thinking well and modelling thinking is based upon the teacher's deep understanding of the subject matter. Assuming that critical thinking is epistemologically based, it is inconceivable that a teacher without knowledge expertise could effectively facilitate critical thinking within that context. The teacher's first responsibility to critical teaching is to be expert in the subject to be taught and then to also have considerable expertise in facilitating and participating in the educational transaction.

To have expertise is to understand the essence of a subject and its nuances. It is interesting to note that experts, compared to novices, tend to be more self-directed (see next chapter) and constructivist in how they search for, and make sense of, new information (Daley, 1999). Experts recognize the importance of the context of professional practice and self-initiated learning to deepen their understanding. Novices, on the other hand, wait to be told what to learn (i.e. other-directed) and assimilate information somewhat fortuitously. All of which points out the importance of teacher expertise both in terms of content and process in an educational environment.

Teachers play a key role in the classroom community by bridging the scholarly and educational communities. The teacher must be externally open and have the expertise to be able to judge the limits of knowledge and not accept and convey it with an inappropriate sense of certainty. Furthermore, the teacher must model reflective scepticism and intellectual humility. They must constantly assess the appropriate balance of interpretative participation by students in the critical classroom community of inquiry. This enormous responsibility and challenge is reflected in the statement by Seixas (1993) that "Ultimately, the teacher is responsible for negotiating the form and content of cultural authority imposed from beyond the classroom, and for defining and modelling the interpretative latitude permissible within the classroom" (p. 312).

The concept of a community of inquiry does raise the issue of the place and role of independent reflection and study. It is important to emphasize again that both collaboration and self-reflection are essential aspects of the complete critical thinking/learning cycle. As such, critical dialogue (discourse) or critical self-reflection, by themselves, will be incomplete in mastering critical thinking/learning. Education must reflect and respect collective purposes as well as individual interests. In addition to discourse, opportunities must be created for students to critically reflect upon new ideas and perspectives as they relate to previous knowledge structures (schemata) and assumptions. In this way, students' cognitive autonomy will be respected and, thus, they will be intrinsically motivated to take responsibility and persist in constructing personal meaning. Critical self-reflection is essential for autonomous thinking in order to escape conformity and the equally dangerous trap of consensus determining all valid knowledge (Habermas, 1971; Mezirow, 1991). While there is a legitimate and crucial place for socially constructed and confirmed knowledge, autonomous thinking provides the openness and vitality to the system to sustain the learning process in a worthwhile and ever evolving manner. Critical discourse and reflection are inseparable components of critical thinking and learning in an educational sense.

Notwithstanding the previous comments, few students have the ability and discipline to rely on critical self-reflection for the purposes of confirming knowledge. As Brookfield (1987a) suggests "It is tremendously difficult to take on the role of an external observer of our own thoughts and actions simply by an act of will" (p. 75). Thus, the teacher and fellow students become essential players in the educational drama. Books by themselves are seldom sufficient to dislodge beliefs and assumptions that most students are not consciously aware they possess. As we have repeatedly argued, students must be given opportunities to iteratively engage in critical reflection and discourse.

In a more practical vein, the first step in facilitating critical thinking is to develop a supportive classroom climate. McPeck (1990a) states "that the attitude of the teacher, and the learning atmosphere in the class, is likely to have real and important effects on the success of nurturing such autonomous thinking" (p. 35); that is, critical thinkers. As a facilitator of critical thinking one must know when to challenge students' thinking without damaging the critical spirit. Students must feel secure as members of a critical community if they are to participate fully in seeking knowledge and truth.

Beyond setting a supportive classroom environment, there are no simple recipes in the quest to facilitate the development of critical thinking. Notwithstanding this challenge, there is a suggested approach to this task. The assumption is that thinking has to be about something and, therefore, learning how to think is accomplished through learning what to think; that is, through developing an understanding of specific content. Constructing meaning goes to the heart of learning to think. If we exclude specific courses whose content is about critical thinking, then we can assume the goal is not to understand thinking in the abstract but to learn how to think in the particular subject domain. Constructing meaningful knowledge is the means to learn how to think. Therefore, thinking is best developed through the challenges of learning specific content. Students who do not approach learning with the purpose of constructing meaning would benefit from explicit instruction in critical thinking operations.

In general, developing critical thinking abilities has to be integral to the construction of meaning within a particular subject domain. But this does not exclude explicit instruction regarding the thinking process. To begin with, critical thinking operations should be modelled and advance organizers provided. Furthermore, phases of the critical thinking cycle as well as the integral judgements and decisions should be made explicit, particularly for novices. Initially, the task of making sense of subject matter may have to be reduced to a sequence of sub-tasks that correspond to the phases of the critical thinking cycle. For example, resolving a problem or dilemma may mean having the students collaboratively define the problem and identify the issues. Once the problem has been understood the task may be to explore for possible solutions or explanations through a brainstorming exercise. Next, groups of students may select and test possible solutions. As students become more advanced, they may individually or in small groups reflect upon the problem before sharing their thinking process in its entirety. A similar strategy for the critical comprehension of written materials is described in Chapter 6.

Through reflection students are provided a model of the phases of critical thinking and an appreciation of particular strategies. Periodically, these metacognitive approaches should be explicitly addressed to encourage students to become increasingly aware of their thinking strategies and approaches to learning. Critical thinkers are metacognitively aware and, thus, are self-directed. Self-direction and cognitive autonomy will depend upon this ability to learn how to learn — perhaps the ultimate goal of education. While students need a coherent model of, and explicit instruction in, critical thinking, it should be kept in mind that the means of developing critical thinking is embedded in the process of understanding a subject domain.

In addition to developing critical thinking abilities and skills, dispositions must also be considered. Fundamentally, educational participants must be explicitly aware of the premises and assumptions of the perspective or argument advocated by oneself as well as others. Participants must be willing and able to follow the reasoning of an argument and be respectfully open to the possibility that either party could be wrong. This will necessitate a good understanding of the knowledge and logic of the subject as well as an appreciation of the specific referential context. Participants in an educational transaction who promote critical thinking must also accept the tentative nature of knowledge and continue to individually and collaboratively examine the meaning and validity of knowledge statements. Dispositions are only developed over time through a constructive and meaningful approach to learning. From a teaching perspective, it is important to consistently model critical thinking and facilitate a critical community of learners.

Conclusion

Educators may not fully agree how to define critical thinking or they may differ in how it should be facilitated. However, most would agree that it is the means to meaningful and worthwhile learning. Thus, it is argued that critical thinking is intimately associated with the process of learning in an educational sense. Critical thinking is essential for constructing meaning from existing knowledge as well as creating new knowledge. Critical thinking is also considered here to be knowledge based and, therefore, is best taught within the context of a discipline. The premise and rationale are that since critical thinking depends upon reasons, and reasons are knowledge based, critical thinking cannot be learned without a basic understanding of the subject matter. As a result, critical thinking is epistemologically (i.e. content) based and, therefore, critical thinking cannot be defined in terms of particular generalizable skills that can be packaged in a separate course and taught as a "fourth 'r'" like reading, writing and arithmetic.

The perspective reflected in the critical thinking/learning model presented in this chapter is that it is a comprehensive process inclusive of higher-order thinking such as creativity and problem solving. Beyond the comprehensive perspective of the model, perhaps its most important distinction is the relationship of reflective (individual) and collaborative (shared) activities. Meaningful learning and continuous knowledge development necessitates an iterative movement between the personal and shared worlds of the student. It was also pointed out that intuition and insight are a part of the critical thinking/learning process and play a role in discovery and the construction of meaning. With regard to the general approach to developing critical thinking in students, it was concluded that this could best be done within the context of learning the subject matter in a deep and meaningful manner. More specifically, this may best be accomplished within a supportive but critical community of learners; where dispositions are shaped through free discussion with fellow students and teachers who honestly and openly model the critical thinking process.

Education is a collaborative activity but learning is the responsibility of the individual. This seemingly paradoxical situation is at the basis of an understanding of the teaching-learning process. The critical thinking/learning model described here suggests that knowledge results from the interplay between individual and socially shared processes and interests. Although critical thinking is a process of the individual making sense of his/her experiences, it is a process that can be facilitated. Construction of meaning may result from individual critical reflection but ideas are generated and knowledge constructed through the collaborative and confirmatory process of sustained dialogue within a critical community of learners. In other words, the student must assume the responsibility to generate ideas and construct personal meaning as well as collaboratively confirm that meaning through discourse with informed others. Knowledge can only emerge from a sustained and serious scrutiny of ideas and claims to truth.

The challenge for teachers is to recognize this "reciprocally constitutive relationship" between the personal and public worlds when facilitating critical thinking and the collaborative construction of meaning and knowledge. Prawat (1999) argues that teachers cannot afford to select a public or private perspective. Teachers "must attend to both public and private ways of knowing at the same time — both group and individual learning, in other words" (Prawat, 1999, p. 72). This is the essence of the teaching-learning transaction and critical thinking/learning model discussed here.

In this chapter, we have emphasized the cognitive perspective and learning theory. The next chapter will begin to focus more specifically on the management of the educational transaction; that is, the theory and explanation of the mechanism (process) of teaching and learning. In this discussion we will explore issues of control and choice for responsible and meaningful learning. The discussion will be organized around the concept of self-directed learning. In a sense, we have approached critical thinking from the inside out. Next we approach self-directed learning from the outside in.

5

Self-Directed Learning

The concept and study of self-directed learning originated in the field of adult education. However, over the last decade other fields of study have shown interest in self-directed learning. Increasing attention has been directed to applications of this concept in formal educational settings. The reason appears to be the increasingly rapid development of new knowledge, coupled with cutbacks in educational funding in a context of global economic competition. As a result of these and other factors, there has been a realization that learning must be more self-directed if it is to be more relevant and efficient, as well as continuous throughout the life-span. In today's social context, students must acquire the habit of taking more responsibility and control in identifying educational goals for themselves and designing appropriate learning experiences. This facility in directing their own learning should then carry on throughout the years of employment in a modern, constantly evolving workplace.

At the same time, we should emphasize that the concept of self-directed learning means more than simply choosing isolating, self-reliant approaches to learning. Self-direction is more than simply controlling the context of learning. It is a complex concept involving a number of social and psychological factors.

To date, few models of self-directed learning have provided a comprehensive treatment of both social and psychological factors. For self-directed learning to be a comprehensive foundational concept in a theory of teaching and learning, it must include contextual, cognitive, and conative (interest/effort) dimensions associated with initiating and sustaining learning activities. Accordingly, self-directed learning is defined here as an approach where learners are motivated to assume personal responsibility and collaborative control of the contextual and cognitive processes involved in constructing meaningful and worthwhile learning outcomes.

Self-Directed Learning Assessed

Self-directed learning may well be the most prominent and well researched topic in the field of adult education (Brockett & Hiemstra, 1991; Long & Redding, 1991). Moreover, the concept is finding a place in other fields of study and practice such as higher education, business, and nursing. While the reasons for this are surely complex, one important reason has to be the intuitively appealing desire to control what we learn and how we learn it. It also fits with the desire and need felt by most adults to continue to learn. These innately human characteristics are inherent in the concept of self-directed learning. As Knowles (1975) has stated, self-directed learning is not an educational fad, but a "basic human competence — the ability to learn on one's own" (p. 17).

The apparent need to "learn on one's own" has certainly been a persistent theme in self-directed learning. For this reason, it is not surprising to find that self-directed learning has its genesis in independent and informal adult learning contexts (Tough, 1971). As such, self-directed learning has largely focused on external issues of control (Brookfield, 1986; Garrison, 1993). An important turning point in conceptualizing self-directed learning occurred with the recognition that it lacked a cognitive perspective. Mezirow (1985) was one of the first to focus upon the cognitive dimension of self-directed learning. He suggested that a critical awareness of meaning and self-knowledge is a key dimension to self-directedness. Similarly, Brookfield (1985, 1986) argued that the full adult form of self-directed learning is realized when the external activities and the internal reflective dimensions are fused.

Long (1989) also suggested turning our attention to the cognitive dimension of self-direction. He identified three dimensions of self-directed learning — the sociological, pedagogical and psychological. Long contends that much of the discussion around self-directed learning has focused on the sociological (i.e. independent task management) and pedagogical (i.e. application in educational contexts) issues. Long expressed amazement at the fact that the psychological (i.e. cognitive) dimension had been generally ignored. He stated that the "critical dimension in *self-directed* learning is not the sociological variable, nor is it the pedagogical factor. The main distinction is the psychological variable, ..." (Long, 1989, p. 3).

While the social context for learning has been and should remain a significant factor in self-directed learning, the lack of focus on the psychological or cognitive dimension, until recently, is somewhat ironic considering the humanistic origins of the concept. In particular, Rogers (1969) specifically used the concept of self-direction in terms of both a cognitive and affective perspective. For Rogers, self-direction was largely about taking responsibility for the internal cognitive and motivational aspects of learning. The emphasis was on cognitive freedom and the ultimate goal was to learn how to learn. Perhaps the time has come to include a discussion of the cognitive/motivational dimensions in a concept of self-directed learning.

Of itself, the phrase self-directed learning invokes both social and cognitive issues — that is, issues of "self-direction" and "learning" respectively. However, in adult education, most of the focus has been on self-direction (i.e. self-management of learning tasks). As such, self-directed learning has been largely defined in terms of external control and facilitation concerns — not internal cognitive processing or learning concerns. Long's (1989) position was that without the psychological (i.e. cognitive) dimension the focus is on teaching, not learning. He argued that: "Pedagogical procedures whether imposed by a teacher or freely chosen by the learner remain pedagogical or 'teaching' activities. Hence we have other-teaching or perhaps self-teaching but not self-learning" (p. 5). This distinction between external control and internal cognitive responsibility issues is the basis of the self-directed learning framework and model presented here.

Meaningful and worthwhile learning must view external task control and cognitive responsibility concerns as integral and reciprocal constructs. For example, self-direction simply focused on task control neglects the critical issues of setting goals that are relevant and meaningful as well as neglecting cognitive strategies and opportunities to question accepted orthodoxies. An adult learner who is fully self-directed has moved beyond simple task control and learned to think critically and construct meaning in ill-defined and complex content areas. As a viable construct, self-directed learning must go beyond task control and include the processes of accepting responsibility to construct meaning and cognitively monitor the learning process itself (i.e. metacognitive awareness). Furthermore, motivational states should also be included, given their mediating effect on both task management and cognitive monitoring of the learning process. A comprehensive self-directed learning model is described below.

A Comprehensive Model

The self-directed learning model described here includes three overlapping dimensions. The three "M's" are management (contextual control), monitoring (cognitive responsibility) and motivation (entering and task) (see Figure 5.1). While each of these dimensions is discussed separately, in practice, they are intimately connected. This creates special problems with ordering the discussion. It is very difficult to discuss one dimension without concurrently considering the others. However, the complexity of an integrated approach would defeat the goal of a parsimonious explication of each dimension. Therefore, since self-directed learning has traditionally emphasized task management and external control, we begin with the more familiar concept of management; that is, the transactional (collaborative) control of external tasks and activities. This dimension encompasses the sociological and pedagogical issues that Long (1989) identified.

Management. The management dimension of self-directed learning within an educational context is concerned with task control issues. Management is concerned with the social and behavioural implementation of learning intentions; that is, the external activities associated with the learning process. (Learning intentions and goal setting processes will be discussed in the section on motivation.) This dimension concerns the enactment of learning goals and the management of learning resources and support. Questions of goal management, learning methods, support and outcomes are collaboratively and continuously assessed and negotiated. For example, learners should be provided with choices as to how they wish to proactively carry out the learning process. Material resources should be available, approaches suggested, flexible pacing accommodated and questioning/feedback provided when needed. In this way, self-management of the learning process will facilitate and energise meaningful and continuous learning.

The term "self-management" is used here to indicate an aspect of external task control specific to the management of learning activities by the learner (which, of

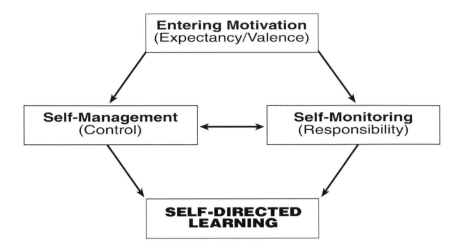

Figure 5.1: Dimensions of self-directed learning.

course, is intimately linked with goal setting and (meta)cognitive strategies). However, this is not a common term. The essence of the concept can be found in the self-regulated motivational literature (Corno, 1994; Pintrich & DeGroot, 1990). While, in practice, contextual self-management cannot be separated from cognitive (self-monitoring) and conative (motivation/volition) control strategies, it is intended to reflect the social setting (resource management) and what learners do during the learning process.

Consistent with a collaborative constructivist view of learning, the individual does not construct meaning in isolation from the shared world. This is particularly true of self-directed learning in an educational context. Increased learner control affects the transactional balance between teacher and learner. From an adult education perspective, Candy (1991) states, "that increasing learner-control demands a negotiated consensus between the parties involved" (p. 243). That is, the control over management of learning tasks is realized in a collaborative relationship between teacher and learner. The teacher assumes considerable responsibility in determining and maintaining an appropriate dynamic balance of external control.

Management has to do with shaping the contextual conditions in the performance of goal-directed actions. While it is possible for some mature learners to rise above a learning context where they have little control, a collaborative learning environment where learner's input can shape goals and activities is more conducive to constructing meaningful knowledge (Prawat, 1992; Resnick, 1991). In an educational context, self-management does not mean students are independent and isolated learners. Facilitators provide the support, direction and standards necessary for a successful educational outcome. Therefore, in what might seem paradoxical, self-management of learning in an educational context is properly a collaborative experience.

Management control of learning activities depends upon a complex array of variables. However, in essence, external management dynamics (task control) is determined contingently by balancing the factors of proficiency, resources and interdependence (Garrison, 1993). Proficiency represents the abilities and skills of the facilitator and learner. Resources encompass a range of support and assistance available in the educational setting. Finally, interdependence reflects institutional/subject norms and standards as well as learner integrity and choice. Sustained collaborative consideration of the many variables associated with these factors, will help determine the appropriate degree of learner self-management.

Control does not translate into social independence or freedom from influence. Educational self-management concerns the use of learning materials within a context where there is an opportunity for collaboration and sustained communication. Self-management of learning in an educational context must consider the opportunity to test and confirm understanding in a critical community of learners. This is an important aspect of knowledge development. Issues of control must balance educational norms and standards (e.g. what counts as worthwhile knowledge) with student choice and the responsibility for constructing personal meaning. All participants must feel comfortable with the degree of perceived and negotiated control of learning tasks and activities. Thus, considerable importance is placed on communication capabilities and opportunities in determining the appropriate balance of control and degree of learner self-management.

Increased learner control through self-management brings with it increased responsibilities, particularly with regard to the learning process itself and the construction of meaning. Perhaps the immediate benefit of increased self-management is increased awareness of the need to make learning more meaningful. That is, the learner takes greater responsibility in monitoring the learning process itself. As will be argued next, it is very difficult to get learners to accept responsibility for meaningful learning outcomes when they have little control of, and input into, the learning process.

To this point in describing the proposed model we have identified the transactional or andragogical aspects of self-directed learning in adult education (i.e. the organization and implementation of the educational experience). The next two dimensions of the model — monitoring and motivation — represent the cognitive dimensions of self-directed learning. These cognitive dimensions recognize perceived cognitive abilities and the importance of learners assuming responsibility for monitoring their cognitive strategies and outcomes.

Monitoring. The monitoring dimension of the self-directed learning model addresses cognitive and metacognitive processes — that is, monitoring the repertoire of learning strategies and quality of learning outcomes (meaningfulness) as well as an awareness of, and an ability to think about, our thinking (plan and modify thinking according to the learning task/goal). Monitoring is the process where the learner takes responsibility for the construction of personal meaning (i.e. integrating new ideas/concepts with previous knowledge). Responsibility for "self-monitoring" reflects a commitment and obligation on the part of the learner to construct meaning through critical reflection and collaborative confirmation. To self-monitor the learning process is to ensure that new and existing knowledge structures are integrated in a meaningful manner and learning goals are being met. It is central to assessing the quality of learning outcomes and shaping strategies for further learning activities.

Self-monitoring is synonymous with responsibility to construct meaning. This may mean adding to, and enriching, existing knowledge structures or the modification and development of new knowledge structures. Responsibility in learning is interpreted to mean a commitment to construct meaning by assimilating and accommodating new concepts with previous knowledge. To be responsible for one's own learning necessitates a willingness and ability to self-monitor the learning process. Responsibility for self-monitoring the learning process, however, is not independent of contextual influences surrounding control of the educational transaction. Self-monitoring is dependent upon both internal and external feedback.

Cognitive and metacognitive processes are involved with self-monitoring the construction of meaning. Cognitive ability is a core variable in self-directed learning. Learners will not succeed and persist in their learning without a set of cognitive abilities and strategies available to them. The extent of self-direction will very much depend upon the learner's proficiency (i.e. abilities and strategies) in conjunction with the contextual/epistemological demands. Bandura (1986) suggests that there are three self-regulated learning processes: self-observation, self-judgement and self-reaction. That is, during the learning process, students self-monitor their progress by observing, judging and reacting to their tasks and activities. Further investigation has revealed 14 self-regulated learning strategies consistent with this and other research (Zimmerman, 1989). Other cognitive skills and strategies related to self-regulation are examined by Winne (1995).

Metacognitive proficiency is very much associated with the ability to be reflective and think critically. Reflective learning encourages the learner to relive the experience with the aim "to develop learners who are capable of monitoring themselves in a variety of situations " (Candy et al., 1985, p. 115). Self-monitoring facilitates a metacognitive perspective of learning and a generalized ability to learn. Models of critical thinking not only help describe the metacognitive processes associated with self-directed learning, but they can be of great assistance in helping students to become metacognitively responsible in their learning (Garrison, 1992). For example, learners must understand whether the requirements of the task are to assess the state of current knowledge, search for additional information, explore new conceptualizations, construct new meaning, or confirm new meaning through discourse/action. To assume cognitive responsibility is to self-monitor the learning processes, assess outcomes, and develop new strategies to achieve intended outcomes.

However, internal feedback alone may lack accuracy and explicitness (Butler & Winne, 1995). Notwithstanding the possibility and value of incidental feedback from serendipitous experience, in an educational setting it is the teacher who can provide efficient and effective feedback for purposes of self-monitoring the quality (meaning and validity) of the learning outcome. The challenge is for the learner to integrate this external feedback with their personal meaning assessment. To be aware of individual and social input and to use it to construct meaning and shape strategies is to self-monitor learning cognitively and metacognitively.

Although self-monitoring is a cognitive process, it is intimately linked to the external management of learning tasks and activities. An interesting and important issue arises with regard to responsibility (monitoring) and control (management). The dilemma is whether responsibility must precede control or whether control should come before responsibility. Although theoretically they go hand in hand, it is very difficult for learners to assume responsibility for their learning without feeling they have some control over the educational transaction. When the teacher controls goals and activities, it places students in the position of being responsible for decisions made by the teacher. Without choice and collaboration, it may well be difficult for students to assume responsibility for their learning.

For example, a lack of self-management (i.e. control/choice) while maintaining a sense of self-monitoring will likely lead to a passive critical state. The student may critically process presented information but is not provided the encouragement or possibly the opportunity to seek additional information or alternative explanations. This can create a closed knowledge system where it is very difficult to challenge the parameters of the educational content and go beyond what is presented; students can only passively and privately assess what is presented because communication with teacher and other students does not allow for critical reflection and discourse.

On the other hand, self-management without self-monitoring does not provide a supportive context for the construction of meaningful and integrated knowledge structures. This process of education without critical thinking could be termed active reproductive learning. Therefore, to ensure the integrity of the educational transaction both self-monitoring abilities and self-management opportunities (i.e. self-direction) are extremely important.

The reality in many formal educational institutions is that control is concentrated in the hands of teachers and administrators. In this situation it is difficult for learners to assume ownership of their learning which, in turn, may encourage short term surface outcomes. This is changing, however, with the increasing demand for lifelong learning (learning how to learn) and network learning (e.g. Internet) opportunities. These trends towards meaningful and relevant learning goals are shifting the balance of control in formal educational institutions.

While it is argued that perceived control should precede responsibility, too much learner control may adversely affect the quality of learning outcomes; or, at a minimum, reduce the efficiency of achieving worthwhile learning outcomes. There is evidence that collaborative control results in more effective self-monitoring and, therefore, improved performance (Butler & Winne, 1995). In addition, self-directed learning controlled by the learner tends to be fortuitously shaped by the environment (organizing circumstance) (Spear & Mocker, 1984). On the other hand, sharing control of learning activities and tasks provides opportunities for instructional support while encouraging students to assume cognitive responsibility.

Finally, absolute learner control may reduce persistence, which will be discussed in the next section.

The inseparability of monitoring and managing the learning process is further complicated by motivational concerns. Motivation is a pivotal issue in self-directed learning. It has an enormous influence on learners assuming responsibility and control of the learning process. When considering motivational influences on learning there is a need to include both a pre-implementation or planning phase and an implementation or action phase.

Motivation. Motivation plays a very significant role in the initiation of interest and maintenance of effort with regard to the achievement of learning goals. Notwithstanding our limited understanding of the link between motivation and cognition, "we do know quite enough to be certain that motivational factors have enormous practical influences on the kinds of cognitive activities that underlie human learning" (Howe, 1987, p. 145). Motivation reflects perceived value and anticipated success of learning goals at the time learning is initiated and mediates between management (contextual control) and monitoring (cognitive responsibility) tasks during the learning process.

To begin to understand the pervasive influence of motivational factors, we need to distinguish between the process of deciding to participate (i.e. entering motivation) and the effort required to stay on task and persist (i.e. task motivation). It is important to note that Dewey discussed these two aspects of motivation in terms of interest and effort or will (Prawat, 1998). Since entering motivation or interest directly influences effort expended on learning tasks, it is important to appreciate how entering motivational states are established. Entering motivation establishes commitment to a particular goal and the intent to act. On the other hand, task motivation or effort is the tendency to focus on, and persist in, learning activities and goals. As Corno (1989) suggests; "Motivational factors…shape intentions and fuel task involvement" (pp. 114–115).

The process of selecting goals/intentions and deciding to participate establishes the student's entering motivational state. In a sense, this is the motivational reserve or fuel that the student possesses when initiating a learning experience. Although much can happen to influence motivation during the learning process, effort and persistence will be greatly influenced by the entering motivational state. The theoretical challenge is to define the variables that influence the decisional process leading to a goal commitment. The decisional process to participate in a learning experience described here is based upon the work of Vroom (1964) and Pintrich (1989) and was influenced by Rubenson's (1987) expectancy-valence paradigm for recruitment (Garrison, 1990). This theoretical framework is relevant here due to its research base; but, more importantly, because of Rubenson's work with this framework relative to participation/recruitment in adult education and Garrison's explication of the paradigm's decision making process using the concept of control.

A student's entering motivational state results from rational intentions (i.e. choice) with regard to selecting learning goals. This is not to say that decisions are

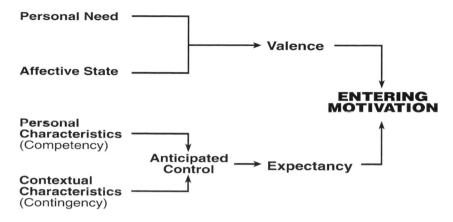

Figure 5.2: Entering motivation factors.

entirely free or voluntary (Stalker, 1993). As we shall see subsequently, contextual contingencies very much shape our choice of goals and decision to participate. Notwithstanding this caveat, establishing the entering motivational state is concerned with choosing goals. It is hypothesized that entering motivation is largely determined by valence and expectancy (see Figure 5.2). That is, students will have a higher entering motivational state if they perceive that learning goals will meet their needs and are achievable. Entering motivation can be perceived as interest — the fusion of attitudes, feelings, abilities and contextual contingencies.

In a learning context valence reflects the attraction to particular learning goals. The factors that determine valence are personal needs (values) and affective states (preferences). Personal need reflects the importance or worth of particular learning goals. Needs and values reflect the reasons for persisting in a learning task. Closely associated with needs are affective states. This set of variables is composed of attitudes toward self (e.g. self-esteem), task (e.g. anxiety), and goal preference.

Expectancy in a learning context refers to the belief that a desired outcome can be achieved. This factor is composed of personal and contextual characteristics that influence goal achievement. Personal characteristics (i.e. competency) reflect the perceived skills, ability and knowledge of the individual while assessing goals. Perceptions of ability or self-efficacy affect the decision to participate as well as the choice of goals and learning environments. Contextual characteristics (i.e. contingency) reflect the perceived institutional resources/barriers as well as ideological and socioeconomic constraints. Together competency and contingency assessments represent the mediating construct of "anticipated control".

Anticipated control is an important perception when assessing expectancy of success and making decisions regarding goal directed behaviour. It is believed that control expectations "influence the direction of much of our behaviour; they help to determine where we invest our achievement energies" (Weisz, 1983, p. 234). Anticipated control reflects the perceived ability and opportunity to exercise control over the learning process. If students are to have an expectation of control, they must have some choice over their educational goals. Providing opportunities for control/choice from the beginning can significantly strengthen the entering motivational state which subsequently influences whether students will become self-directed and persist in their learning tasks.

Maintenance of intention during the learning process brings into focus the second motivational phase — task motivation. To direct and sustain motivation students must become active learners. As noted previously, task motivation is integrally connected to task control and self-management. In addition, task motivation is conceived as being closely associated with the issue of volition. Volition is concerned with sustaining intentional effort (i.e. diligence) which influences persistence and task performance. In "the context of learning, volition refers to bringing discordant affective and executional preferences in line with one's task goals" (Kanfer, 1989, p. 381). Corno (1993) argues that volition is a key aptitude for educational success. Its function is metamotivational in directing and sustaining effort toward learning goals. This metamotivational mechanism is necessary if learners are to assume responsibility for the achievement of desired educational outcomes and represents a direct link to the self-monitoring dimension of self-directed learning.

Motivation to assume responsibility in learning is influenced by external conditions and internal states. While extrinsic motivation may well complement and enhance intrinsic motivation, externally imposed tasks and criteria can also reduce the "will" to assume responsibility for learning. The challenge is to have students internalize external goals and rewards which are often more dominant during the entering stages of learning. To encourage intrinsically motivated learning, students must see opportunities to share control and to collaborate in the planning and implementation of the learning process. For example, in an educational setting, students should be provided with an opportunity to at least understand why specific objectives are worthwhile if not select relevant objectives from amongst options as well as shape approaches and select appropriate learning tasks. It is imperative that we create the conditions where students become increasingly motivated by authentic interest and effort/will to construct personal meaning and shared understanding (worthwhile knowledge). Motivation and responsibility are reciprocally related and both are facilitated by collaborative control of the educational transaction. Issues of motivation, responsibility (monitoring) and control (management) are central to a comprehensive concept of self-directed learning. Learners are motivated to assume responsibility for constructing meaning and understanding when they have some control over the learning experience. Moreover, it is also suggested that self-direction is consistent with deep and meaningful approaches to learning. Biggs (1988) states that a "self-conscious and planful approach to learning thus requires, first, that students are *aware* of their motives and intentions, of their own cognitive resources, and of the demands of academic tasks; and second, that they are able to *control* those resources and monitor their consequent performance" (p. 187).

The reality is that a significant number of students in higher education have not learned or been given the opportunity to accept responsibility for their learning and to approach learning in a deep and meaningful manner. This is not addressed, however, by simply demanding that students teach themselves. Unstructured educational environments do little to encourage students to be reflective and to accept responsibility for their learning. Cognitive autonomy and pedagogical control are predicated upon possession of the cognitive and conative abilities as well as contextual resources appropriate to the demands of the educational task. Although cognitive autonomy is largely the responsibility of the student, this autonomy does not imply social independence. Somewhat paradoxically, cognitive autonomy may well depend upon collaboration and external support. The issue is whether students have the opportunity to collaboratively control the management of learning tasks.

The continuous process of maintaining the delicate balance between internal monitoring (responsibility) and external management (control) issues central to sustaining motivation is discussed next.

A Transactional Perspective

Transactional issues surrounding managing, monitoring and motivating learning in an educational setting are influenced by many contextual factors. From a macro-contextual perspective the educational process is indirectly influenced by institutional and community norms. While the primary focus here is on the immediate educational transaction, it is important to keep in mind that the participants possess a wide range of personal values which may reflect larger social and family values and influences. Moreover, specific institutional contingencies may have a direct influence through administration, teachers, and the peer group on the nature of the educational transaction. This diverse set of values and expectations makes understanding the dynamics of the educational transaction challenging and necessary.

Facilitating self-directed learning in an educational context necessitates a dynamic balance on at least two levels. At the macro level, an educational transaction interconnects teacher, student and curricula. An educational transaction in its best sense must recognize legitimate teacher, student and curricula values and standards. Issues of control, responsibility and persistence must be addressed. Therefore, educationally, self-directed learning is realized within a critical community of learners where rights and responsibilities must be observed. At the micro level, the dimensions of self-direction discussed previously (i.e. management, monitoring and motivation) predominate. The maintenance of a dynamic educational balance among issues of control (management), responsibility (monitoring) and persistence (motivation) is realized through sustained communication.

The purpose of the discussion here is to address the complex and dynamic elements in an educational transaction as well as demonstrate the challenges in maintaining an appropriate balance amongst competing factors. There is no ideal balance around issues of motivation, monitoring and management. Each situation is unique in that an individual may be extremely self-directed in one context but not in another. Educational self-direction is contingent.

From a monitoring perspective, "the beneficial consequences of self-regulation [i.e. self-direction] can only be obtained when there are sufficient cognitive resources available" (Kanfer & Ackerman, 1989, p. 663). However, cognitive proficiencies must be complemented by motivational dispositions (interest) and states (effort/volition). Responsibility also applies to teachers in facilitating learning competencies. Construction of meaning by the student can be facilitated considerably by a responsible and competent teacher. For example, a teacher's command of the curricula as well as their willingness and ability to model a critical thinking/learning approach can enhance the proficiency of students to learn in a meaningful way.

From a management perspective, the issue of control is a primary consideration. Control is contingent and assessed collaboratively. It is not absolute and it does not mean freedom from influence. Contingent control reflects the appropriate independence afforded a student. Independence must consider the teacher's legitimate role as educator (reflecting societal norms) as well as the student's needs and abilities. Greater teacher direction and less student choice may represent a reduction in independence but be entirely justified. At the same time, a sense of independence is important if students are to exercise choice. Given the collaborative nature of education the real issue is the nature of the interdependence (i.e. shared control) of teacher and student.

External control is shared in an educational transaction and is not associated with power over others. It has everything to do with the conditions of constructing meaning in a collaborative and critical community of learners. More specific to self-directed learning, control directly influences effort and "an ability to keep the goal activated during the performance of goal-directed actions: to wait for an appropriate opportunity to act, to correct activities in midstream, and to stop one's activity when the goal is reached" (Lutkenhaus, Bullock & Geppert, 1987, p. 146). Successful self-directed learning is not achieved independent of contextual contingencies and control strategies.

Contingent control necessitates an awareness of surroundings and the possession of a repertoire of capabilities, knowledge and good judgement in taking action as well as being accountable for and adaptable to the consequences of intended actions. Since students seldom have the awareness, capabilities and accountability necessary for full independence, the teacher's role becomes an important necessity. In addition, the teacher must possess the awareness and expertise to complement and enhance the control characteristics of the educational transaction. The control responsibilities of the teacher are to initiate effort, provide a goal and possibly an advance organizer for the learning task, determine and encourage awareness of learners' existing knowledge, have a repertoire of learning methods and techniques, and, most importantly, maintain dialogue and feedback regarding knowledge development.

In any educational transaction, the contextual support and guidance is crucial. Learning resources include personal guidance as well as learning materials. Reliance on non-human resources (i.e. pre-packaged self-instruction) without the opportunity for sustained communication with a teacher and fellow students may represent a reduction of student choice, responsibility and persistence. This approach reduces communication along with the opportunity for personal guidance and critical discourse. For some educational purposes this approach may be justifiable; however, a dynamic balance must be maintained between teacher guidance and structural support if students are to be encouraged to negotiate goals and meaning on a sustained basis. Since the primary goal is to deepen understanding and develop worthwhile knowledge, resources must be such that they facilitate cognitive responsibility within a critical and collaborative learning context.

Balancing contextual (control/management), cognitive (responsibility/monitoring), and conative (interest/effort) issues have practical implications for designing and managing an educational transaction. For instance, allowing students to choose learning goals and activities without sufficient subject knowledge is questionable. However, this may be appropriate if the student possesses sufficient additional abilities and resources to support self-directed learning. Similarly, students should not be required to become more self-directed than they feel comfortable with. Students may feel overwhelmed if they are placed in a situation where they are expected to take more control than they are ready for or capable of accepting. Conversely, students who have the ability and resources are not always afforded the opportunity to make decisions regarding their educational goals and activities. The result may be complacency and short term surface learning. That is, students simply acquire the necessary information to pass the exam without critical examination and the realization of deep understanding. In reality, educational decisions are far more complex and dynamic than just depicted. As such, the issue of communication is crucial to establishing and maintaining self-directed learning as needs change during the course of the educational experience.

In its most elemental form the process of education is communication between teacher and student. While communication between student and instructional materials may play an important role in transmitting information, in itself it does not provide for clarification of meaning or critical discourse that goes beyond the prescribed content. As such, sustained two-way communication between teacher and student will normally mediate the one-way communication between student and curriculum materials. In addition, communication between teacher and curriculum materials may occur as they are redesigned to better meet changing needs and conditions of the educational transaction. However, it should be noted that the most powerful communication is likely to occur when several elements (e.g. teacher/student, student/curriculum materials, student/student) interact concurrently.

The transactional nature and essence of an educational experience places great importance on the communication process. Understanding how to facilitate communication is of central importance in understanding teaching and learning. The conditions necessary for worthwhile educational communication are:

1. students having an awareness and agreement with the educational goals;
2. students able to access relevant information and knowledge;

3. students who have sufficient interest to be critically open to new ideas and perspectives;
4. students who are willing to make the effort to act rationally and reflectively;
5. teachers who are able to facilitate a collaborative and reciprocal transaction;
6. teachers who will model critical reflection and discourse;
7. teachers who have expertise in their subject;
8. teachers who are ethically responsible and respectful.

These are the parameters of an ideal educational transaction.

We have noted the difference between one-way and two-way communication. Communication in an educational sense is seen here as being intentional and reciprocal. True communication is a collaborative activity requiring the co-ordinated action of the participants in order to achieve mutual understanding (Clark & Brennan, 1991). Store and Armstrong (1981) make an important distinction between judgemental and explanatory feedback. Worthwhile feedback goes beyond simply confirming right or wrong; it is explanatory in that it provides for mutual influence and reasons why a student may be right or wrong. The following describes the reciprocal nature of the communication process in an educational transaction:

> In educational terms, this role-alternation would imply that students act not simply as receivers and processors of teacher-messages but also as generators and senders of messages (about themselves, their ideas, their perceptions, their experiences) which the teacher values and allows to change his [her] personal perspective on the student, the subject under discussion, his [her] own feelings, or some other feature of the situation. (Rowntree, 1975, p. 285)

Open communication is also central to facilitating self-directed learning. However, open communication and self-direction can only flourish when learners are encouraged to assume responsibility in a context of shared control and choice.

Responsibility and control. In various ways it has been argued that responsibility and control issues are central constructs for self-directed learning in an educational context. To fully represent the educational transaction, self-directed learning must not only concern itself with andragogical control and self-management but must also concern itself with cognitive responsibility and self-monitoring issues. To paraphrase Dewey, the challenge in an educational transaction is a coherent balancing of formation from without with formation from within. Conceptualiza-tion of the educational transaction must integrate cognitive and contextual factors to encourage meaningful and worthwhile learning. Cognitive responsibility and pedagogical control are complementary and inseparable conditions for meaningful, worthwhile, and continuous learning.

Cognitive responsibility for learning has much to do with critical reflection.

Responsibility for learning suggests a commitment and willingness to construct meaning through the critical questioning, analysis and integration of new ideas and values. From a self-directed learning perspective, responsibility is a critical metacognitive self-monitoring process. Without a metacognitive awareness of learning strategies it is not possible to learn responsibly. Responsibility for learning means an authenticity to self and accountability with regard to what is meaningful. As Thomas and Harri-Augstein (1985) state, "Self-organised learners expect to go on learning, to make independent judgements and to question" (p. 331). While there may be a predisposition with self-regulated learners to accept responsibility, this will be greatly influenced, positively or negatively, by contextual control issues. As such, the primary concern is the process of constructing meaning from the educational experience. There is a difference, however, between personal meaning and public knowledge.

Personal meaning must have a social confirmation process if it is to achieve the status of knowledge. Meaning may be the responsibility of the individual but knowledge is constructed in collaboration with others. Education is a collaborative process for the purpose of personally constructing and confirming knowledge. Avoiding misconceptions is achieved through a critical community of learners, which include teachers and students. Therefore, issues of collaborative control must be considered concurrently with issues of individual responsibility. A clear differentiation must be made between cognitive autonomy and social autonomy. Responsibility to construct meaning may ultimately be that of the learner, but control of the transaction must be shared if there is to be an "organic union" of facts and ideas as well as personal meaning and public knowledge. How to ensure the proper balance of control that will facilitate responsible and critical learning is the question that all educators must struggle with. It is not intuitively obvious how to encourage students to assume responsibility while accepting support and direction from others.

Control must include both the opportunity and ability to make decisions. Students should have the opportunity to make decisions without coercion. However, that decision may be to choose to give up considerable control if ability or confidence is perceived to be lacking. Assuming responsibility for learning is dependent upon contingent control. That is, the opportunity to collaboratively determine the resources and independence commensurate with ability and educational task. Too much or too little control can both diminish the quality of the educational learning experience. There is no contradiction between collaboration and self-directed learning. Taking responsibility and control of one's learning (i.e. self-direction) does not mean independent and isolated self-discovery.

Self-directed learning is a necessary aspect of a true educational experience that unifies individual cognitive responsibility and collaborative control issues. Self-directed learning also reflects metacognitive and metamotivational factors to be considered in the context of an educational transaction. These same issues were addressed in the previous chapter on critical thinking around issues of individual and socially shared worlds. Notwithstanding that self-direction and critical thinking evolved from distinct literature bases, educationally the primary difference between the two is that of emphasis. The connection between these constructs is found through responsibility and control issues. Whether one thinks in terms of critical thinking (inside-out) or self-directed learning (outside-in) will depend upon one's perspective and the specific educational context and concern; however, the underlying and unifying concepts of personal responsibility and collaborative control are inherent to both perspectives and models.

Teaching and Motivation

Perhaps the fundamental question addressed in this book is how do we as teachers create the conditions where students are motivated to take responsibility for constructing meaning from their educational experiences and, thereby, achieve the intended outcomes. It has been argued that motivation to assume responsibility for one's actions, and persist in a learning event, flows from a sense of control and the opportunity to collaboratively make decisions. The role of the teacher is to provide guidance and support, yet allow students to be actively engaged in educational decisions. Teachers must consider both external and internal conditions. Extrinsic motivation complements and enhances intrinsic motivation. It is important not to deny external goals and rewards but, instead, facilitate their internalization. Externally imposed tasks and success criteria can de-motivate and alienate students from the educational process if they unduly limit opportunities to control learning tasks and make responsible decisions. The challenge for teachers is to facilitate the internalization of extrinsic motivators.

According to Entwistle (1981), "interest and intrinsic motivation are likely to foster a deep approach, and an active search for personal meaning" (p. 259). Deep and surface approaches to learning exhibit a strong correlation to intrinsic and extrinsic motivation respectively. The deep approach to learning is internal to the knowledge, experience and interests of the learner. On the other hand, the surface approach to learning is a process in which "material is to be impressed on the memory for a limited period and with the specific intention of satisfying external demands" (Entwistle & Ramsden, 1983, p. 195). Since the focus of this book is upon deep and meaningful forms of learning in adult and higher education, a primary concern is how students derive intrinsic motivation to learn.

While the goal is not to deny or eliminate external motivation to learn, the downside of excessive reliance upon external motivation must be addressed. Excessive reliance on extrinsically motivated learning encourages expedient solutions, tends to reduce transferability, may increase anxiety due to loss of control, and does not fully develop self-determination in students; however, the most serious result may be decreased intrinsic motivation (Ryan, Connell & Deci, 1985; Wlodkowski, 1985). Learning based upon interest or intrinsic reasons is more enjoyable but, most importantly, it generates sustained motivation, leads to accepting responsibility for learning, and ultimately the ability and confidence to continue to learn and cope with a variety of learning situations beyond the classroom. In short, intrinsic motivation mediates and is a consequence of relevant and meaningful learning.

In an educational context, Corno and Rohrkemper (1985) define intrinsic motivation "as a facility for learning that sustains the desire to learn — through the development of particular cognitive skills" (p. 53). Corno and Rohrkemper (1985) believe that there are two key features of intrinsic motivation to learn in classroom education. The first is for the student to assume some responsibility for learning which results from developing a sense of personal control. Responsibility includes a recognition that accomplishments are due to one's own efforts and an expectation of a successful outcome. Intrinsic motivation to learn is the result of students becoming deliberate participants in the learning process. Secondly, intrinsic motivation to learn involves an ability or competency to learn new concepts. In addition, Corno and Rohrkemper (1985) suggest that challenge and curiosity are two other variables closely related to competence and represent important goals for educators.

However, becoming a self-directed learner requires learning support. Considerable support and guidance in the classroom is necessary for students to become self-directed learners. They need to have developed the competence and responsibility to achieve their educational goals. Effective classroom teaching involves consideration of students' expectations as well as students adapting to learning tasks. In other words, "effective classroom teachers walk a fine line between imposing and relinquishing control over student learning, and they know when to move back and when to step forward along this continuum" (Corno & Rohrkemper, 1985, p. 75).

From the student's perspective, the motivational impact of an educational event is determined by their interest in the short and long term goals (extrinsic motivation) and the meaning the individual attaches to the event (intrinsic motivation) through their efforts. That is, communication or feedback can be either explanatory or confirmatory (i.e. right or wrong), depending on subtle elements of the transaction. Explanatory feedback represents events that allow choice while confirmatory (i.e. controlling) feedback represents events that impose a particular way to think or feel. Explanatory feedback provides support and guidance in developing cognitive competencies and self-direction. Developing self-directed learning may depend upon external support to increase competency and control. That is, providing structure, guidance and limits may provide explanation and, thereby, be functionally informative rather than controlling. Therefore, self-directed learning may involve a student choosing to give up control. However, students must be participants in the decision making process if they are to assume responsibility for their learning. Self-directed behaviour implies acting out of awareness and choice as opposed to obligation or coercion.

Because of the pressing demands of examinations and grading, students are not often motivated to approach learning in a deep and meaningful manner. Generally, too much learning is of the surface, reproductive nature which is precipitated by external demands. Murray (1991) concluded from an extensive review of college teaching effectiveness research that teachers do make a difference in student learning but the greatest teacher effect may be influencing student motivation.

Teachers have an indispensable role to play in engaging students in learning and in helping them to become self-directed and intrinsically motivated.

More specifically, there are useful techniques to develop self-direction and intrinsic motivation. One technique, suggested by Corno and Rohrkemper (1985), is to have the teacher explicitly model cognitive strategies as well as highlighting difficult aspects of the performance. Another is to ensure clear goals regardless of whether they are prescribed or emerge from student-teacher collaboration. Content should be challenging but the essential ideas should be addressed first. Notwithstanding the need for guidance and support, if intrinsic motivation and self-direction are goals, then intrinsic motivators and student control must be maximized. In short, students must be shifted from extrinsic to intrinsic motivation. Development of higher cognitive abilities such as critical thinking is founded upon intrinsic motivation resulting from self-direction of the learning process.

Motivation is not something teachers do to students. It is inherent in meaningful approaches to learning where teachers consider the needs, expectations, and abilities of students as well as educational norms and demands of the subject. Intrinsic motivation for learning follows from a student's sense of control and responsibility. It is a consequence of the conditions of learning and the quality of the interaction. Intrinsic motivation is influenced by the learning climate and authentic, purposeful teacher-student and student-student dialogue. Ausubel, Novak and Hanesian (1978) stated, in reference to intrinsic motivation, that "although not indispensable for limited and short-term learning, it is absolutely necessary for the sustained type of learning involved in mastering a given subject-matter discipline" (p. 397). Intrinsic motivation is essential for continuous, lifelong learning and is a long-term outcome of self-directed learning.

Motivation is the foundation of increased cognitive engagement in learning and sustainment of effort. Sternberg (1994) states that "Perhaps no single personal attribute is more important to success or learning than is motivation" (p. 227). Without a minimal threshold of entering motivational strength it becomes less likely that students will achieve intended outcomes. A complex set of expectancy-valence factors involved in pre-implementation decisions establish the entering motivational state. The entering motivational state, established as a result of deciding to participate in the educational process, is seen to be different from the motivation to persist. However, once a commitment is made, the primary focus is upon the when and how of initiating learning tasks and achieving the intended educational outcomes.

Self-direction can enhance learning when the transactional elements (management, monitoring and motivation) are in dynamic balance. Monitoring, management and motivational variables need to be assessed in concert to maintain an appropriate and dynamic balance. Self-directed learning depends upon this dynamic balance. Maintaining this complex balance is a serious challenge to all teachers. Without maintaining this self-directed balance, the worthwhileness and integrity of the educational transaction may be compromised. Maintaining such a complex balance is achieved through sustained communication and the mutual respect of teacher and student.

Conclusion

The self-directed learning model described here attempts to integrate management (contextual), monitoring (cognitive) and motivational (conative) dimensions of the educational experience. The self-directed learning model has important implications with regard to the quality of educational outcomes and cognitive development. The reason is that students are motivated to become more meaningfully engaged in their learning (i.e. assume responsibility) when there is choice and they have the opportunity to make relevant decisions (i.e. control). The fundamental argument for understanding and facilitating self-direction is its potential to improve the quality of learning outcomes in the short and long terms. That is, learning is more meaningful, worthwhile and students learn how to learn. Inherently, self-directed learners assume responsibility for, and control of, their learning which, in turn, motivates and reinforces continuous learning and development.

Self-direction is contradictory to the transmission of information from the teacher or text to students without interpretation and the construction of meaning. As seen here, self-directed learning is consistent with a collaborative constructivist view of learning that encourages students to approach learning in a deep and meaningful manner. Richardson (1994) contends that constructivism is a "meaning-making theory" and that most constructivists believe that the traditional transmission model of learning does not promote deep understanding because new information is not well integrated with prior knowledge. Constructing meaning and collaboratively confirming understanding is at the heart of the proposed self-directed learning model.

Meaningful learning outcomes would be very difficult to achieve if students were not self-directed in their learning. Taking responsibility to construct personal meaning is essential to self-directed learning. At the same time, taking responsibility for one's own learning does not mean making decisions in isolation. The challenge for teachers is to create the educational conditions that will facilitate self-directed learning. Choosing and committing to particular learning goals is an important initial phase of self-directed learning. Goals must be valued, well defined and realistic. The probability of achieving this state is increased when students are collaboratively included in setting learning goals. As Thomas and Harri-Augstein (1985) state, "if they do not negotiate a shared purpose, the learner and the teacher are each likely to draw different inferences about the learning that has, or has not, been achieved" (p. 309). Moreover, with shared purpose, there is a concomitant increase in interest and effort to sustain learning activities.

During the learning process consideration needs to be given to transactional and motivational issues. Corno (1994) suggests that "effort is a function of person-situation interaction, and occurs when available external and internal resources combine" (p. 232). These resources include teachers and materials as well as the cognitive abilities and motivation of students. The challenge for teachers is to create the conditions where "mindful investment of effort" is realized by students. Through collaboration and control students learn to monitor their thoughts. The likely order of things is that shared control leads to intrinsic motivation and then to responsibility.

In conclusion, self-directed learning described here is seen as an important if not necessary process in achieving worthwhile and meaningful (i.e. quality) educational outcomes. Self-direction is seen as essential if students are to achieve Dewey's (1916) ultimate educational goal of becoming continuous learners and possessing the capacity for further educational growth. Learner interest and opportunities for control promote responsible, self-directed learning. Opportunities for self-directed learning, in turn, enhance metacognitive awareness and create the conditions where students learn how to learn and will continue to learn.

Self-directed learning and critical thinking are manifestations of the same process — learning. The difference results only in perspective and how we wish to think about the learning process. The analogy is the apparent contradiction of light being both particle and wave. Learning also can be seen in a similar manner in that, from one perspective (outside in), it takes on the characteristics of the self-directed learning model. On the other hand, looking from the inside out, learning may take on the characteristics of the critical thinking model. While on the surface the two models may not have much in common, when viewed through the concepts of constructivism and collaboration as well as responsibility and control, they are complementary and consistent. That is, there is a unity to the learning process and, depending upon our needs, we can think about the process in different ways. One emphasizes the management of the transaction and the other the management of cognition.

Having described and discussed the models of critical thinking and self-directed learning in previous chapters, the next challenge is to translate these theoretical issues and concepts into practical approaches and strategies associated with the teaching-learning transaction.

PART II: Approaches and Strategies

6

Approaches to Teaching

The transactional approach is based on the interaction of teaching and learning, the yin and yang of the educational process. The previous two chapters have discussed the learning process from the two perspectives most associated with higher and adult education — critical thinking and self-directed learning respectively. The present chapter is focused on the other half of the central transaction, namely teaching. What framework should guide the selection of teaching strategies that will ultimately result in an increase in the quality and quantity of learning? What principles should guide the actions of the teacher? What makes for teacher effectiveness?

Research on teacher effectiveness in higher education began as early as the 1920s. However, systematic and sustained inquiry into the role of teachers in higher education has emerged only in the last thirty years (Meyer & Muller, 1990). The reason for this long period of neglect, at least at universities, is quite simple: teaching was not considered very important. Faculty were hired based on their training in research and their demonstrated potential to excel in it. Research achievements, after all, were what made the reputation of a university — and the careers of individual academics. No training in how to teach was required; teaching was just a rather bothersome chore that professors had to perform, and they could perform it well enough to get by just by teaching as they had been taught (Ellner & Barnes, 1983).

Therefore the lecture method remained dominant, even though its effectiveness was called into question. There were few alternative models of teaching available, and most professors, during their time as students, had never seen such alternative models in action. Needless to say, institutions made little effort to promote better teaching, and the efforts that were made were not very effective. Few resources were (and are) directed to these operations. The result of all the factors mentioned above is that good teaching is not well understood in higher education, and rarely demonstrated.

In marked contrast to higher education, the field of adult education has traditionally placed a premium on teaching effectiveness. The role of the educator in adult education is somewhat different than in higher education, as adult learners are usually willing and able to take more responsibility in directing their learning, thereby leaving to the educator a facilitation and mentoring function rather than an instructor role. Nevertheless, this facilitation role has to be fulfilled effectively, for the excellent reason that adult educators do not usually have a captive or even semi-captive clientele: if they teach (or facilitate) ineffectively, they will soon have no students.

Adult students, with their awkward habit of demanding competent teaching, have recently been showing up in greater numbers in institutions of higher education. This may be one reason why such institutions have begun to show more concern about the quality of their teaching. But they face something of a dilemma: while it is now generally recognized and accepted that teaching is more than lecturing, and that teaching should be more highly valued and rewarded, it is not always clear just what constitutes effective and responsible teaching. Too few teachers in higher education understand why they should change, or in what direction they should change. The present chapter aims to establish a framework to assist them in conceptualizing their problem. Later chapters will suggest some solutions.

To begin to establish this conceptual framework, this chapter begins with a summary of research on effective teaching in general. The discussion then shifts to research focusing on teaching practices aimed at facilitating higher-order cognitive learning — that is, teaching that is motivated by a concern for a specific learning outcome, namely for students to become critical and continuous learners.

Research on Teaching

Prior to the 1970s, it seemed reasonable to study teacher effectiveness by focusing on specific teacher behaviours. This was a logical deduction from the then powerful behaviourist school of psychology, which tended to view education as a linear process in which one adjusted stimuli in order to produce desired responses. One of the stimuli that could be manipulated was teacher behaviour, particularly presentation techniques. Techniques for giving feedback to students so as to produce desired responses were also given some attention, as were classroom management techniques. However, little attention was given to the values and beliefs upon which teachers base their decisions. There was even less attention paid to student thought processes, and the desirability or worthwhileness of the proposed learning outcomes. Most studies of effective teaching focused upon the lecture method and "relied almost exclusively on final exams and recall as cognitive outcome measures" (Murray, 1991, p. 169).

Interestingly, it was students' opinions about teaching styles that formed the basis of early studies of teaching effectiveness in higher education. When responding to structured questions regarding actual teaching situations students had experienced (usually variations of the lecture method) the consistent finding was that students preferred teaching characteristics associated with effective presentation of information (Feldman, 1976, 1988; Murray, 1991; Sherman, 1987). Considering that the lecture was (and is) the dominant instructional method, it is not surprising that presentation characteristics such as an enthusiastic delivery style and clear organization of material emerged as effective teaching behaviours. What was missing, or relegated to second status, were teaching characteristics associated with critical reflection and discourse as well as the creation of a respectful, supportive and collaborative learning climate — exactly the characteristics that were demanded by learners in adult education seminars.

There is, obviously, a strong relationship between the teaching method being employed in a given situation and criteria used to judge teaching effectiveness — by students and others. Murray (1991), notes that characteristics such as enthusiasm and clarity were judged most effective with lecture or lecture-discussion methods. He then raises the crucial question "whether teaching behaviors identified as effective in these studies can be shown to be similarly effective with other methods of teaching, such as small-group discussion" (p. 152). Interestingly, two reported studies using small group discussion and measuring critical thinking gains showed above average gain for students who interacted with the teacher and fellow students.

As to the generalizability of effective teaching characteristics associated with the lecture method, an interesting thing occurs when students are allowed to think outside the box of a presentation approach to teaching. When students were asked in a non-structured manner where they could freely list ideal or important teacher characteristics, they present quite another impression of the effective teacher. They provide characteristics that reflect a preference for facilitation skills such as the ability to establish respectful relationships, open and challenging discussions, and helpful support in constructing meaning (Feldman, 1976). The question is, why do students shift their criteria for effective teaching from facilitation skills to presentation skills when confronted with traditional teaching methods.

Criteria used by students to judge teaching effectiveness appear to change depending upon the educational conditions. Preferred teacher behaviours shift from facilitation to presentation characteristics when the reality of the classroom is present. Perhaps this should not be surprising considering that reality for most students is to attend a lecture and assimilate prescribed course materials for purposes of examination. If students are to be evaluated on prescribed content, then it seems reasonable to expect that they would value teacher characteristics related to presentation. That is, if reproducing information on examinations is the standard of assessment, then presentation characteristics that relate relevant content in a clear and interesting manner would be most valued by students.

Others have consistently associated the presentation characteristics of organization/clarity as well as enthusiasm/stimulation with effective teaching (Donald, 1985; Sherman et al., 1987). However, as a result of the focus on presentation techniques (i.e. lecturing), students' ratings, and lack of clarification of teacher intentions and measured outcomes, the generalizability of these findings has been questioned (Donald, 1985). It is argued here that measures of effective teaching should be designed so that they are appropriate to the nature of the intended learning outcomes, rather than relying on student ratings, which tend to be closely linked to presentation techniques.

Another issue worthy of consideration is the variability, from one discipline to another, of what constitutes effective teaching. This adds another dimension of complexity to understanding effective teaching. The relationship between different approaches to teaching and success in promoting learning in various disciplines is obviously complex, and is not well understood.

In an extensive study of 2208 students in 66 departments, Entwistle and Ramsden

(1983) concluded that the effects of teaching have to be understood within the context of the discipline in which it takes place. They suggest that since different disciplines have different demands there is no general recipe for better teaching. They go on to state:

> In arts, students should be encouraged to search for personal meaning, which seems to depend on empathy and openness from staff, informal teaching discussion methods, freedom for students to explore their interests, and yet, because of that freedom, the setting of clear goals and standards. In science and social science, good teaching seems to depend more on operation learning, on relating evidence and conclusion, and on the appropriate use of a certain amount of initial rote learning to master the terminology. (p. 209)

It was also found that for the sciences certain prerequisite knowledge is necessary for deep learning, while in the arts it would appear to be student interest.

Similarly, Sheffield (1974) found differences among students in the physical sciences, biological sciences, and humanities with regard to what they regarded as effective teaching characteristics. Students in the physical sciences noted whether main points were stressed and formulated at their current level of understanding, and whether teaching aids were used effectively. Biological science students valued currency of content, clear organization of this content, and evidence that the teacher was well prepared for the presentation. Humanities students approved of teaching that showed a sense of humour, enthusiasm, and encouragement of questions and students' expression of opinions.

Thus, it would seem that effective and responsible teaching must consider disciplinary variation. In particular, in some subject areas, for example the sciences, it seems to be more important for teachers to assist students in acquiring foundational skills and knowledge, rather than to provide them with freedom and choice. However, that is not to say that education in the sciences should be totally prescriptive. In all situations students must have an appropriate degree of control if they are to assume responsibility for the construction of knowledge that is both personally meaningful and socially confirmed. To foster this type of learning, students should be encouraged to reflect upon even basic information so that they will make the connections which are necessary in constructing a comprehensive and coherent mental framework that will facilitate further learning.

Besides the important work by individual scholars discussed above, another approach to understanding effective practice in college teaching involved the bringing together of a task force of "scholars who had contributed much of the research over the last five decades on the impact of the college experience" (Gamson, 1991, p. 6). Their challenge was to build upon the previous 50 years of research on college teaching and learning in order to identify the practices, policies and conditions of effective undergraduate education in the form of a minimum number of principles. The result of this collective effort was the "Seven Principles for Good Practice in Undergraduate Education" (Chickering & Gamson, 1987). These principles assert that good undergraduate educational practice:

1. encourages student-faculty contact;
2. encourages cooperation among students;
3. encourages active learning;
4. gives prompt feedback;
5. emphasizes time on task;
6. communicates high expectations;
7. respects diverse talents and ways of learning. (Chickering & Gamson, 1991, p. 63).

Sorcinelli (1991) examined each of the Seven Principles within the context of other validating studies. Recognizing the diversity of research, disciplines, contexts as well as the generalizability of the Seven Principles, Sorcinelli acknowledged the difficulty of reviewing the literature related to each principle. Notwithstanding these challenges, she concluded that the results "of research on student-faculty contact, prompt feedback, and active involvement in learning are especially encouraging" (p. 22). However, it is worth mentioning that with regard to feedback, Sorcinelli (1991) cites research which suggested "that the long-term effects of prompt feedback depend on the quality of the tests (for example, tests for memorization versus critical thinking) and the quality of the feedback (for example, encouraging and informative in terms of pinpointing the source of student errors versus an overall grade or general comment)" (p. 19). Similarly, high expectations and time on task must take into account the quality of the learning outcomes students are asked to achieve.

This concern for overall quality in the teaching/learning process represents a sharp departure from previous research that was concerned only with classroom management and presentation skills. In this more broadly focused research, it is important to note the emphasis placed on active involvement of teachers and learners, and the quality of the assessment provided to the learners. These factors interact to facilitate quality learning opportunities and outcomes. In particular, the congruence of intended outcomes and the nature of the educational process is an area of increasing concern in current research on teaching and learning. In a later chapter we shall examine in more detail the overwhelming influence of the nature of assessment on the quality of students' approaches to learning.

In summary, the desirable teaching characteristics identified in the higher education literature have generally assumed as a given the lecture method, without taking into consideration variability of intended outcomes. While some of these identified characteristics have intuitive appeal, the ambiguity that exists with regard to educational goals (e.g. disciplinary variation) may result in an incongruity of process and outcome. For example, presentation characteristics associated with lecturing may not be consistent with facilitating critical thinking and continuous learning. The question at this point concerns the relative importance of presentation and facilitation teaching characteristics and, perhaps more importantly, the influence of intended learning outcomes on meaningful and worthwhile approaches to learning. Few studies have examined effective teaching for critical thinking or addressed other issues of higher-order cognitive outcomes. As a result, we know little of what makes good teaching for achieving "higher order thinking and problem solving skills" (Hannaway, 1992, p. 5). That will be the focus of discussion in the next section.

Beyond Presentations: Teaching for Higher-Order Outcomes

Much of the research reviewed above has been concerned with how learners can be assisted in their efforts to acquire information, and for that limited purpose it points the way toward useful strategies on the part of teacher and learner. However, we are assuming the ultimate purpose of higher education is to assist the student to develop higher-order thinking abilities, and to become a self-directed learner. When viewed with those higher-order learning outcomes in mind, existing research on higher education is considerably less satisfactory.

Until recently, few educational researchers have investigated the relationship between intended outcomes of learning and the processes used to achieve these outcomes. The small amount of research that has been published to date indicates that intended outcomes, as made explicit to students through assessment procedures, drive the selection (by both teachers and learners) of teaching/learning methods. In the following sections we will argue that selection of higher-order learning outcomes, with learning assessment procedures appropriate for such outcomes, favours the use of collaborative constructivist teaching and learning methods.

Outcome-process issues. There is a growing interest in establishing connections between learning outcomes and effective teaching. In fact, it may be argued that identifying teaching practices that will have a high probability of realizing certain desired outcomes is the ultimate goal of research on teaching. However, "few studies of college teaching have actually described the cognitive processes that occur in classrooms" (Fisher & Grant, 1983, p. 47). Fisher and Grant (1983) conducted a study of 40 undergraduate classes and analysed audio tapes of classes throughout the term to determine which cognitive processes (factual recall, analysis, synthesis, evaluation) were being used. The disappointing if not discouraging conclusion was that classroom discussion was rarely used to encourage higher-order thinking. Regardless of contextual characteristics, professors did most of the talking and simply conveyed information without analysis, synthesis or evaluation. It was suggested that knowledge of subject matter "may be necessary but not sufficient to aid students in developing higher-order cognitive processes" (Fisher & Grant, 1983, p. 58). In other words, as important as content expertise is, teachers must also have a coherent conceptual framework of the teaching and learning transaction consistent with the desired and intended learning outcomes.

Smith (1983) also explored the relationship between process and learning outcomes. The focus was on active student involvement and its effect on critical thinking and the perceived value or influence of the course, the discipline, and education in general. A direct relationship between processes of instruction and outcomes was found. The conclusion was that "student participation, peer-to-peer interaction, encouragement, and high-level student participation were directly associated with the outcomes of instruction, and most particularly and consistently to the influence of the course and to critical thinking" (Smith, 1983, p. 110). This suggests that active and verbal student participation encourages thinking and develops higher levels of cognition.

The importance of assessment. Perhaps the most important influence on students' approaches to learning is related to what is being assessed. Assessment reveals to students what is valued and rewarded. This directly impacts students with regard to what is crucial to their future — grades — and largely dictates how they study and what the quality of the learning outcomes will be.

Entwistle and Tait (1990) note that previous research on effective teaching based upon general student ratings emphasizes presentation skills. However, in subsequent interviews students explained that outcome assessment procedures emphasizing recall of factual material led them to define an effective teaching process in terms of presenting clearly structured material at the right level and pace. That is, their approach to learning was of a surface nature when the assessment instruments indicated that surface learning was what was required in the course. In such cases, they rated teaching effectiveness as high when the teacher assumed full responsibility for organizing and presenting content in a way that could be easily reproduced on the exam. On the other hand, when a deep or understanding approach to learning is required, as indicated by what was being assessed, then effective teaching is defined in terms of facilitation; that is, relevance, choice, full explanations, appropriate assessment, and empathy (Entwistle & Tait, 1990).

The influence of assessment on approaches to learning and the quality of learning cannot be over-emphasized. In attempting to explicate the nature of understanding (i.e. quality of learning), Entwistle and Entwistle (1992) found that variations of understanding (breadth, depth, structure) were influenced by individual and environmental circumstances. In particular, they suggested that examination requirements substantially influenced the type of understanding students sought. They state that, "Perhaps the most worrying features of the findings were, firstly, the way in which the examination distorted the efforts of the students to achieve personal understanding and, secondly, the limited extent to which some types of examination question actually seemed to tap conceptual understanding" (Entwistle & Entwistle, 1992, p. 15).

Ramsden and Entwistle (1981) studied the effects of the larger educational environment (course organization, assessment, and teaching methods) on students' approaches to learning. In comparing meaning/understanding and reproducing approaches to learning, they found departments that rated highly on good teaching (being helpful, well prepared and committed, and allowing freedom in learning) have students who are meaning oriented. On the other hand, departments "with the highest mean scores on reproducing orientation were seen to have a heavy workload and a lack of freedom in learning" (p. 368). The conclusion was that improving the quality of what is learned will require changes in teaching; in particular, it will require helpful, prepared and committed teachers who will provide choice and avoid overloading the students.

Others have also found substantial relationships between approaches to learning, learning environment, and the quality of learning outcomes. Trigwell and Prosser (1991) also suggest that encouraging deeper approaches to learning is related to good teaching, clear goals and choice in learning. However, they cautioned that "teaching strategy such as creating an opportunity for students to ask questions is likely to be unsuccessful if the teacher's intention behind the strategy is just to be seen to be creating an opportunity, rather than to be genuinely encouraging students to ask questions" (p. 264). In other words, teachers must have a clear conception of their teaching, have a strategic plan to facilitate deep understanding, and be sincere.

The message is that teaching cannot be viewed in isolation from expected outcomes. There must be congruence between process and outcome before effective and responsible teaching can emerge. Not only do responsible teachers ensure that learning activities and assessment are congruent with outcomes, but they encourage students to assume responsibility to construct meaning for themselves by creating a supportive and interactive learning environment. Furthermore, responsible teachers are committed to their profession and give teaching high priority (Barnes & Ellner, 1983; Andrews, Garrison & Magnusson, 1996).

If the goals are analysing, integrating and evaluating information (i.e. critical inquiry), then discussion methods appear to be more relevant and effective (Barnes & Ellner, 1983; Kulik & Kulik, 1979). However, the discussion method is inappropriate if the instructor's questions only demand recall of content and the goal is to transmit pre-packaged information. In reviewing alternatives to the lecture method, Kulik and Kulik (1979) provide the caveat "that teaching by discussion is neither more nor less effective than teaching by lecture when the criterion of effectiveness is learning of factual information" (p. 71). This again emphasizes the necessity of considering outcomes before making generalizations regarding characteristics of effective teachers and practices of effective teaching. Clearly there is a place for presentational approaches to teaching, such as lecturing, when the goals are to structure information so that it can be successfully implanted in the long-term memories of students. However, when higher-order thinking is the desired outcome, then constructivist methods are more appropriate.

Constructivist views of teaching. Constructivist views of teaching are about encouraging students to assume responsibility to construct meaning for themselves. In this type of teaching, greater expectations and demands are placed on teachers due to the enormous range of issues which demand judgements and decisions. Teaching is no longer seen as the simple transmission of information; nor is it simply shifting the responsibility for learning to the student. Specific methods and techniques used within this general approach will depend upon the abilities of the learners and the nature of the task. This is the challenge presented to educators in adult and higher education when they recognize the complexity of the educational transaction in developing higher cognitive abilities in students. To meet this challenge demands responsive and responsible teaching.

Responsible teaching is essentially encouraging students to accept the task of constructing meaning for themselves. Responsible teaching will provide students with choice and support in making educational decisions. It will also provide feedback in terms of confronting the validity and worthwhileness of the learning outcomes. Responsible teaching means constantly assessing understanding and the appropriate balance of control in the teaching-learning transaction. It is as much about authenticity and caring for the student as it is about an obligation and passion for the curriculum. The integrity and quality of educational decisions with regard to balancing student and curricular concerns manifest responsible teaching. Making judgements and decisions with awareness of their possible immediate and long-term implications is the hallmark of a responsible and professional teacher.

However, the first step and most difficult obstacle to responsible teaching is for teachers to reflect upon the essential issues and purpose of higher education. Prawat (1992) argues that if educators are to move away from traditional transmission approaches and adopt a constructivist perspective, four sets of beliefs must be addressed which represent obstacles for conceptual change. First, there is a tendency with traditional approaches to view learners and content as separate (non-interactive) and fixed entities. This leads to an over-emphasis on the packaging and delivery of content and an under-emphasis on teaching and assessing students' understanding. Prawat (1992) states that "this static concept is in striking contrast with current epistemology, which views the generation of disciplinary knowledge as a social process carried forth by communities of discourse" (p. 366).

The second set of beliefs, which Prawat terms "naive constructivism", is to equate activity with learning and placing faith in students to structure their own learning. While attempts should be made to connect subject matter to the student's experience (a hallmark of Dewey's philosophy), these experiences must be carefully designed and judged according to their contribution to a continuity of knowledge development. That is, it is important to ensure that the activities are authentic educational experiences and do not simply emphasize enjoyment value.

The third set of beliefs concerns the separation of learning and application as well as understanding and problem solving. According to Prawat (1992), the "major problem with this view from a constructivist perspective is that it assumes that knowledge is independent of the situations in which it is used and acquired, a premise that has been strongly challenged by constructivists" (p. 374). Meaning through knowledge-knowledge and knowledge-context connections is enhanced when applied in a specific context. Just as experience must be interpreted from a conceptual framework, so too must theoretical conceptions be grounded by examples of experience for it to be meaningful. As was discussed in Chapter 4, it is a mistake to separate critical analysis from content and contextual contingencies.

There is little evidence that critical thinking and problem solving skills and abilities generalize to other contexts (McPeck, 1990b; Prawat, 1992).

Prawat's fourth set of beliefs relates to a fixed view of curriculum with preset means and predetermined ends. The alternative view favours "a more interactive and dynamic approach to curriculum, believing that it should be viewed more as a matrix of ideas to be explored over a period of time than as a road map" (Prawat, 1992, p. 358). This is consistent with the view that education should proceed from the whole to the parts. This will facilitate possible changes of direction during the educational transaction. In essence, the quality of learning and understanding must not be subverted for the sake of having to cover a prescribed curriculum. A constructivist approach to learning is about making connections and constructing meaningful concepts that serve the goal of continuous learning.

Teachers generally intend to promote higher cognitive levels of learning but implicitly encourage or explicitly reward surface and strategic approaches to learning. The problem, according to Bowden (1988), is that teachers are not aware of the contradictions between their espoused theory and theory-in-use. One major reason for this situation is related to believing in the development of higher cognitive processes but then providing excessive amounts of information and assessing for recall; or grading for a particular biased perspective; or reinforcing a non-reflective/subjective reaction. If the educational process is to change, teachers must become aware of these contradictions. Institutional constraints may prevent the full application of espoused theory; however, students should be made aware of the constraints and solutions negotiated with regard to assignments and exams. Teachers must understand the challenge of effective teaching and be encouraged to make pragmatic judgements while maintaining their ideals. Although compromise is a reality, teachers must understand and be able to defend their ideals if these beliefs are to provide direction and guidance.

In considering what might be desirable conceptions of teaching, Ramsden (1988a) states that if "learning is about changing one's conceptions, then teaching is about discovering students' conceptions and helping them to change their conceptions" (p. 21). Instead of viewing teaching as a treatment, a "more desirable conception is of teaching as diagnosis prior to treatment" (Marton & Ramsden, 1988, p. 276). Diagnosis, of course, necessitates assessment of learning outcomes. As has been stated before, perhaps "the most significant single influence on students' learning is their perception of assessment" (Ramsden, 1988a, p. 24). Therefore, a desirable conception would be to view assessment as an integral and sustained function of responsible teaching.

Another conception of good teaching is to provide time for reflection and discussion. This will mean a significant reduction in the quantity and range of content covered. Ramsden (1988a) suggests that if "we want students to know more, we will probably have to tell them less" (p. 26). This statement has meaning on two levels: from the perspective of quantity of material covered as well as the nature of the teaching-learning process (e.g. less lecturing). Teachers must be realistic about what can be meaningfully assimilated in a given period of time and they must provide opportunities and encouragement for students to assume responsibility to construct meaning for themselves. That means less content transmission and more time for exploration, reflection and critical discourse (i.e. critical inquiry). Without the time and expectation to reconstruct information in a meaningful way, it is not surprising that students resort to memorization.

Consistent with the previous discussion of good teaching, Marton and Ramsden (1988) have suggested the following specific teaching strategies:

1. Make the learners' conceptions explicit to them.
2. Focus on a few critical issues and show how they relate.
3. Highlight the inconsistencies within and the consequences of learners' conceptions.
4. Create situations where learners centre attention on relevant aspects.
5. Present the learner with new ways of seeing.
6. Integrate substantive and syntactic structures.
7. Test understanding of phenomena; use the results for diagnostic assessment and curriculum design.
8. Use reflective teaching strategies. (pp. 277–280)

Most importantly, these strategies should be directed toward constructing or acquiring the "big idea", not only to create interest and effort but to provide order to complex subject matter. It is essential that learners not become overwhelmed with non-essential facts and information but, instead, first focus on the core idea and organizing concept. Once the organizing concept is understood, it can be expanded by anticipating applications and implications. Through this testing process learners can enhance their understanding by rounding out the concept through direct and vicarious experiences as well as acquiring additional facts and information.

Responsible teaching and meaningful learning must start with both the teacher and student becoming aware of the student's preconceptions and then helping them to become conscious of other conceptions. It is important that the teacher first appreciate and focus upon the essence of a particular conception before moving to peripheral issues. Integrating new conceptions with previous conceptions will necessitate highlighting inconsistencies as well as engaging students in shifting their focus to relevant aspects of the phenomena. New insights cannot often be expected to occur spontaneously and, therefore, it is important to present students with new conceptualizations. At the same time, it is necessary to provide opportunities to explore connections among information and ideas if meaningful and coherent conceptions are to result. Students should be given the opportunity to act upon, express their conceptions along with diagnostic assessment if understanding is to be validated. And, finally, teachers should constantly reflect upon their judgements and decisions in order to provide a dynamic educational transaction.

This perspective is based upon a transactional view of teaching and learning. A transactional view of teaching depends upon the insight of teachers to determine learning paths the student may take to change or enhance existing conceptions. This transactional view concerns diagnosing and facilitating conceptual under-

standing. Teachers should attempt to understand students' conceptions and encourage students to reflect upon their conceptions. Finally, teachers must provide
the time for students to reflect upon current and new conceptions. This will likely
necessitate a reduction in the quantity of subject material in favour of increased
interaction and the focus on higher quality learning outcomes. However, focusing
on broader concepts and an organizing framework can mitigate the effect of this
reduction in quantity of material covered. This approach will also sustain learning
beyond the classroom.

Collaborative teaching and learning. The previous section emphasized the cognitive
aspects of facilitating the construction of meaning. However, development of
understanding and knowledge is not only about individual, internal processes, but also
about the process of confirming that understanding and knowledge through
experience and application in context. This checking and confirming of the knowledge
that has been constructed internally is done most effectively when the learner
interacts with other individuals in a collaborative teaching-learning transaction.

Reciprocal teaching, outlined by Brown and Palincsar (1989), is one socially
shared (i.e. collaborative) constructivist approach to teaching and learning. Although this research was conducted with younger students, it is reasonable to
assume that the ability to monitor and manage one's own comprehension in a
socially supportive context would similarly benefit older students. Brown and
Palincsar (1987) themselves see a connection of their research to critical thinking.
Reciprocal teaching emerged from a rejection of fact oriented, inert knowledge and
the embracing of a fundamentally different form of knowledge acquisition where
the learner establishes ownership of what is learned. In other words, the learner's
goal is to assume responsibility for constructing knowledge that is personally
meaningful and yet collaboratively understood.

Brown and Palincsar (1987) developed reciprocal teaching in the context of text
comprehension (although it is generalizable to other forms of transmitting
information) and the belief that it is very much related to critical thinking. They
state that the "procedure was designed to be a simplified, concrete version of
essential critical thinking skills, with the teacher modeling the types of processes we
believe that expert learners engage in frequently on their own volition" (Brown &
Palincsar, 1987, p. 127). The process attempts to externalize internal dialogues and
critical thinking processes to provide cognitive support as well as provide an
opportunity to "witness others' enactment of each of the roles, roles that
correspond to thinking strategies that they must subsequently perform independently and silently" (Brown & Palincsar, 1989, p. 401).

The teacher in reciprocal teaching carries a heavy responsibility. The teacher is
a subject matter expert who must identify the essence of the subject, resolve
ambiguities and dilemmas, explore implications, and confirm knowledge acquisition. The role of the teacher is to provide; (1) a model of expert behaviour, (2) clear
instructional goals, and (3) appropriate control and feedback (Brown & Palincsar,
1989). When combined with the intent to facilitate critical thinking and meaningful
learning, these roles exemplify the responsible teacher.

Modelling is a key feature of a collaborative constructivist form of teaching and learning. In reciprocal teaching, the teacher must first model expert behaviour and be "able to model mature comprehension activities, thus making them overt, explicit, and concrete" (Brown & Palincsar, 1989, p. 417). Modelling allows students to see knowledge experts reason through problematic situations and "also contextualizes the use of both domain-specific strategies and metacognitive control strategies showing how experts can exert conscious control over their thinking processes in order to attain particular, meaningful goals" (Kintsch, 1993, p. 32). Students are also allowed to model cognitive strategies for other students under the guidance of a teacher. From observing these activities a teacher may become aware of the precise difficulties students may encounter with the content.

Brown and Palincsar (1989) make it very clear that the teacher is in charge and group membership is not democratic. The teacher's responsibility is to keep discussion focused on the content by practicing four strategic activities. The concrete strategic activities that must be practiced routinely are questioning, clarifying, summarizing, and predicting. The authors state that "Attempts to state the gist of what one is reading, and asking questions of clarification, interpretation, and prediction are activities that both improve comprehension and permit students to monitor their own understanding" (Brown & Palincsar, 1987, p. 84). The group monitors its progress and jointly attempts to construct meaning. However, the teacher relinquishes only as much control as the students are capable of handling and is always ready to provide direction and assume leadership when it is appropriate.

Students are encouraged to gradually assume control of the strategic comprehension activities depending upon their capabilities. Collaboration increases strategic and metacognitive awareness. Control and feedback are adjusted to the students' existing level of competency and gradually encouraged to take responsibility for constructing meaning. Scaffolding, a key concept in reciprocal teaching, refers to temporary support that enables students to use higher cognitive skills which would be difficult to learn independently. Scaffolding provides support when needed but gradually removes the support as students gain competence and responsibility. Reciprocal teaching is a collaborative learning environment where interactions with peers and teacher guide students to perform at higher cognitive levels by providing the appropriate support but gradually encouraging them to assume greater control and responsibility for learning.

Reciprocal teaching, with its consideration of both internal and external aspects of the teaching-learning process, has much to offer higher education. It is a collaborative (group) discussion based educational process that focuses upon the development of critical thinking and meaningful learning. As such, it takes a balanced and realistic approach to control issues. It is stated that "reciprocal teaching is both a co-operative learning group jointly negotiating the understanding task and a direct instruction forum wherein the teacher attempts to provide temporary scaffolding to bolster the ... [student's] inchoate strategies" (Brown & Palincsar, 1989, p. 417). Sustained teacher and student discourse is an excellent means for developing critical and continuous thinking and learning.

Towards Effective Teaching

The study of effective teaching in higher education has largely been atheoretical and described in a technical manner, ignoring the teacher's perspective and beliefs regarding the educational process. However, what teachers think affects what they do. Frequently, teachers are not aware of the implicit beliefs that define their teaching orientations. Reflecting upon their own practice and approaches may make these beliefs explicit. However, whether their beliefs are implicit or explicit, teachers' educational judgement is strongly influenced by their views of teaching and learning. These beliefs may "constitute an important obstacle in attempts to change normal patterns of classroom interaction" (Prawat, 1992, p. 356).

It would seem that if we are to understand and change teaching practices in adult and higher education, then we must start by making explicit our intentions and conceptions of teaching and learning. Ideally, these conceptions can be made explicit through reflection and discussion within the teaching/learning process. This would help students to understand these conceptions, and therefore to approach their learning in an appropriate manner.

However, students themselves also hold conceptions of teaching that can undermine well intentioned teacher conceptions. While researching the effect of teacher conceptions on teaching behaviour, Larsson uncovered a paradox. He discovered two basic teacher conceptions, but found that these conceptions did not always translate to practice. The first conception is a traditional one where teaching is essentially packaging information for students to absorb without much interpretation. The second conception was to have the students develop deep or real knowledge by having them take responsibility for interpreting and structuring subject content. The difficulty for teachers trying to apply the second conception was that the students generally held the first conception of teaching, and opposed any deviation from it. In effect, a paradox existed in that "the students use their control to press the teacher to exert control over them" (Larsson, 1983, p. 360).

When interpreting these findings, Larsson pointed to exams as the steering system for the students. Success from the students' perspective was dependent upon the teacher interpreting and structuring content that would reveal the criteria upon which they would be tested. Assessment according to the second conception of teaching was problematic for both teachers and students. As Larsson (1983) concludes, "When students have an instrumental intention, i.e. have the rewards in focus rather than the content, they tend to adopt a surface approach to the learning material" (p. 364). This reinforces our previous comments regarding the relationship of outcome and process. More specifically, if the outcome measure is information recall then students will expect and adopt a surface or reproductive approach to learning.

The teaching conceptions described by Larsson were confirmed in a study by Gow and Kember (1993). Using a combination of qualitative and quantitative methods they "identified two main orientations to teaching — learning facilitation and knowledge transmission" (p. 20). Those oriented to learning facilitation "conceive teaching as a facilitative process to help students develop problem solving skills and critical thinking abilities ... [and teaching] is likely to involve interactive class sessions" (p. 28). On the other hand, those oriented to knowledge transmission focus on the subject and envisage teaching as the clear presentation of the subject matter. Gow and Kember (1993) also associate the facilitation orientation with deep (meaningful) approaches to learning and knowledge transmission orientations with surface (reproductive) approaches to learning. Therefore, they conclude that "if it is considered desirable that students adopt meaningful approaches to learning, it seems to be important to direct initial attention towards the lecturers' conception of teaching" (p. 31).

Given the diversity and complexity of educational contexts, conceptions and beliefs are central to understanding and influencing effective teaching practice. In addition, due to this diversity and complexity, there is almost a total absence of accepted truths about teaching; the professional knowledge of teachers is more accurately described as belief structures (Kagan, 1992). Pajares (1992) states that "Few would argue that the beliefs teachers hold influence their perceptions and judgements, which, in turn, affect their behavior in the classroom, or that understanding the belief structures of teachers and teacher candidates is essential to improving their professional preparation and teaching practices" (p. 307). Therefore, changing teacher practice must begin by understanding the personal educational beliefs of teachers and encouraging them to confront these beliefs with regard to worthwhile student outcomes as well as cognitive and contextual contingencies.

Whether they are implicit or explicit, teaching conceptions and intentions guide practice. Teaching conceptions and intentions are expressed in terms of what is taught, how it is taught, and what outcomes are valued. The enormity of the challenge is evident when we consider all the elements of the teaching and learning transaction.

> The relations between teachers' understanding of subject matter, the way they approach their teaching, and their perceptions of teaching and learning contexts and situations, and how these factors relate to the quality and experience of students and their learning represents, for us, the next major development for our understanding of teaching and learning in higher education. (Prosser & Trigwell, 1998, p. 266)

If teachers are to act with awareness — i.e. reflectively and critically — then every "teacher has a professional obligation to formulate and articulate a rationale for his or her instructional world. Developing that rationale requires reflection about personal theories, knowledge of formal theories, and blending of the personal and the formal" (Rando & Menges, 1991, pp. 13–14). And, perhaps most importantly, this rationale must be articulated for the students.

Effective and responsible teaching goes beyond content expertise. While content expertise is an important first step, it does not tell us how to facilitate meaningful and worthwhile learning in our students. Effective teachers are willing to assess their values and beliefs and are constantly refining their conception of teaching and learning. Furthermore, given the diverse and changing context of learning, teachers are challenged daily to translate their intentions into successful practice. This will require the full attention of teachers.

Although it is dangerous to generalize about teaching practice, the following principles are associated with effective and responsible teaching as discussed above. Effective and responsible teachers:

1. give high priority to teaching;
2. are prepared and enthusiastic;
3. are experts in their subject;
4. have a flexible repertoire of methods and techniques;
5. are realistic about workload;
6. value critical reflection and discourse;
7. create a supportive learning climate;
8. communicate and negotiate expectations;
9. model critical thinking;
10. assess fairly and frequently.

As if this were not enough, for teaching to be effective, it also demands dedication and must be given the highest priority. There is little chance that teaching excellence and quality outcomes will be achieved without a sustained focus on, and concern for, the teaching-learning transaction. Teaching is too complex and challenging to be approached with less than a full commitment. The mark of a responsible teacher is one who is willing to give this kind of commitment and develop the skills and ability to facilitate quality learning experiences.

It is very difficult to be an effective and responsible teacher if facilitating learning is not an essential component of your professional self-concept. In addition, it is important to understand that critical thinking is facilitated through choice and responsibility. Teachers must also possess the technical skills of designing learning activities that create opportunities for assimilation, reflection and application. Being a subject expert will enable teachers to select the essential concepts while still providing time to construct meaning. Of course, communication and collaboration are the foundational elements of an authentic and facilitative learning environment. Finally, students must be recognized for their cognitive development and realization of intended outcomes.

However, a caveat is in order with regards to the application of these principles. They cannot be applied blindly — they must be tempered with considerable professional judgement. As valid as these principles may be, they do not reflect the complexity and unpredictability of the educational transaction. Teachers must integrate these principles into their particular approach to teaching. Professionally, teachers must question their assumptions and develop a coherent framework of teaching and learning. Such a framework will provide a conceptual map when responding to the needs of students and other contextual contingencies.

At the same time, it is not sufficient for teachers to simply have a coherent conceptual framework. Brookfield (1990a) states with regard to teaching responsively, "Although you are guided by a clearly defined organizing vision, you change your methods, content, and evaluative criteria as you come to know more about the ways these are perceived by students" (p. 30). Moreover, your vision and intentions should be communicated and implemented with the understanding and co-operation of students. In this way the congruence between expectations (i.e. outcomes) and learning activities (i.e. processes) can be validated on a sustained basis. To teach in a responsible and effective manner, we must communicate what kind of learning we value, diagnose students' misconceptions, and facilitate the construction of meaningful knowledge.

Conclusion

Responsible and effective teaching is a complex process where content, setting, and both teacher and student outcome expectations are addressed. As a result of this inherent complexity, it is imperative that teachers reflect upon their personal beliefs. Most importantly, teachers' beliefs and conceptions of learning should be open to discussion and negotiation in the classroom. Teachers must be clear about their intentions and share them if students are to responsibly construct meaningful knowledge.

It is argued that a collaborative-constructivist view of teaching and learning is not only consistent with developing higher cognitive abilities and meaningful learning, but it places considerable responsibility on the teacher to make difficult educational judgements and decisions on a sustained basis. Among others, two issues typically contradict and undermine a collaborative-constructivist approach to teaching and learning. The first relates to the overwhelming influence of assessment on approaches to learning. It is disingenuous rhetoric for educators to advocate quality of learning through deep approaches and then assess learning quantitatively through recall; or assess only from the teacher's ideological perspective. The second issue is excessive workload or content and not providing sufficient time for students to construct meaning through critical reflection and discourse. One of the most difficult tasks for a teacher is to decide on the essential concepts and not be distracted by extraneous information. This requires considerable content expertise.

Collaborative methods externalize the critical thinking process and help students become less ego-centric by confirming personal meaning through discourse. Without collaboration and mutual understanding there is an increasing likelihood of reproductive learning and alienation. Conversely, collaboration is only effective when complemented by constructive, reflective moments. These may be moments stolen during the collaborative process, or extended periods of concentration in a private, undisturbed setting. Generally, both opportunities for reflection are necessary for deep and meaningful learning outcomes.

Responsible teaching must consider worthwhile outcomes and the appropriate methods and techniques that will facilitate students to take responsibility to construct meaning for them. The design and technology of responsible teaching and quality learning is primarily influenced by collaborative-constructivist assumptions. These assumptions encourage students to mindfully participate in the collaborative educational experience while assuming responsibility for reflectively constructing personal meaning of the experience.

Responsible teaching, as described above, is still not the norm in our higher education systems. The following comment by the editor of a periodical focused on the improvement of higher education is about the situation in the United States, but it could be generalized to other countries as well:

> ... when students arrive from high school, they expect college will be difficult and that they'll study hard. Within weeks of arrival, as they sit through their university's "lecture and text" survey courses, they soon learn that eight to 12 hours a week with the books is all they need for an A or B. Once set, that pattern is never broken: study hours stay flat over the four years. Analyses of syllabi and senior portfolios show why: most of the teaching they encounter is of the "let me tell you, then I'll test you" kind — a nice recipe for convenience, but death for deeper learning. (Marchese, 1998, p. 1)

Organizing higher education for the convenience of professors wanting to focus on their research and students wanting more time for extra-curricular activities is hardly responsible teaching. The following chapters discuss alternatives to alter the balance of control and for both teacher and student to assume responsibility for achieving deep-meaningful learning outcomes.

7

Learning Activities

The previous chapter was intended to provide a comprehensive and coherent framework for teaching and learning. Operating from within such a framework, teachers can critically assess why particular learning activities may or may not be appropriate in their particular context. (This is often best done in collaboration with the students.) Teaching decisions that will guide the teaching-learning transaction should be made in context, using not only a theoretical framework of educational values and beliefs, but also situational knowledge about content, the students, and the institution.

Learning activities must be selected in the light of both types of teacher knowledge. Once selected, each learning activity must be assessed, on a sustained basis, as to its appropriateness for achieving the intended learning outcomes. Therefore, responsible teaching is dependent upon an understanding of the purposes and strengths of various learning activities.

Student Learning Activities

In order to provide a rational basis for the selection of particular techniques, we begin with a classification of educational learning activities. This classification is useful in revealing the essence and strengths of different learning activities. This approach presumes that selection of learning activities should be based upon intended learning outcomes. An understanding of these outcomes will facilitate the selection and assessment of techniques at the design phase and during the implementation process. In particular, it will demonstrate that learning activities serve different functions in the educational process.

Learning activities are classified using a two dimensional matrix (see Figure 7.1). The dimensions are the cognitive nature of the learning task (exploratory or confirmatory) and the social or transactional nature of the task (individual or group). Since reflection is an essential and integral aspect of all educational learning activities, it is placed centrally in the matrix. Starting with the cognitive dimension, exploratory or inquiry activities represent learning often associated with information acquisition and assimilation. Confirmatory activities represent learning that is most often associated with knowledge integration and application. The transactional dimension of the matrix is concerned with whether learning is individual or group focused. Individual activities reflect a greater emphasis on reflection while group activities reflect an emphasis on interaction and collaboration.

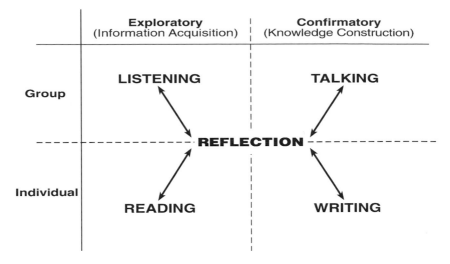

Figure 7.1: Meaningful learning activities.

It is important to emphasize that there is no clear separation between exploration and confirmation. They are part of a comprehensive and coherent perspective of knowledge construction. It is also important to emphasize that the individual is never completely separate from the group in an educational setting. Notwithstanding the limitations of a categorical scheme, the usefulness of this matrix is in the identification of four fundamental activities. The four activities are listening, reading, talking and writing. Just as education focusing exclusively on exploration or confirmation is incomplete, each of these learning activities is insufficient in itself. For learning to be meaningfully relevant and educationally worthwhile different types of activities will most likely be found in combination.

In an educational context, learning activities are designed for specific purposes and supported by knowledgeable teachers. Listening and reading are useful information gathering activities. They are legitimate and important activities during the initial phases of constructing meaning. Talking and writing may take on greater importance as learning advances. From a transactional perspective, listening and talking are group activities likely to be quite limited in time, while reading and writing provide extended opportunities for reflection. Nevertheless, to be constructive, the appropriate mix of activities must be determined.

Listening. Perhaps the most pervasive instructional technique in higher education is the lecture where the major "activity" of the student is to listen. Listening in an educational setting generally takes place in a group context that is outwardly passive. This places considerable importance on the relevance, organization and presentation of the lecture in order for the student to make sense of the information conveyed. The student's ability to create meaning from a lecture depends upon their prior knowledge, as well as the actual content of the lecture.

But speech, as compared with print, is ephemeral. If the student is not able to make sense of each utterance in the lecture within a few seconds of its being spoken, it will have been of no value to that student. Without further confirmation activities, such as the option of asking the lecturer to stop and explain a point that was not clear (not always practicable in large lecture classes), the personal meaning constructed by the student from the lecture may well be incomplete or distorted.

Yet for various reasons, some valid and some invalid, the lecture remains a standard method of organizing a learning experience and relating to students. Ideally the specific learning task should determine when the lecture might be appropriate. The lecture may be defensible for conveying information to a large audience but it is usually necessitated by administrative or economic reasons (e.g. the need to have large classes). This is particularly true if the information to be assimilated by the students is not readily available in other formats or easily understood. On the other hand, it places considerable emphasis on listening abilities. A serious challenge for the lecture method is to facilitate critical reflection and meaningful knowledge construction. While listening may be enhanced when the lecturer attends to presentation characteristics such as enthusiasm and clarity (see Chapter 6), other facilitation techniques such as concrete examples are required.

Hodgson (1984) studied the lecture method and found that the quality of the learning was associated with certain characteristics of the lecturer's presentation. In particular, the student was enabled to experience the lecture content vicariously either through the lecturer's enthusiasm or by an interesting illustration or example. The evidence also indicated that vicarious experiences could serve as a bridge or transition between surface and deep approaches to learning. Hodgson (1984) concludes that through vicarious experiences "it becomes possible for the lecturer to help students to go beyond the outward demands of a learning situation and make connections between content of the lecture and their understanding of the world around them" (p. 102).

A successful lecture, however, places considerable responsibility on the teacher to maintain cognitive engagement. Although there are inherent limitations with the lecture method, a number of scholars have made useful suggestions about how to lecture well. Consistent with the previous suggestions, Eble (1988) states that lecturers should seek "unrelentingly for precise examples and illustrations" (p. 80). This can be accomplished by alluding to actual situations or personal experiences. Other suggestions include restricting the number and scope of ideas or topics considered, beginning by stimulating surprise or curiosity, being spontaneous, pausing after ten minutes for reflection and questions, and varying presentation style.

Lecturing and listening are usually associated with large classes. Large classes present the teacher with the challenge of how to engage students in meaningful learning given the reliance upon passive listening abilities. At the same time, much can be done within the lecture format to increase cognitive involvement. The key is to stimulate and sustain mindful reflection during the presentation. Along with examples and vicarious experiences, one of the most useful techniques is to provide a context or framework in which students can actively organize the information presented. This can be accomplished by explicitly providing a conceptual model or relating current content to previous knowledge structures. Another obvious but effective technique is to pose questions rhetorically or take questions from the students. In either case, wait-time for reflection and formulation must be provided. As Tobin (1983) states, wait-time "has been shown to have a consistent effect on the quality of verbal interaction in classrooms" (p. 35).

Lang, McBeath and File (1994) suggest that the lecture may be effective when the teacher is introducing a topic, when dealing with factual subject matter, when preparing for another method, or when time is limited. However, excessive reliance on the lecture has its limitations. The lecture is not recommended when content is complex or abstract, when affective outcomes are important, when content needs to be integrated, when thinking skills are valued, or when long term retention is desired. It would seem, therefore, that the lecture has serious limitations. Certainly, it is inadequate as a stand-alone method. It is clear that if the goal is to facilitate critical thinking and achieve deep, meaningful learning outcomes, the lecture is not the method to use. Even when it could be justified in the contexts noted above, few teachers have the presentation skills to be effective lecturers.

One of the main reasons for the limited usefulness of listening is the severely limited opportunity that it provides the learners to act upon and test (other than vicariously) their understanding. Listening by itself can not provide critical feedback or diagnose problems encountered by the learner when constructing knowledge. Another limiting factor is the lack of student control of the pace of instruction or information flow, often resulting in a lack of time to reflect upon and assimilate this information so as to construct meaningful concepts. Reading as an educational activity shares the first weakness, though not the second.

Reading. Much learning occurs independently as students read and study on their own. As mentioned previously, advantages of reading, as compared to writing, are the explicitness of the written word and the control afforded the student. Olson (1977) contends "that there is a transition from utterance to text both culturally and developmentally and that this transition can be described as one of increasing explicitness, with language increasingly able to stand as an unambiguous or autonomous representation of meaning" (p. 258). Given the developmental level of adult and higher education students, it would seem reasonable to rely on readings for the transmission of information to be assimilated. Reading provides extensive opportunities for reflection, which is important for integrating information in a meaningful manner. For this reason reading may be a more active learning activity than listening, and may provide for a higher level of cognitive processing.

The use of text materials is so ubiquitous that many teachers may not have thought about the purpose of reading assignments — at least not explicitly. Often readings are assigned to convey information that presumably cannot be covered in class. However, apart from allowing students to acquire information efficiently, the strength of reading is the opportunity it provides for reflection upon this information. This has implications for teacher procedures. An assigned reading before a topic has been introduced may serve quite a different function than an assigned reading after a topic has been introduced. It is, therefore, extremely important to make our expectations clear when it comes to assigned readings. We must make it clear why the reading is important, how it should be read, and how it relates to classroom activities (Meyers & Jones, 1993).

A reading assigned prior to classroom treatment has a major educational advantage, in that it may reduce reliance on the lecture to transmit relevant information. When reading an article, ideally students should reflect upon key concepts or issues and come to class prepared to raise questions, critically analyse concepts, and discuss issues. In this way, prior reading may be used to set the stage for a lecture that focuses on clarifying difficult concepts or controversial issues. Here the teacher should attempt to ground the concept by relating it to either their or the students' experiences. Supplemental readings assigned after a class, however, must be approached cautiously. They should not overload students with time consuming work where the relevance to the course themes is not apparent. Readings should relate to future topics, assignments or assessment. If they have little apparent relevance, they will not likely be read. For this reason, the amount of reading expected both before and after class should be realistic with regard to time available to students. The reading that is assigned should be done reflectively and be reinforced in the classroom.

One challenge when using reading as a learning activity is sustaining task motivation. For this reason, considerable thought should be given to supporting reading activities through appropriate following-up in the classroom. If class sizes are small enough, it may be particularly effective to have students take responsibility for summarizing and leading the discussion on a particular reading. This certainly would provide incentive to prepare for the class, even for those students who do not have to provide the summary, because they will be expected to contribute to the discussion.

However, before asking students to take on such a classroom responsibility, teachers need to explicitly state their intentions and model the activity. That is, teachers should explain and demonstrate how students are to go about critically reading an article. Relevant study questions may initially provide needed guidance and a transition to classroom discussion. The best approach, however, is for teachers to identify their strategies through modelling — i.e. by sharing and discussing with the students their metacognitive strategies and techniques when reading an article for meaning.

As with all learning activities, it is important to recognize the inherent limitations of reading when used in isolation. As indicated previously, reading is an individual activity particularly suited for acquiring information and reflecting upon it. At the same time, it must be remembered that textual material does not respond to students' questions. Responding to questions that arise during reading becomes the responsibility of the reader. While it is good to cause the student to reflect in this way, students are generally limited in their ability to fully grasp the meaning of new subject material and resolve dilemmas in isolation. The more interactive activities of the educational transaction, talking and writing, have a distinct advantage in supporting critical discourse and facilitating the confirmation of meaning and knowledge construction.

Talking. Talking or speech offers the potential for sustained communication. The tendency of speech, as compared to written language, to be ambiguous or unclear is mitigated by sustained discourse. Clarification of meaning and intent is made possible through questioning and feedback. Verbal discourse can facilitate consensual meaning by providing opportunities for feedback and correction. We use the term talking in the context of critical discourse, which means that all participants have an opportunity to contribute without discrimination. Furthermore, it assumes that ideas will be challenged and explored collaboratively. Talking and shared writing provide an opportunity to consensually confirm meaning and knowledge.

Talking externalizes thought, and in so doing provides an opportunity for students to understand and recognize possible inconsistencies, narrowness of perspective, or incompleteness in their thought. Those that have taught or presented ideas publicly know the extent to which the necessity of speaking facilitates clarity of thought, particularly when speaking to a critical audience. The critical audience should include oneself. Fulwiler (1987) argues that the "intersection between articulate speech and internal symbolization produces comprehensive meaning" (p. 5). Thus, talk has both an internal and external audience.

This talk should not be confined to teacher and student. As desirable as a one-on-one teacher-student tutorial situation may be, it is not realistic (for reasons of class size) in most institutions of higher education. However, beyond pragmatic considerations, student-student discourse may well be more effective at times. It can provide a more secure and unrestricted environment for students to explore ideas that are not well developed. When the teacher is present, students may try to reflect back what they feel the teacher wants to hear, they may not be comfortable challenging the teacher, or they may simply be too nervous to express themselves adequately.

If authentic critical discourse is the task objective, then it is essential that the proper climate be set (see subsequent section) and that the teacher model critical discourse. To model critical discourse the teacher must encourage students to challenge ideas, including the teacher's. Teacher authenticity is the foundation of a critical community of learners. It is not sufficient to say that critical analysis is valued and then be defensive when one's own assumptions or ideas are questioned. The issue is maintaining open communication. Teachers must listen carefully if deep and meaningful learning is to occur. That means that teachers must make judgements about when to contribute or intervene. Too much or too little teacher intervention or contribution can be detrimental to the quality of the discourse and the learning outcomes.

The teacher's role in classroom discussion needs further comment. Discussions have different purposes. For example, a small group discussion in a physics class may prove very useful in exploring problem solutions and improving problem-solving abilities. While control must be given to students if they are to accept responsibility, the physics class may require the teacher to take greater control in order to provide support and guidance, and thus avoid too much frustration. Judgements must be made as to how much scaffolding and preparation is appropriate. On the other hand, a sociology class discussing values and beliefs related to social policy could be quite different. Here teachers must be very careful not to have a hidden agenda and excessively control the discussion. Participation must be open, honest and on an equal basis with the students. Trust must be established where the teacher may challenge positions but student disagreement is respected — particularly with regard to the position or perspective of the teacher.

Discussion can be facilitated in large groups through question and answer, but this provides limited opportunity for participation and the systematic treatment of an issue or problem. For these reasons, the most effective use of questioning may be to facilitate the activities of small groups. Discussion questions will, of course, depend upon the specific content and cognitive level of the educational objective. Different types of learning will influence task instructions, student preparation, and the teacher's role in small group learning (Cohen, 1994). For example, ill-structured (higher-order) knowledge tasks will require different instructions, preparation and roles than tasks focused on lower levels of cognition. Group discussion is generally better suited for higher-order cognitive task demands where students have the necessary foundational knowledge. In this situation, the teacher's role is facilitation of the discussion. Guiding questions should encourage analysis and synthesis of subject matter.

Discussion is not appropriate for every situation or equally useful for every subject. However, it is very useful for providing "a context where the students can voice their specific questions, confusions, and doubts and where they can put ideas together, frame hypotheses, and be assisted in their ability to learn on their own" (Eble, 1988, p. 85). Clearly, discussion is about stimulating thought and motivating students to make connections about information. The success of the discussion method is based upon how well it facilitates critical thinking and understanding. To the degree that it provides students with the opportunity to assume responsibility for constructing meaning and knowledge, the discussion method can be an ideal collaborative learning experience.

Talking as discussion or critical discourse has the potential to clarify meaning and consensually develop knowledge. The emphasis is on the collaborative process of constructing and confirming knowledge. However, the inherent deficiency of talk is our inability to hold in mind more than a very few ideas simultaneously during a discussion. Fulwiler (1987) suggests that with speech or talk, "we can't extend, expand, or develop our ideas fully because we can't see them" (p. 5). Writing, on the other hand, is a reflective activity that allows the individual to cognitively and visually hold several ideas at once and create a coherent conceptual structure.

Writing. Writing is an effective means to facilitate higher-order thinking. The reason is the inherent need to be reflective during the writing process. White (1993) argues strongly that "writing as an advanced skill becomes both the means and the expression of critical thinking and problem solving" (p. 106). Fulwiler (1987) expresses the conviction that "writing is basic to thinking about, and learning, knowledge in all fields as well as communicating that knowledge" (p. 1). Similarly, Bereiter and Scardamalia (1987) state that:

> Writing, especially expository writing, offers an opportunity for students to work actively and independently with their own knowledge. They can clarify meanings, find inconsistencies, discover implications, and establish connections between previously isolated fragments of knowledge. (p. 362)

Writing is integrative in that it strives for coherence through reflective thinking. To write reflectively is to construct meaning. Writing can be a time where exploration and confirmation merge.

Applebee (1984) suggests that the role of writing in thinking is often attributed to the opportunity to rethink and revise over time, the explicitness of the written word, the active nature of writing, and the resources available for organizing thoughts. For all these reasons, writing can be a disciplined and rigorous process for reflecting upon the consistency, coherence and validity of one's thoughts. The self-reflective knowledge interest of emancipation, as outlined by Habermas and discussed in Chapter 2, can be greatly facilitated through the writing process. Writing can be a valuable activity in encouraging students to search for authentic insights as well as becoming cognitively autonomous and responsible.

Unfortunately, too many writing assignments are not intended to have students construct new meanings. Too often the purpose is recitation and not reasoning. Bereiter and Scardamalia (1987) have made a distinction between knowledge telling and knowledge transforming. Knowledge telling is a natural process of recalling or generating readily available content; that is, there is little reflective thinking. Knowledge telling "preserves the straight-ahead form of oral language production and requires no significantly greater amount of planning or goal-setting than does ordinary conversation" (Bereiter & Scardamalia, 1987, pp. 9–10). On the other hand, knowledge transforming, as the phrase suggests, involves the reworking of knowledge or the formation of new thoughts during the writing or composing process. It is the critical thinking process that distinguishes knowledge transforming. When the critical thinking process is embedded in the knowledge telling process, knowledge transformation results. Knowledge transforming involves both a content (knowledge and belief issues) and rhetorical (clarity of expression) problem space.

White (1993) makes a similar distinction between knowledge telling and transforming when he discusses writing as product and process. Although we should think of writing as both process and product, "when we look at writing in the context of critical thinking and problem solving, the writing process becomes far more important than the product" (White, 1993, p. 107). Writing as product emphasizes imitation and conformity (i.e. mechanical correctness). On the other hand, writing as process emphasizes reflective thinking and knowledge construction. The process model includes the overlapping activities of invention, drafting, rethinking, connecting, revising and editing (White, 1993). Only at the end is mechanical correctness emphasized through the editing activity. It should be noted that there is a close parallel between the process model of writing and the phases of the critical thinking model.

While there is a role for recitation or knowledge telling, the real challenge for adult and higher education is in transforming knowledge through reflective writing. This will necessarily include problems of knowledge development and composition − not just summarizing one's current knowledge or that of others. Not dissimilar to Bereiter and Scardamalia, Biggs (1988) identifies surface-telling and deep-reflecting approaches to writing. He expands upon writing as knowledge transformation (deep-reflection) by emphasizing the cyclical thinking process and labelling it reflective writing. With regard to reflective writing, Biggs (1988) states that "the product itself adds to the content space ... so that revision in this case involves a more fundamental examination and moulding of basic meaning and structure" (p. 191). Furthermore, Biggs notes the parallel between the two basic approaches to writing and the deep and surface approaches to learning in general. Reflective writing necessitates an intentional, deep, motivational, and strategic approach to learning.

A deep-reflective approach to writing will include developing and using self-directed learning strategies. Composition strategies or abilities are not sufficient. Self-directed strategies are required for knowledge transforming writing. Self-directed strategies include "a structure for setting goals to be achieved through the composition and for monitoring progress toward those goals, for identifying obstacles, solving problems, and so on" (Bereiter & Scardamalia, 1987, p. 250). The basic self-directed learning mechanisms are planning, monitoring and revising. Students must be encouraged and supported in taking responsibility for these metacognitive activities if deep-reflective approaches to writing are to be facilitated.

Writing tasks will differ in terms of the depth of processing. For example, summarizing an article may be a first step in facilitating critical thinking, but by itself, it will only enhance recall of information. On the other hand, writing an essay exploring two or more perspectives on an issue will enhance understanding through an examination of the conceptual connections. Biggs (1988) emphasizes the intentional or motivational aspects of writing in order to clarify the purpose of the writing activity. Depending on the motivational intent (i.e. surface-telling or deep-reflecting) of the writing activity, the ensuing monitoring and revising activities will differ accordingly. In particular, there are strong differences with regard to revision between surface-telling and deep-reflecting approaches to writing (Biggs, 1988). Revision is an integral part of the deep-reflective approach to writing and includes rethinking and rewriting text. For a detailed discussion of essay writing suggested references are Biggs (1988) and Fulwiler (1987).

Facilitating writing activities are crucial for the development of meaningful knowledge structures. Bereiter and Scardamalia (1987) list five elements in developing knowledge transforming approaches to writing. First, they emphasize the importance of making students aware of the full extent of the writing process including planning, monitoring and revising. Second, the "thinking that goes on in composition needs to be modelled by the teacher, who can thereby show the problem-solving and planning processes that students are often unaware of" (Bereiter & Scardamalia, 1987, p. 363). Third, students should be involved in developing self-directed strategies. Fourth, students need to be challenged within a supportive environment. Fifth, the students need to understand the purpose, nature and function of the writing process.

Reflective writing is intentional, autonomous, rigorous and explicit. As a result, students must be prepared and have the time to reflect upon the content of interest. Most importantly, they have to persist through all the stages of writing. Students may be encouraged to submit preliminary drafts of papers. To encourage awareness of the developmental process of writing a paper, teachers may assess drafts according to their stage of development. For example, writing at the initiation, composition or revision stage should be assessed accordingly. Continued support and guidance is necessary because students generally do not have the critical and compositional skills required for written assignments in higher education. From a teaching perspective it must be realized that writing is the most demanding and reflective educational activity students are asked to engage in. Well-designed writing activities can provide an opportunity for reflection and encourage the necessary discipline to further stimulate reflection.

Reflection

Reflection is an integral part of all learning activities if they are to be educational. Bereiter and Scardamalia (1987) define reflection as "a dialectical process by which higher-order knowledge is created through the effort to reconcile lower-order elements of knowledge" (p. 300). This examination and reconciliation of ideas and concepts with facts and information figures in all the educational activities discussed. Reflection is central to critical thinking and learning.

The process of reflection and constructing meaning is valuable across the disciplines. It is just as important to develop conceptual understanding in physics as it is in psychology. By focusing on confirming conceptual understanding through discourse or written assignments it is also possible to diagnose learning difficulties. These confirmatory learning activities communicate to students that the goal is understanding and not simply memorizing various problem types. Problem solving itself should be a reflective activity in the same class as written assignments. Therefore, it should be made clear that it is not just an instrumental activity (i.e. get the right answer) but is an opportunity to make conceptual connections among items of information, and, thereby, increase one's depth of understanding.

An activity for encouraging sustained reflection is the use of student learning journals. Brookfield (1990a) describes learning journals as "private records of how students feel about and make sense of their learning" (p. 34). Journals should not be restricted to reflections on course content. It is very useful feedback to the teacher for students to reflect upon the learning process — the highs and lows of the experience. Entries can be made at the end of class or after class. It is important that students write the journal for themselves. This may initially be a problem when students know that the teacher will read and comment upon it. In order to reduce this focus on the teacher as audience, it is recommended that credit be assigned but all students get the same grade if entries are made regularly. Fulwiler (1987) provides a full discussion on the use of journals for the purposes of facilitating expressive writing.

Another technique to encourage reflection is the critical incident. Critical incidents are significant events in a student's life which are briefly reported either orally or in written form after reflection. These events are related to concepts or issues in the course and are often used to introduce a new topic. The purpose is to probe the students' values and beliefs in order to make them more explicit. In this way students can better build upon and integrate new concepts into existing knowledge structures. In short, they become aware of their assumptions and existing knowledge structures. Specific examples of how to write and use critical incidents can be found in Chapter 8.

Conclusion

Effective teachers have a repertoire of learning activities. Moreover, selection of specific activities is context dependent. Therefore, the successful application of a particular learning activity will depend upon a number of factors related to content, student, teacher and institution. The previous discussion has attempted to look at these learning activities largely from a learning perspective in order to understand the purposes and reasons for the design and implementation of learning activities.

The central role of reflection in an educational learning setting was also discussed. Reflection is seen as an essential part of all learning activities if students are to construct lasting meaning from the activities. A coherent and comprehensive view of the teaching-learning transaction is required to make the necessary educational judgements regarding content, desired outcomes and appropriate learning activities. The next chapter provides practical guidelines and specific strategies for the selection and application of learning activities that teachers may find useful in designing relevant, authentic and meaningful learning experiences.

8

Teaching Strategies

A basic assumption of this book is that the teaching-learning transaction is a collaborative constructivist process that must be viewed in its totality. The previous chapter looked at the transaction largely from the students' perspective with regard to intended outcomes. We now turn to the learning activities from the perspective of the teacher who assumes responsibility for facilitating a meaningful and worthwhile educational experience. Using the previously outlined learning activity framework, the present chapter provides practical strategies, techniques and suggestions for facilitating a learning experience.

Before going further, let us say why we use the word facilitation to describe teacher activities and responsibilities within a proper educational experience. In a collaborative constructivist transaction the student accepts the ultimate responsibility to construct meaning and understand specific content. However, this process is shared and examined through sustained discourse in a dynamic community of learners. A community of learners is formed and guided largely by the teacher. In this community of learners, worthwhile goals can best be achieved when the teacher acts as a facilitator, providing guidance and support as required.

By using the term "facilitator" we do not intend to diminish the legitimate role of the teacher. Consistent with discussions in previous chapters, we see the teacher's role as that of an educational and subject matter authority, but one who is non-authoritarian in terms of transmitting ideas as well as implementing and shaping the educational process. That is, the teaching and learning transaction is collaborative and control is shared appropriately. Given the importance of encouraging questioning and accepting the basic uncertainty of all knowledge, the role best exhibited by the teacher is that of a facilitator. One of the most important overarching responsibilities of the facilitation role is creating an environment that will support a critical community of learners.

Classroom Climate

Critical reflection and collaboration are dependent upon a supportive classroom climate. A continuous process of challenging ideas and assumptions is best encouraged and facilitated in a climate of trust. Critical analysis of ideas and assumptions requires a degree of risk taking on the part of students and teachers. Thus, an open educational transaction is dependent upon respect for individuals and ideas as well as collaborative support in exploring new perspectives. Sisco

(1991) suggests that climate setting is a metaphor for effective teaching. Your approach as a teacher is evident in the climate you set and the approach to learning students take will be consistent with that climate.

Perhaps the most important principle in creating a climate that supports a critical community of learners is the authenticity of the teacher; that is, the teacher should be genuine and open. This engenders trust emotionally and academically as well as encouraging active participation. It is not appropriate for teachers to say they value critical discourse and then cut off discussion; or suggest that they are supportive but then not make themselves available to students. A teacher's authenticity will be judged by the congruence of their words and actions. Teachers must model critical reflection in their teaching if they expect students to acquire a similar approach to learning. It is also essential that the teacher convey confidence in the ability of the students to succeed. This means trusting students to make educational choices and encouraging them to accept responsibility in constructing meaning. This is initiated by sending clear and consistent expectations to students, particularly at the start of the course.

However, climate setting is not just about academic issues. Creating a trusting environment must also include psychosocial concerns of students as well. Teachers should try to get to know their students — even in large classes. Although it is a good idea for teachers to be open and reveal something of themselves as the course proceeds, they should realize that this is not the primary concern of students during the first session. At the start of a course students are interested primarily in academic issues surrounding the course (Garrison & Brook, 1991, 1992). Getting acquainted is a very important issue in climate setting but it must be seen as a developmental process occurring throughout the course.

Consistent with a developmental perspective, groups exhibit a pattern or dynamic over time. Pratt (1981) suggests that groups have beginning, middle and ending phases. Each of these developmental phases has its characteristics that influence learning. During the initial phase students need structure (clarity of expectations) and need to feel included. The middle stage is a productive period but may be marked by challenges and conflict. Conflict is not necessarily negative. It may be a normal aspect of group development, demonstrating that students are taking responsibility for their learning. Attempts to influence and challenge should be met with understanding and negotiation. When group cohesiveness and accomplishment have been achieved, endings become a particular challenge. Issues that should be addressed at this stage are review of achievement, provision for emotional closure, and preparation for transition (Pratt, 1981).

There are several advantages gained through acknowledging the co-operative dynamics of groups. Fellow students can model and support learning. Groups provide for an opportunity to share and test ideas. They encourage active listening and learning. Through all of this, groups can facilitate individual responsibility for learning. Establishing a climate conducive to the above places considerable responsibility on teachers. As noted previously, authenticity is integral to the role of an educational leader. In general, authenticity requires a group leader "to be task-oriented and to apply oneself passionately to what one has contracted to do in relation to others" (Singer et al., 1975, p. 157). In this context, authenticity is established collaboratively through negotiated expectations.

Because the group has a power to shape individual behaviour, teacher and students need to be aware of potentially oppressive dynamics as well as positive collaborative characteristics. Within groups, the dangers of coercion and in-doctrination must be considered along with the benefits of critical discourse and knowledge (re)construction. One way to ensure a positive developmental process is to encourage the sharing of leadership roles and make use of subgroups. At various times, teachers must be prepared to relinquish leadership functions and encourage students to assume leadership roles. This will help move the group through periods of conflict and on to more collaborative and productive roles and activities.

First and Last Sessions

Somewhat surprisingly, little has been written about the importance and design of the first and last sessions of a course. While much has been written about setting climate, few explicit guidelines exist as to prevalent issues and concerns that should be addressed in the first session. Yet, student satisfaction with the first session in voluntary adult education courses is crucial for continuance. Common practice in adult education is to focus on the psychosocial issues and devote considerable time to getting acquainted. On the other hand, the first sessions in higher education are almost always content and expectation focused. The position here is that both areas are important and neither extreme is likely to address the concerns of students during the first session.

Consistent with approaches in higher education, the first session is crucial in setting clear and consistent goals and expectations for the course. In order to avoid ambiguity and misunderstanding, Pratt (1984) identifies four questions that should be the focus of the first session. Questions related to purpose (reasons for attending), expectations (workload), roles (teaching/learning approaches), and content can be the basis for agreement between teacher and student. By discussing these issues, incongruency between process and outcome can be addressed while establishing a collaborative and supportive climate. Time spent during the first session clarifying and negotiating these issues will reduce tensions and unproductive conflicts later.

One study of first session student and teacher expectations in higher education (degree and non-degree courses) found that the overwhelming concerns were with course content and expectations as well as teaching expectations and qualifications (Brook & Garrison, 1995; Garrison & Brook, 1992). This is an important finding in that a common practice in adult education is to first focus on student introductions and creating a community of learners. However, as important as community development is, this takes time and can frustrate students if their other academic needs are not met. Addressing course and teacher concerns does not preclude student introductions without it being a nuisance or threatening.

A suggested technique that can address both academic and social climate setting has students form groups of four or five for the purpose of listing questions about the course or the instructor. At this time, students informally introduce themselves before collectively listing the questions that they have for the teacher. Students can organize their questions around purpose, expectations, role and content. Although the focus is on academic issues, the students naturally develop a rapport with some of their fellow students. Students will begin to feel more confident in raising concerns within a small group setting. However, it is very important during the first class that students be engaged in the course content and leave with the sense of having accomplished something substantive.

Each participant brings expectations based upon their knowledge and experiences. Teachers' expectations may be more explicitly defined through a curriculum planning process. However, time should be given to assessing and clarifying teacher and student expectations with regard to workload, roles, and learning outcomes. Teachers must evaluate not only student expectations but also their current state of knowledge. It has been argued previously, if students are to accept responsibility for their learning, then choice, negotiation and agreement must be part of the process. This process is dependent upon a responsible and collaborative process of assessing students' current goals, motivation and knowledge.

Choice is essential in developing critical thinking and problem solving. Choice also implies considerable self-direction in monitoring and managing the learning process — all of which creates challenges with regard to designing and implementing assessment. Students may emphasize different areas of the curriculum and progress through the curriculum in different sequences. However, if critical thinking is to be the intended process, then opportunities must be created to provide feedback to students during the learning transaction in order to enhance student self-direction.

While there has not been much discussion in the literature about specific design issues for the first session (other than climate setting), next to nothing has been written about the last session and the importance of closure. Closure becomes particularly important when efforts are made to create a supporting climate and a collaborative community of learners. Emotional bonds are created and the end of a course can represent a significant loss to the participants.

One author who has addressed the importance of the last session, although briefly, is Apps (1991). He states that the last session may be as important as the first session. Unfortunately, the last session has traditionally "been devoted to a final examination, an end-of-session form, and a rush to include information that you had intended to cover earlier" (Apps, 1991, p. 83). This certainly is typical of most higher education courses and too many adult education courses. Apps suggests that the worst thing to do is dump more information on the students at the end of a course. Instead, the last session should be a celebration of learning. If the group has bonded, an opportunity for the students to arrange a lunch or dinner should be provided. Also, if students wish to continue their learning beyond the last session, consideration could be given to setting up a computer conference or some other systematic way for students to maintain contact with each other after the "official" end of the course.

To avoid an anti-climatic let down, a very useful activity (both cognitively and psychosocially) is to review the main ideas and concepts that have been acquired. An opportunity should be provided to discuss what was learned, including ideas beyond the formal curriculum, and possible application beyond the classroom. One approach would be that each student do a concept map of what they learned (see next section) and then share it with the class. If the class is large or anonymity is an issue, students can be divided into small groups to consider issues such as what were the best and worst aspects of the course as well as what should be kept and changed. A spokesperson can report back for the group. This can be an opportunity for the teacher to get some feedback both in terms of content relevancy, learning activities and their own presentation/organizational skills.

Another important, if not essential, means of teacher feedback is completing an end-of-course feedback or evaluation form. These are often required in higher education. They should include open-ended questions in addition to objective (forced-choice) ratings. End-of-course assessment is crucial for revising various aspects of the course in preparation for the next time it will be delivered. It may also be used to evaluate the teacher for merit or employment purposes. The end-of-course assessment should provide specific information but be easy to complete, meaningful, worthwhile and confidential. More information with regard to constructing an end-of-course assessment can be found in Chapter 9.

Presentations and Lectures

The lecture has been described by some sage as being a method of transferring information from the notes of the professor to the notes of the student — without it passing through the mind of either. Unfortunately, as with many facetious statements there is a strong element of truth in this one. The reality is that the lecture is very teacher-centred and best suited for transmitting information and not particularly suited to facilitating critical thinking. Notwithstanding this limitation, much can be done with the lecture to motivate students to reflect upon the content being transmitted — that is, encourage students to be self-directed and critical learners.

Considering that the main purpose of the lecture is transmitting subject matter, the most important task and challenge is to identify the essence of the topic or subject at hand, thereby limiting the amount of material that must be assimilated by the student. Equally importantly, the lecture should provide some order to the material so as to provide a meaningful framework in which students can organize their thoughts as well as analyse and incorporate new ideas. This has been noted previously as a major responsibility of the teacher as a content expert. As important as this task is, it is not sufficient for a successful lecture.

The attention span of students is limited to not much more than ten minutes. Ideally the lecture would have the students fully engaged and vicariously ex-periencing the topic of discussion. This can be facilitated by the presentation skills of the lecturer. These skills will be manifested through enthusiasm, sharing of personal experiences, humour, insights, use of examples, and modelling of critical thinking. This is an enormously difficult challenge that most teachers are not likely to master. Those who are not natural performers can try making their lectures more interactive (this is not an oxymoron).

Teachers who must lecture in order to convey information to a large class can take opportunities to shift some of the responsibility to the students to engage actively in assimilating the content being transmitted. That is, they can make their class less teacher-centred. Perhaps the first step is to realize that there are means of transmitting information other than the lecture. Reading materials can be used effectively to prepare for a lecture or further explore content. One should also take the time to ask questions (even if rhetorically) and to allow students to ask questions. Consideration should also be given to integrating other learning activities such as discussion groups and writing/reflection assignments.

Another useful tactic, if one must lecture, is to be very well prepared and make use of the best tools available. One of the most useful of these tools is an electronic slide presentation (e.g. PowerPoint). While this may add some colour and glitz, its real strength is that it encourages the teacher to think about the key points and to be clear as to the organization and timing of the lecture. Another important tactic is to relate to, or interact with, your class before, during and after the lecture. This will not only convey a genuine sense of caring but will also encourage students to provide feedback.

However, the best advice remains, don't lecture. In this regard, Eble (1988) believes that the teacher should first "think in terms of discourse — talk, conversation — rather than lecture. Second, respect silence, both the teacher's and the student's. Third, shift from a total dependency on verbalizing to other means of animating, illustrating, and reinforcing talk" (p. 68). The point is that while large classes may seem to necessitate use of the lecture method, one does not really have to descend to an industrial approach and massification of the classroom. As has been noted, much can be done to mitigate the downside of a lecture.

One of the most powerful methods of overcoming the loss of identity and sense of personal importance that is common among students in higher education is to engage the students cognitively in a critical incident activity. The critical incident is an activity where students are encouraged to reflect upon relevant personal experiences that have particular significance to them. Their reflection is guided by specific but non-threatening questions. Students are given "a set of instructions that identifies the kind of incident to be described and asks for details of the time, place, and actors involved in the incident and the reasons why the event was so significant" (Brookfield, 1990b, p. 179). Critical incidents may become informal mini-case studies. Students may voluntarily share these reflections verbally or submit them in writing. When shared verbally, individual awareness and collective clarification is achieved regarding the entering state of understanding. Whether shared through written assignments or verbally, these incidents can be of great benefit to the teacher in understanding students' knowledge and emotional states as well as for students to reflect upon their current knowledge.

Not only do critical incidents encourage students to reflect upon their experiences and knowledge structures, it is a means for the teacher and students to assess understanding and sources of misconceptions. This is core to a collaborative constructivist and deep-meaningful approach to teaching and learning. It can provide a baseline for teacher and student as to the current state of the student's knowledge. It brings students in touch with gaps in their understanding and actively involves them in relating to and making sense of the subject matter at hand. However, it presupposes that the students can relate to and have had some experience with the topic.

One example, taken from an instructional development course, would be to ask the students to take a few moments to reflect upon a recent situation where they believed themselves to be practicing critical thinking. Questions to guide this reflection might be: What were the distinguishing characteristics of critical thinking? What precipitated such thinking? What risks were involved? What was done to facilitate this activity?

The critical incident activity can be adapted to various areas of study by simply changing the issue that students will be asked to reflect upon. For example, if the topic were organizational communication, the guiding questions for the students' reflections might include: How does communication occur within an organization that you are very familiar with? What is an instance in which internal communication failed? What does this failure suggest about the usual pattern of internal communication? Can you suggest a change in this pattern that might have prevented this failure?

As a verbal technique, the critical incident can be used effectively in a large group setting to orient both teacher and students as well as involve and encourage students to think about their own perceptions and assumptions. After giving the class five or ten minutes to think about the incident, students are asked to volunteer to share their experience. After four or five of these some general observations can be made that are central to the lecture. This approach can also be used during the lecture as a change of pace or the end of the lecture to provide feedback. Variations and further explanation on the use of the critical incident can be found in Brookfield (1990b, 1995) — one of which will be discussed in the section on facilitating discussion.

Considering the importance and challenge of taking notes during a lecture and trying to make sense of fast-paced verbally delivered information, a technique worth exploring is concept mapping. This is a technique that encourages students to take responsibility and control of their learning, which in turn, facilitates self-directed learning. It goes to the heart of students' taking responsibility for constructing meaning. Knowledge construction is about making connections, structuring ideas and developing coherent frameworks that facilitate further learning. More specifically, concept mapping has the student hierarchically representing the connection of key concepts with linking words that can be used to explain their understanding to others.

Constructing personal meaning through a concept map requires concentration and time. It is a work in progress that may find its genesis in a lecture or be refined during a lecture after an initial reading of a topic. The key is to distinguish concepts from linking words. Concepts are events or objects that can be observed while "linking words specify the relationships between concepts" (Fraser, 1996, p. 22). Examples of linking words or phrases are: consists of, illustrates, is different from, influences, results in, and requires. An excellent way to teach and encourage the use of concept maps is to model it during a lecture. However, the value is in having the students create their own concept maps, not memorizing the teacher's. For additional explanation and uses of concept maps see Fraser (1996).

Reading Assignments

In traditional classroom teaching and learning, reading assignments are an important means of presenting information and ideas. Next to classroom presentations and lectures, students rely most heavily on textbooks and other print materials. At the same time, the literature on teaching and learning says little about the use of print materials. In adult and higher education, print materials are primary sources of course content. These materials generally provide the foundation for the teaching-learning transaction but they are no substitute for a critical community of learners. Parenthetically, the industrial model of distance education employs the prescriptive self-instructional course packages to provide both content and instruction. Its weakness, of course, is the lack of critical treatment of content and opportunity to clarify understanding through communication.

As noted in Chapter 4, the assumption here is that critical thinking is domain-specific and context-dependent (McPeck, 1990a). While subject matter is crucial to facilitating critical thinking, it must also be approached with a sceptical attitude. Critical thinking is about constructing meaning and confirming understanding and possibly reconstructing knowledge. The content of subject matter and problems posed shape thinking. This why it is so important that the teacher have expertise in the subject being taught and why greater attention should be given to the selection of reading assignments and the use of text materials. Reading assignments provide an important opportunity for sustained reflection that is difficult in a classroom environment. Furthermore, written text is generally more precise and explicit, so provides a valuable complement to verbal discourse.

As important as reading assignments are, we must keep in mind that students do not have unlimited time, motivation or ability to assimilate vast amounts of material. As we have emphasized previously, it is generally better to provide less material but expect more thoughtful and deeper assimilation and accommodation of the content than would be possible with an excessive reading load. Reading assignments must be integral to the course and classroom lectures, discussion and assessment. More often than not, the students' inclination is to ignore "optional" readings. Moreover, classroom activities must add to the understanding that students have gleaned from their readings. It serves no purpose to present the same material at the level at which it has already been assimilated by the students before class.

Reading assignments must be central to classroom activities. They can serve multiple purposes. Beyond preparing students for more in-depth classroom treatment, readings can:

> ...describe in depth the topics and issues we only have time to outline during class. They can present theory, allowing us time in class to consider examples and spell out complexities. They can be used as points of agreement and contrast. They can stretch and challenge students' thinking abilities. (Meyers & Jones, 1993, p. 125)

The use we make of readings will depend upon many factors such as the discipline and the specific subject matter itself, the developmental stage and abilities of students, and the point at which the readings occur during the course. For example, readings will be used differently according to whether they are being used in a science course or a humanities course, an introductory undergraduate course or one at advanced graduate level, and whether they are assigned near the beginning or near the end of the course. Regardless of how we intend to use reading assignments, the readings must be relevant to intended outcomes, expectations as to the reading assignment must be clear, and modelling of how to approach the assignment should be provided.

Relevance of reading assignments is crucial if we are to reasonably limit the amount of material students are expected to digest. Not only should expectations be clear, as described previously, but readings should be used for a variety of purposes (e.g. overview or critique). Finally, direction and guidance must be provided in the form of strategies and study questions. To be truly facilitative, the teacher should consider explicitly modelling how to approach a reading assignment and explain the strategies that might be used. In the final analysis the student must take responsibility to extract meaning from the reading assignment. With proper preparation, they should be given the control to devise their own strategies, and when appropriate, select readings of particular interest.

As is the case with writing assignments (to be discussed subsequently), the task given to the student as a reading assignment may progressively move from summarizing and identifying key ideas, to critiquing and translating ideas into a new context or area of practice. Another technique to focus attention, as discussed previously, is to ask students to construct a concept map. Whether the results of a reading assignment are submitted in written form or presented orally, feedback and discussion should follow. Again, to ensure that reading assignments are relevant, they should explicitly be addressed in the classroom. In this regard, one approach is to have students take turns presenting and leading the discussion of a particular reading of their choice.

A particular and special reading assignment is the case study. The case study is an opportunity to analyse and resolve a realistic dilemma or problem. The case provides "opportunities for inquiry — inquiry bounded by experience, framed by theory, generating possibilities, and informing practice" (Harrington & Garrison,

1992, p. 721). Students are expected to make judgements and decisions on contextually-based problem information. Since the case describes complex and ambiguous situations, there is no one correct solution. Cases are a simulation of reality, and, therefore, perceptions and proposed actions must be anchored in the data provided by the case description (Marsick, 1990). Because cases simulate reality, practical knowledge and transfer is enhanced. A case study also creates an opportunity for inter-subjective understanding and knowledge confirmation.

Use of case studies is consistent with the view that knowledge is socially situated. That is, "the specificity and localism of cases as instructional materials may not be problematic for learning; indeed, they may be far more appropriate media for learning than the more abstract and decontextualized lists of propositions or expositions of facts, concepts, and principles" (Shulman, 1992, p. 24). The narrative and story line of a case may make it easier for students to appreciate the complexity of actual situations and construct meaning in ill-structured domains. Students learn to construct flexible meaning structures instead of rigid decontextualized schemata.

Preparing a case is a challenging process. Meyers and Jones (1993) suggest several rules. First, the case should tell a story, much like a well researched news report. Secondly, like a good story it should develop the main characters. Finally, the length and detail of the case should be consistent with the time available for analysis and discussion as well as the ability and knowledge level of the students. A full description and discussion of case design is beyond the scope of this chapter.

A good source of cases in adult and higher education are the students. One can have students develop a case from their own experiences as an assignment. For this to be effective students must have analysed cases and have guidelines to facilitate their development. A good start to writing cases is to begin by studying examples and forms of cases. Readings suggested for these purposes are Christensen and Hansen (1987), Fenstermacher and Soltis (1992) and Shulman (1992).

Using cases effectively requires extensive teacher preparation and a clear idea of what is to be accomplished. Case studies are essentially about critical thinking and problem solving involving the application of knowledge to the complexity of real-life situations. The case study represents a process of critical reflection and shared inquiry of genuine problems that parallels the critical thinking cycle. Therefore, it is a powerful means to facilitate critical thinking and increase the metacognitive awareness of students. Each of the phases of the critical thinking cycle can be used as suggestions in approaching the case. For example:

1. Define the problem, its causes, and contextual contingencies.
2. Explore the issues and gather relevant information.
3. Begin making connections and sense of the data.
4. Generate explanations and test implications.
5. Provide a coherent integration of events and construct a resolution.
6. Relate resolution and findings to accepted theory.

All phases may not be relevant in a particular case, but students should have some metacognitive awareness of the complete cycle to assist in developing strategies to approach and resolve the case.

Using the case study method requires considerable student preparation to realize its full potential and intended learning outcome. In addition, students must have some knowledge and experience related to the topic. Students can prepare for a case discussion by reading the case and writing a short summary. Appropriate questions may also be provided that will guide the students in the analysis of the case. A more formal analysis in the form of a written assignment may be requested after the case has been discussed in class.

Much thought should be given to the teacher's role in sharing students' analysis of the case. It is also important to allow students to relate the case to their own experiences. Therefore, students should be allowed to share their personal narratives in order to integrate the vicarious experience of a case with previous experience. Obviously, an open and secure learning environment must be established if students are to identify issues and defend them. Teachers must also be well prepared to guide the discussion without allowing it to digress, but on the other hand not dominating the discussion. Questions should be designed to raise issues, be probing, link issues and insights, and request an assessment or overview of the discussion. Examples of suggested questions and approaches can be found in Kleinfeld (1992) and Meyers and Jones (1993). Consideration should also be given to initiating discussion in small groups. We will explore in the next section strategies for facilitating group discussion that would apply here.

Critical Discussion

Critical discussion or discourse is an essential process in critical thinking and meaningful learning. This is particularly true in complex and ill-defined content areas. In groups, critical discussion can encompass the full critical thinking cycle. Such discussion can focus on identifying and defining issues or problems, it can identify key information and ideas, it can synthesize ideas, and it can apply and test solutions or resolutions. Open discussion in a supportive climate can also encourage the development and use of intuition and insight, leading to unanticipated learning outcomes. The reasons for this are that group discussion allows students to listen and integrate ideas as well as critique and offer new perspectives or solutions. Both reflection and active collaboration are possible, and essential, for full participation and educational effect.

Use of discussion groups is a quintessential adult education method for facilitating learning. There are many good reasons for this, such as the active participation and facilitation of deep and transformational learning through critical discussion. It also respects the needs, experiences and knowledge of adult learners. While discussion groups are certainly a significant aspect of higher education, the lecture still dominates. Unfortunately, discussion groups are too often seen as a waste of time that detracts from assimilating additional and excessive subject material. Equally important, students in higher education have been conditioned to passively listen and take notes. Moreover, they have successfully moved through the educational system without questioning this approach.

Critical group discussion is a powerful and perhaps essential means of encouraging students to assume responsibility to construct deep and meaningful understanding of a subject. One of the key reasons is that an appropriate balance of control can be realized, particularly in small group discussions. It is a distinct shift from the excessively teacher-centred approach often associated with the lecture and higher education. Discussion certainly can shift the balance of control in a positive direction.

To use critical discussion effectively, it is important to understand the reasons for its use. We have previously noted the close connection of discussion with higher-order cognitive learning outcomes. It is also very powerful in allowing students to affectively get in touch with their own interests and experiences. Thus, it can bring together the cognitive and affective domains to create real passion and motivation for learning. Consistent with this, Brookfield (1990a) provides four purposes for using the discussion method. The first purpose is to provide a diversity of perspectives; second, to externalize assumptions regarding one's values and beliefs; third, "to see the world as others see it" (p. 192); and fourth, to learn to cope with complexity and ambiguity.

A successful educational discussion requires considerable teacher and student preparation. This will include selecting from the course of studies an appropriate topic amenable to discussion. That is, the topic requires reflective thought and judgement and is not one to which there is a "right answer." Planning for a critical discussion will also require some preparation on the part of students. This is likely to be the reading of relevant materials. Both reading and discussion can also be aided by appropriate focus questions. Understanding appropriate conduct also requires preparation on the part of both teacher and students. Such conduct would include scepticism balanced by a respect for the thoughts of others; listening and considering what others have said — especially divergent or contrarian perspectives; being prepared to share thoughts, experiences and feelings but trying to link these comments to the flow of the discussion; and generally, trying to contribute to an atmosphere conducive to open communication and critical discourse. Finally, consideration should be given to the size of the discussion group(s). An ideal size may be six to eight students; with a group much larger than 15 break-out groups should be used.

The facilitator of a discussion, whether it is in a large or small group, must outline to the group the purpose, structure and guidelines as they begin the process. During the discussion, the facilitator must intervene in a timely fashion both to encourage wide participation among students as well as to draw attention to key issues that might have been missed. Modelling behaviour can be very important if the students have not had much experience with critical discussion. It is important to understand when the goal has been accomplished and not draw the discussion out when interest wanes. At this time, it is necessary to sum up, make connections to previous material, and provide a transition to the next learning activity. During the summary is a good time for the teacher to add his or her comments, experiences and insights.

Judging how much guidance or direction to give requires striking a balance between flexibility and purpose. How much freedom or direction to give will depend upon several factors. First is the purpose of the discussion. Is the discussion at the early (i.e. identifying issues), middle (i.e. searching for resolution) or late (i.e. evaluating conclusions) phase of the critical thinking cycle? Second, in terms of the group dynamic, are the participants just getting to know each other or have they reached a stage where they are prepared to take responsibility and control? Third, the developmental level of the students and their subject matter expertise will also be an important factor to consider when facilitating the discussion.

It is as much a mistake for a teacher to abandon responsibility and control over the direction of the discussion as it is to direct it to the extent that spontaneity and open participation are eliminated. The risk, on the one hand, is digression and confusion and, on the other, domination and withdrawal. Discussion must have some uncertainty and freedom to explore new ideas and connections. If the discussion is overly structured and deterministic, it will be perceived as being less than genuine or even manipulative. In any case, it will do little to facilitate critical and higher-order thinking. Not surprisingly, facilitating a critical discussion requires considerable skill and experience. Judgement is required to know when to encourage and when to challenge students.

Finally, it should be noted that a key goal of critical discussion is to build in students the confidence they need in order to question "received" knowledge, as well as their own perspectives, assumptions and understandings. This is not an obvious and natural process in an educational context. Guidance, exemplary practice, and encouragement are essential components. When done well, critical discussion can go a long way to build skill in critical thinking as well as confidence and self-esteem in terms of expressing one's thoughts.

Writing Assignments

Writing can encourage critical reflection, constructing meaning, and metacognitive awareness. However, accomplishing these outcomes will depend upon the provision of a clear purpose and sufficient support. At times, depending on the nature and level of the subject, content mastery will be the goal. Moreover, since knowledge reconstruction or transformation must start with a good grasp of existing content, it may be worthwhile to start with short writing assignments that teach students how to extract the salient issues from course materials. In facilitating critical thinking, Meyers (1986) believes that students "should begin with simple operations, such as summarizing, recognizing basic issues, identifying key concepts, and learning to ask appropriate questions" (p. 72). In this way, students can build toward the higher-level critical thinking skills necessary for deep-reflective writing.

Written assignments without mutually understood objectives and guidelines can be counter-productive. When assigning a paper it is important not to be too vague or too specific. In either situation, the risk is that deep-reflective writing will not be encouraged. Broad and vague assignments often lead to rambling thoughts and cursory thinking. On the other hand, assignments that are too specific risk being trivial and may not encourage divergent thinking and the linking of relevant ideas and experiences. As well, topics should relate to specific course objectives and encourage the consideration of personal experiences. Clarity of purpose and expectations can also be achieved through scaffolding and modelling. As discussed previously, a good scaffolding technique is to start with small assignments that build the necessary skills for a major paper or project. The other technique is to model critical thinking skills. In this regard, examples of well-written assignment papers can be a useful guide.

As noted, writing assignments are very helpful to stimulate reflection and the construction of meaning. However, their length must be appropriate for the purpose, and the number of writing assignments should be realistic in terms of the time available and what is required for a quality product. Time is almost invariably too short and expectations too high for end of term papers. Long papers at the end of a term can be as problematic for deep-meaningful learning as trying to cover too much content in a course of studies — particularly in undergraduate or introductory courses. Moreover, there is less opportunity for constructive feedback. For these reasons, term papers generally result in a simple summary of what has been covered in the course. Communicating the nature of the writing assignment and guiding the process can be enhanced with the expert input of the teacher by shaping the approach to the topic (e.g. defining the problem), locating sources of information, providing insights, and incorporating personal experiences.

Designing short writing assignments for specific purposes is congruent with facilitating critical thinking. Unfortunately, as Meyers (1986) notes, we have few appropriate models. Writing assignments can demonstrate the progression of the thinking process and not just the answer or solution. Meyers (1986) also points out that writing assignments "in critical thinking should give students opportunities to puzzle over issues, to sort things out, and to formulate their own independent judgements" (p. 69). The reality is that critical thinking is best developed gradually, developing competence at each phase of the critical thinking cycle. Therefore, writing assignments that facilitate critical thinking should be short, focus on real problems, and sequentially build appropriate competencies such as recognizing key ideas, identifying assumptions, critiquing arguments, integrating ideas coherently, and offering solutions to dilemmas or problems. Another advantage of short assignments is that constructive feedback can be provided to students in a timely manner.

Initial writing assignments for developing critical thinking abilities might ask for a one or two page document summarizing the content of an article or chapter. The demand here is to select the key ideas according to their importance and attach some meaning to them. Short analytical assignments can follow this. Such assignments might analyse the assumptions and theoretical basis for the document, provide another perspective upon which to view the problem, focus on the logic of the argument, analyse the implications of the thesis being advocated, or compare and contrast two theses. All of these emphasize different aspects of critical thinking.

The key challenge is to fully engage students in the writing assignment. A very powerful way to make assignments meaningful and useful is to go beyond simply acquiring theory and have the students apply their knowledge to the contexts that they know well. This may be the workplace or their personal lives. In any case, it will sharpen critical faculties and fully engage the students in a meaningful and worthwhile learning experience. One assignment that is ideally suited to this purpose is the project.

A project can require incorporation of all phases of the critical thinking process, from defining the problem to implementing a plan of action. A project can provide a balance of reflection and action as well as independence and guidance. However, the teacher must ensure that students have the time and ability to complete the project. For this reason, the project should be a focus of attention from the beginning of the course. Students need to submit an outline for feedback and assurance that it can be completed.

For larger projects, collaboration should be considered. Collaborative projects provide an invaluable opportunity for students to be exposed to new ideas and perspectives, clarify their thoughts and test new ideas. The primary risk is that not all collaborators contribute to the outcome; however, even in this situation, the passive participant may well vicariously learn valuable critical thinking skills related to conceiving, implementing and evaluating a practical application. Structure and guidance is required to maximize the benefits of collaborative projects (see Meyers & Jones (1993) for guidelines and examples).

The final writing assignment to be discussed here is the student journal. Use of the student journal as a writing assignment is common in adult education but it is less frequently used in higher education. Journals can be used appropriately in almost any type of course or subject. The strength of the journal is as "a place to practice writing and thinking" (Fulwiler, 1987). It is a place to relate public knowledge to personal thoughts and experiences, which makes it more than just a notebook.

As with any analytical writing assignment, journals encourage students to critically reflect upon course content and construct personal meaning. To do this they should be used three or four times a week to record the students' educational experiences. Moreover, to take full educational advantage of journals, they should become part of the classroom activity and be shared with the community of learners. Initially, it may be useful to provide time in class for students to write in their journal. This will provide opportunities to guide students as to what is expected.

Depending on the purpose, student journals can be used for formal feedback, checked in a cursory manner, or selectively reported on by the student verbally in order maintain privacy. They can be used as a catalyst for other writing assignments or projects. Use of the journal to get students to express their understanding of any idea or concept will encourage deep-meaningful learning without the undue pressure or anxiety that often accompanies other writing assignments. Fulwiler (1987) provides a detailed discussion of student journals.

Conclusion

Collaboration complements reflection in the thinking/learning process. Both require a supportive classroom climate. Classroom climate is based upon the authenticity of the teacher and the trust he or she engenders in the students. Critical reflection and collaboration requires an acceptance of students in their exploration and testing of ideas. Both academic and psychosocial climate must be nurtured, beginning with the first session. It was also noted that incongruent and inappropriate evaluation methods would likely cause a rapid deterioration of the classroom climate.

Of course, none of these learning activities are sufficient in and of themselves. The real challenge for the teacher is the creative combination and integration of learning activities appropriate for the intended learning outcomes. Issues of responsibility and control should be discussed and clarified. Expectations and assignments should be open to negotiation. Finally, teachers should model appropriate behaviour and ensure that the educational activities and assessment are congruent with intended learning outcomes. In this way, teachers will be seen to be authentic and have the expertise to exercise appropriate educational judgements.

9

Assessment and Grading

> If we wish to discover the truth about an educational system, we
> must look into its assessment procedures. (Rowntree, 1977, p. 1)

Perhaps nothing about education makes teachers and students feel more insecure
than assessment. Assessment makes students feel pressured by their teachers;
assessment makes teachers feel pressured by their colleagues and the institutional
bureaucracy. All the while, too few of the participants in the educational enterprise
understand the effect of assessment on teaching and learning.

The relationship between classroom assessment and student outcomes makes it
"one of the most potent forces influencing education" (Crooks, 1988, p. 467).
Assessment affects students in that it indicates to them what is important to learn,
raises or lowers their level of motivation, predisposes their approaches to learning,
and encourages or impedes the development of higher-order cognitive abilities.
Unfortunately, given the powerful influence of assessment on educational outcomes, it "appears to receive less thought than most other aspects of education"
(Crooks, 1988, p. 467).

Learning Assessment

Assessing learning for purposes of measuring achievement is described as a
systematic process of selecting, collecting, interpreting, and communicating
findings to focus learning activities and enhance the quality of learning outcomes.
While there are different purposes for learning assessment, the two primary
purposes are diagnosis of misunderstanding (i.e. feedback) and certification of
competence (i.e. evaluation). Both assess learning but from learner and teacher
perspectives. Therefore, assessment is fundamentally concerned with obtaining
valid data about students' understanding and competence in terms of intended
educational goals.

While such a definition may seem reasonably straightforward, the actual process
of assessing understanding and grading achievement is not so simple. To guide the
discussion a classification of learning assessment is provided (see Figure 9.1). This
classification should assist in clarifying terminology, purposes and appropriate data
associated with learning assessment.

First, we see assessment as accomplishing two broad overlapping purposes —
feedback and evaluation. Feedback provides informal guidance as to the progress
of learning. Such feedback can be explanatory or confirmatory, depending upon the

		Qualitative (Diagnostic)	Quantitative (Measurement)
PURPOSE	**Feedback** (guidance)	**Explanatory**	**Confirmatory**
	Evaluation (grading)	**Formative**	**Summative**

Figure 9.1: Forms of learning assessment.

nature of the data gathered. That is, it can make a qualitative judgement regarding how well meaning has been constructed, or a quantitative measure of basic ideas and information. Explanatory feedback sets the stage for diagnosis of misconceptions and negotiation of meaning. Confirmatory feedback, on the other hand, conveys to the student simply whether a response is right or wrong. When the purpose of the learning activity is transmitting basic information and simple ideas, this may be appropriate and efficient. However, for less well-structured and complex subject areas, this form of feedback is not particularly useful. In such instances, students are usually asked to make connections among basic information and ideas; therefore, confirmatory feedback should be followed by explanatory feedback in the form of reciprocal communication.

Evaluation provides a more formal judgement as to the quality of meaning constructed and the achievement of curricula goals. This form of assessment can be either formative or summative, depending on whether the focus is on diagnosing understanding or measuring achievement. Formative evaluation, like explanatory feedback, makes a qualitative judgement for purposes of assessing understanding. On the other hand, summative evaluation makes a quantitative measurement of content goals. Formative evaluation is an inherent aspect of the educational process while summative evaluation is a measure of learning outcomes.

As we have stated, feedback as a means to guide learning activities is different from evaluation of achievement for purposes of grading. Feedback data should focus first and foremost on basic understanding and meaning structures. At the same time, assessment in the form of feedback or evaluation must be congruent with and reinforce intended and worthwhile learning goals. Feedback guides students toward such goals or standards. These standards are then evaluated by means of grades. According to Glaser and Silver (1994):

> As assessment and instruction are more closely linked, achievement measurement will be integral to learning rather than imposed by some external shaper of students' fates". (p. 412)

It is difficult for students to cope with inappropriate assessment practices. As Ramsden (1992) warns, "Unsuitable assessment methods impose irresistible pressures on a student to take the wrong approaches to learning tasks" (p. 68). Deep-meaningful approaches to learning are not facilitated by testing that assesses only surface information and content. When students are rewarded for memorizing and reproducing as well as being burdened with an unrealistic workload, they cannot be blamed for simply trying to cope with a dysfunctional learning situation. In this situation, the intelligent strategy is to just try to pass the exam and get a good grade. Without relevant feedback along with time and opportunity for reflection, there is less chance of meaningful and lasting learning.

If teachers are to facilitate students' learning of what we value as knowledge, then there must also be a corresponding shift in what and how we provide feedback and evaluate intended outcomes. Incongruence between educational assessment and promoting critical thinking and self-direction will create confusion in how students ought to approach learning. For example, quantitative norm-based tests with multiple-choice formats may create a particular problem. It is difficult to measure students' reasoning processes and knowledge constructs with selected response formats. To exacerbate the challenge of facilitating meaningful learning and measuring understanding, teachers are pressured by their students and other external factors to teach to the test. In the worst case, as Glaser and Silver (1994) state, the "widespread use of multiple-choice assessment has contributed to a 'dumbing down' of instruction, in which skills tend to be taught in the form required for performance on the assessment rather than for more realistic or natural applications" (pp. 404–405).

Unsuitable assessment methods are often associated with excessive workloads. That is, teaching is excessively focused on delivering content with little discretion as to what is important or what might motivate students to construct deep meaningful constructs. Quality learning in an educational sense must be concerned with acquiring the central concepts and constructing connections among the essential concepts. Unfortunately, the excessive focus on the amount of material "covered" tends to create a preoccupation with grades at the expense of understanding. While grading may serve a purpose, it is important that teachers understand the influence of grades on approaches to learning and ultimately the quality of learning outcomes. A balance must be struck between the need to facilitate meaningful learning (i.e. sustained guidance) and the institutional demands for normative standards (i.e. comparative and discriminating grades).

The quality of educational outcomes is judged from the perspective of both meaning and worthwhileness. Worthwhileness is concerned with selecting key concepts that will support future learning and provide the foundation for the construction of more complex and integrated knowledge structures. Although worthwhileness has a broader social implication, it goes directly to the issue of content and workload. In this sense worthwhileness reflects what is essential. It is not possible to study every aspect of even a narrow content area. Within a particular subject area, decisions have to be made as to what is essential for understanding if students are to have the time to approach their learning in a meaningful manner.

On the other hand, meaning has a narrower focus. The students' motivation and strategies for making connections between new and current knowledge determine meaning. Constructing meaning is greatly influenced by assessment. By itself, rote memorization and mindless replication of content can diminish the quality of learning and increase the perception of irrelevance. Basic information must be organized in a coherent manner for meaning to be perceived and maintained. A quality educational transaction integrates the concerns of both teacher and student through issues of worthwhileness and meaning respectively. Worthwhileness and meaning are conceptual descriptors of the quality of education, while workload and assessment shape the quality of learning outcomes in practice. The essential challenge for teachers is to design workload and assessment to make knowledge construction worthwhile and meaningful to their students.

We cannot ignore the reality that much assessment in higher education is about formal assessment and grading. Unfortunately, however, most of the insecurity and frustration with assessment is associated with grading. The key to relieving this frustration is to appreciate that assessment must be consistent with stated goals. For example, to advocate the development of critical thinking and then test for recall is inappropriate and will cause frustration and failure in achieving higher-order learning outcomes. On the other hand, if assessment is consistent with intended goals, then grading can provide useful evaluation. However, the first priority is to use assessment to diagnose understanding; second, to facilitate and motivate; and finally, to assign a grade.

Assessment is inherently linked to good teaching by revealing misconceptions (i.e. meaning) and measuring students' understanding and achievement. This, in turn, can provide useful feedback to guide subsequent educational design and teaching decisions. Ramsden (1992) suggests that assessment "is about several things at once" (p. 182). He goes on to say:

> It is about reporting on students' achievements and about teaching them better through expressing to them more clearly the goals of our curricula. It is about measuring student learning and it is about diagnosing specific misunderstandings in order to help students learn more effectively. It concerns the quality of teaching as well as the quality of learning: it involves us in learning from our students' experiences, and it is about changing ourselves as well as our students. (p. 182)

Assessment is a challenging and uncertain process. Teaching and learning must utilize various forms of assessment in a coherent and strategic manner. This includes feedback (i.e. guidance) and evaluation (i.e. grading). Educational practice must also recognize the necessity for standards. Assessment results (i.e. diagnosis and measurement) need to be compared to some standard or comparable group of students if they are to be meaningful and useful educationally. Ramsden (1992) argues that assessment is a "series of relations between the person whose work we are assessing, the quality of the outcomes he or she demonstrates in comparison with others, and our own understanding of what students know and do not know" (p. 187). The relativity and complexity of the task argues for considerable flexibility and professional judgement when selecting assessment methods.

Too often "the tests widely used today are fundamentally incompatible with the kinds of changes in educational practice needed to meet current challenges" (Resnick & Resnick, 1992, p. 37). That is, these tests do not assess for higher-order cognitive abilities such as critical thinking as well as relevant knowledge that can meet the challenges of complex external settings. The reason they are incompatible is that too often assessment instruments use easily administered and scored "selected-response" formats, which makes it very difficult to assess learning beyond recall or recognition of basic facts. The alternative is to include opportunities for "constructed-responses" where "the student produces an answer or furnishes an 'authentic' response to a given stimulus" (Erwin, 1991, p. 55). The best examples are critical essays, projects, portfolios of developed work, and performances.

Feedback

We envision the assessment process in terms of three phases — expectation, transaction and outcome. Assessment in the expectation and transactional phases are viewed as primarily a feedback concern. On the other hand, the outcome phase is discussed as an evaluation concern.

Issues related to expectations or intentions assess what teachers and students bring to the educational context. Both teachers and students have specific responsibilities and bring expectations with regard to learning activities and assessment that need to be clarified and brought into alignment. Transactional forms of assessment are essential for meaningful approaches to learning. Explanatory and confirmatory feedback is focused in the transactional phase. This is manifested in terms of facilitative feedback regarding meaningfulness and understanding achieved. Students need to share the meaning they have constructed and have it assessed fairly. From the students' perspective, they need to assess the implications of this new knowledge in terms of previous knowledge structures. Teachers can also use this information to assess their approaches and methods in order to make pedagogical adjustments.

The educational transaction is constructed around learning activities. These learning activities have been described previously as consisting of four essential types — listening, reading, talking and writing. It is through these activities that the teacher has the responsibility to ensure sustained reciprocal communication in order to gather sufficient qualitative and quantitative data to provide relevant and authentic feedback to guide the learner in constructing meaning and confirm understanding. Feedback for both teacher and learner is essential to facilitate learning. Transactional feedback goes to the heart of a worthwhile educational experience. As the term transactional suggests, such feedback goes both ways. Moreover, assessing authentic understanding and providing feedback is a challenging process. Providing and receiving this feedback is discussed, below, in the context of the four learning activities.

Listening. The predominant classroom learning activity in higher education is the presentation or lecture. The lecture relies largely upon listening skills where concentration is difficult to maintain. Due to the limitations of the lecture for meaningful learning (see Chapter 7), feedback becomes particularly important and challenging. Implementing interaction and feedback in a presentation is essential to keep students mentally active.

A good presenter becomes very adept at visual feedback by reading the audience. This can be enhanced by rhetorical questions combined with appropriate pauses. However, perhaps the most effective way to mitigate the inherent limitations of presentations is to combine them with other complementary learning activities, such as opportunities for questions and answers as well as mini-discussion groups reporting back to the large group. Written feedback can also be used during and after the presentation. Written questions can be picked up during the presentation and simple questionnaires asking what was the least clear point can be handed in after the presentation and addressed at the next lecture.

Reading. Reading assignments can be a very effective technique to introduce students to a topic before it is introduced in a class lecture or discussion. Assessing comprehension can be achieved by having the students do a brief presentation as to the main points of the reading. This will provide considerable motivation to read the document carefully and reflect upon its central message. Most importantly, however, this gives all participants feedback as to possible misconceptions and points missed. Feedback from reading assignments can also be obtained through short written papers. Assessing reading through written responses may be best used as students become more advanced or proficient in a topic.

Talking. Dialogue and critical discourse are considered here to be central to adult and higher education. As noted in the previous learning activities, they are dependent upon some form of verbal communication to provide the qualitative feedback necessary to assess comprehension and understanding. Moreover, a collaborative constructivist philosophy of the educational transaction clearly suggests a strong reliance upon discussion and the sustained and immediate feedback it provides. Other learning activities (i.e. reading, listening and writing) are not complete without some form of discourse and discussion to assess assimilation and accommodation.

Discussion is a core learning activity when higher-order learning outcomes such as critical thinking are valued. The primary reason is the immediate diagnostic feedback provided by the teacher and fellow students, not to mention self-assessment by the students themselves through the process of formulating their thoughts for expression. Discussion provides an informal means of peer assessment to complement teacher feedback. Students who are listening are encouraged to vicariously enter into the discussion, thereby assessing their understanding. This may then prompt further clarification from the group.

To provide the high quality feedback inherent in critical discourse necessitates establishing a supportive and secure environment for students to express themselves (see Chapter 8). For this reason, using participation as a formal evaluation measure is suspect and must be approached cautiously. The problem is that it encourages students to speak when they may not have anything to contribute. On the other hand, students may become overly self-conscious and worry about looking foolish. Verbal discourse should be spontaneous and free-flowing but at the same time guided by the teacher.

Writing. Writing assignments are also a well-used learning activity in adult and higher education, although they are used more often for evaluative rather than feedback purposes. Writing assignments with written confirmatory feedback are appropriate for assessing and guiding the assimilation of basic knowledge. Here short quizzes can be effective. On the other hand, short answer and essay assignments provide an opportunity to assess understanding. Explanatory written feedback to the students can be useful but time consuming for the teacher in diagnosing conceptual understanding. The full benefit of written feedback, however, is gained by further verbal clarification of the assessment to ensure nuances have been communicated.

Writing is essential to facilitate and assess critical thinking. The main reasons, as discussed previously, are that written language is more precise and there is time for reflection when communication is in writing. Moreover, with written assignments, feedback can be used as guidance to revise and increase the depth and quality of understanding. The permanent nature of writing is a distinct advantage over verbal discourse with regard to time and the ability to reflect and revise. Writing is well suited to facilitate critical thinking.

Generally, it is best to assess frequently using a variety of methods. For example, critical thinking assignments should begin with short tasks such as identifying and defining the problem or issue, summarizing the main ideas, contrasting perspectives, and then progress to major critical papers and practical projects. This provides more opportunities for feedback and an understanding of expectations. All students need to have critical thinking modelled in order to feel comfortable as to what is expected. This is doubly important when we consider that critical thinking varies according to the nature and level of the subject matter.

With regard to content areas such as mathematics and science that involve quantitative manipulations, care should be taken to "always include questions requiring explanations in prose" (Ramsden, 1992, p. 211). Writing assignments are essential for accommodation of new information and restructuring knowledge for deeper understanding. Quantitative feedback can conceal misconceptions. Finally, it is important to remind students frequently, through the use of appropriate and authentic feedback, that what will be rewarded is demonstrated understanding. Ultimately this will provide a more accurate reflection of the student's learning.

The normative aspects of assessment should be used judiciously when collaborative learning is valued. Collaborative learning approaches may be undermined by an overemphasis on competitive grading. Peer- and self-assessment methods are particularly useful as informal feedback and to encourage students to assume responsibility to construct meaning. Use of peer- and self-assessment to assign grades, however, must be approached with considerable caution. In addition to concerns about validity of grades, it may have undesirable consequences on collaboration and co-operation.

Self-assessment. A useful if not necessary means of guiding the transaction is the students' own judgement of the quality and substance of their learning. Student self-assessment is the process of reflecting and writing about their learning experience. Self-assessment is very closely associated with the development of critical reflection and self-direction. However, it is important to emphasize that self-assessment does not replace the need for other forms of assessment such as explanatory feedback on critical essays, projects and exams. From a transactional and teaching perspective, self-assessment creates an impetus for dialogue and feedback as well as a need to diagnose misunderstandings.

From the students' perspective, self-assessment can facilitate self-directed learning. Kusnic and Finley (1993) argue that with regard to the process of written self-assessment:

> ... students strengthen their skills of analysis, synthesis, and evaluation; work to make sense of what they have learned and explore its relationship to their previous knowledge and ideas; become more conscious of their values and more cognizant of the ways in which they form values; deepen their learning and build connections between themselves and the content of their studies; and develop the skills, competence, and authority required for effective lifelong learning. (pp. 6–7)

This is the essence of a constructivist approach to learning. From a constructivist perspective, formative assessment and feedback should be emphasized with the intent to facilitate self-directed and continuous learning.

Evaluation

Evaluation of outcomes is a more formal activity, and the final phase of assessment. Traditionally, outcome evaluation has been seen as a form of summative assessment and grade assignment. Evaluation of outcomes is intended to measure the success of the educational transaction. This is why it is crucial that assessed outcomes are congruent with initial expectations. For better or for worse, students will use this information to reassess their expectations and approaches to learning. The strength of outcome evaluation in shaping approaches to learning should not be underestimated. If outcome evaluation is used as a means to assign grades, it will have an overwhelming influence on the nature of learning. For this reason, outcome evaluation and grading must reflect initial expectations and intended learning goals.

Maintaining high standards in grading is justified when evaluation is congruent with course aims (content), expectations are clear from the beginning, and students feel the teacher is effectively facilitating their learning. Students should perceive the teacher as an ally in understanding the course content. However, harsh or unfair grading does little to motivate students to approach learning in a meaningful manner. Nothing puts a chill over the classroom environment faster than an exam seen to be inappropriate or seen to be graded unfairly. Assessment should provide feedback and evaluation that will encourage students to take responsibility for their learning and continue learning. Poor or inappropriate assessment results can have a profoundly demoralizing impact on both students and teachers. Therefore, considerable care and attention should be given to assessment strategies and instruments.

Test design. Traditional tests that measure declarative knowledge (i.e. basic information) are pervasive in higher education. Perhaps the reason is that higher education has been largely concerned with conveying basic foundational ideas and knowledge associated with a particular discipline. This has been reinforced with overriding cost and efficiency concerns. In introductory courses this may be valid but too often quantitative tests are used inappropriately in advanced courses where higher-order learning outcomes are intended.

The inappropriate use of information recall tests is less common in adult education programs due largely to the fact that most adults do not have to, nor will they, tolerate inappropriate assessment. Adult students are very aware of what they wish to achieve from a course of study and will voice strongly their displeasure with learning activities that are incongruent with desired outcomes — including testing. Moreover, adult education is usually focused on immediate practical goals and problems that require higher-order problem solving activities and which are difficult to assess with objective tests. So the question is, when should objective tests be used and how should they be designed.

As noted, objective tests are designed to assess factual and foundational knowledge. For this reason, they have a place in assessing entering knowledge when initiating a course of studies as well as for periodically assessing the acquisition of foundational ideas. Summatively, objective tests can be used to measure acquisition of basic facts, ideas and standard procedures. They also lend themselves well to assigning grades — whether the grades are valid or not. However, even in introductory courses, they are not well suited to measuring depth of understanding and higher-order thinking abilities.

It is important to know when to use objective tests as well as how to design them. Having discussed the first issue we will provide some basic guidelines as to how to design such tests when appropriate. Moran (1997) provides what he calls well-established guidelines for writing individual test items. These guidelines are:

- Write all items in the simplest, most direct language.
- Avoid ambiguities.
- Avoid clues to correct answers.
- Solicit a review of the test from a colleague.
- Continually upgrade a file of test items. (p. 49)

Writing objective or quantitative test items is challenging and requires considerable up-front design effort.

The most common quantitative tests in adult and higher education, and those we will focus on, are multiple-choice and short answer written responses. Multiple-choice tests are designed for recognizing and selecting the correct option relative to the stem. In theory, multiple-choice items can be used to measure both factual knowledge and understanding. The reality is, however, that measuring understanding with a multiple-choice test is very much more demanding and limited. Multiple-choice items can reveal misconceptions, but the diagnosis is difficult, as it must be gained from inference based upon limited information. Compared to written or oral explanations, this method of diagnosing misconceptions is indirect and suspect.

Selected-response formats such as multiple-choice tests are usually norm-referenced for the purpose of comparing and ranking students. This raises a problem because this type of assessment provides little formative feedback to improve the quality of learning and teaching. If assessment is to be a useful tool for facilitating meaningful learning and critical thinking, then criterion-referenced and self-referenced assessment measures should be considered. Criterion-referenced assessments reflect a particular standard of achievement with regard to content mastery. On the other hand, self-referenced measures serve the purpose of demonstrating learning and development to the individual student.

Suggestions for writing multiple-choice test items are to make the options as short as possible, randomly assign the correct response among the options, and ensure there is only one correct answer. Statistical procedures can be very helpful in identifying items that are not clear and can provide test reliability measures. At the same time, validity measures are open to interpretation. That is, what exactly do the test results reveal with regard to the kind of knowledge and level of understanding that is reflected by such test scores?

Short answer questions that measure recall of basic information have problems similar to those associated with multiple-choice items. The one difference is that short answer questions go beyond simple recognition and require the students to provide their own response. While this may provide an additional challenge to the student, it is more difficult to score as it introduces a qualitative dimension. This, of course, is an advantage in terms of providing students with the opportunity to demonstrate some degree of understanding.

Short answer questions that go beyond fill in the blank can be used as short, structured essay type questions. These questions are better suited to measuring high-order cognitive achievement. At the same time, it must be clear to students what is being asked for in terms of information recall and depth of understanding.

Another consideration is providing choice to learners in terms of which short answer questions they will answer. For reasons discussed extensively around control and choice, we do recommend providing students with choice and the opportunity to demonstrate what they know as well as revealing deficiencies.

Usually the objectives in a course will shift from basic information acquisition to critical analysis and synthesis activities. As these objectives shift so too will the methods of assessment. Short answer assessments may be useful early in a course while critical papers and projects will likely be more appropriate nearer the end. A similar progression may occur in the quantitative subjects where basic concepts and typical problems are assessed before students are asked to apply these concepts and solve more complex problems in different contexts. Assessment should be frequent and grades based upon a number and variety of evaluation instruments. It is recommended that between four and six measurements be obtained during a course of studies using a variety of assessment methods that reflect intended objectives.

If assessment practices are to provide valid and useful feedback to students, then the marking criteria need to be clear and consistently applied. Generally these criteria should be communicated to the students in advance of the exam. Teachers must also be available to discuss the results of an exam or paper in order to clarify comments and improve students' approaches and strategies. In terms of papers and projects, it is very important to provide qualitative feedback (i.e. insightful and explanatory comments) if students are to gain more than a grade from the exercise.

Consideration should also be given to attitudinal and social dispositions. Teachers should be very clear as to the purpose of the examination or graded assignment and help students prepare for an examination. The teacher should genuinely help the students do the best they are capable of doing. It makes no sense to try and confuse, misdirect or trick the students as to what is expected and what will be tested. If at all possible, major or final exams that count for the majority of a course grade should be avoided. Finally, a useful method that can enhance the affective dimension, such as personal satisfaction, as well as reveal developmental progression over a period of time is the performance portfolio.

Performance portfolios. In many adult and higher education courses and programs, objective testing that only provides quantitative data and feedback may be inappropriate. For reasons of content or student expectations, many legitimate learning outcomes cannot be adequately measured through conventional tests. In such situations, serious consideration should be given to assembling a collection of work that clearly demonstrates development and learning in terms of desired outcomes. Performance portfolios can provide a collection of work upon which to judge the achievement of learners. These portfolios are particularly useful for judging the accomplishments of students from a qualitative perspective associated with abstract and creative endeavours.

Performance portfolios have traditionally focused on examples of a learner's acquired higher-order abilities and skills. These examples could include written and visual assignments, project/lesson plans, assessment of projects, research studies, multimedia materials, and journals. It is important that each of these examples or products have been assessed and relate directly to stated learning outcomes. Clear directions should be given as to what should be included and how they will be judged. This will make it possible to do a summative assessment of accomplishments. That is not to say that students should not have some control over or input into specific learning activities they will include in the portfolio.

Portfolios can be very motivational and satisfying for learners to display and explain what they have accomplished. This may be a good time for self-assessment. A written self-assessment may well be part of the portfolio and be a good method of initiating the discussion. It also provides an opportunity for the student and teacher to discuss future directions and goals. The teacher should take a facilitative and mentoring approach to such meetings. This is a collaborative process where the teacher also has an opportunity to receive feedback on how the educational experience might be improved. Educators should also give consideration to teaching portfolios that would demonstrate their own professional development (Moran, 1997).

Teaching evaluation. To this point the discussion has been on student assessment. Learning assessment is intended to focus students' efforts to efficiently and effectively achieve the intended educational outcomes. However, as a form of two-way communication, feedback must be reciprocal. Therefore, it is essential that students have an opportunity to assess teaching methods and techniques for the purpose of providing data and direction for improving the teaching side of the educational transaction. This can be done with simple evaluations, asking what students liked best and least after each class. This can be enormously helpful to the teacher and also gives the students a sense of control.

Notwithstanding continuous formative self-evaluation in the form of teacher notes along with daily student evaluations, a very useful technique is administering a post-course teaching evaluation form. Questions should include both selected response and open-ended formats. Areas of evaluation could include course content and materials, teacher preparation and knowledge of the subject, opportunity to influence goals and assessment, teacher presentation and learning activities, learning climate and facilities, opportunities to apply knowledge, and what would make this course better.

Conclusion

Assessment practices reveal what is valued educationally and will shape learning activities accordingly. The primary purpose of assessment is to aid and direct learning activities. If the educational goals are associated with meaningful learning and critical thinking, then assessment should be associated with the performance of these skills and abilities. Furthermore, assessment should itself be a learning experience. In this regard, it has little to do with ranking students according to fragmented and decontextualized information. Assessing for meaning and under-standing should occur in the context of writing essays, solving relevant problems, working on projects, and generally exploring and constructing meaning that reveals the student's full range of achievement.

Assessment is an integral aspect of the teaching-learning transaction and considerable attention must be given to this process. The reasons are that it explicitly reveals what is considered important and how a student's achievement will be judged and possibly graded. While assessment will reveal deficiencies, it must be demonstrated that these results are to be used developmentally to facilitate deeper understanding. With regard to grading, students should be provided the opportunity to demonstrate the extent of their knowledge, not just the extent of their ignorance. It is all too easy to demonstrate students' ignorance, given the explosion of information and knowledge in any field or sub-field of study.

Methods of assessment have an overpowering influence on how students approach learning. Assessment of the quality of an educational outcome must be congruent with the intended goals. Assessment should be seen first as a formative technique providing information that will guide the transaction. Grades must reflect achievement that is consistent with the agreed goals of the course. Unfair grading will do little to ensure that students continue to approach their learning in a deep and meaningful manner. To avoid dysfunctional incongruencies between intentions and learning approaches, assessment methods must consider the educa-tional transaction in its entirety.

10

Distance Education, Design and Technology

There are a number of reasons why even those educators who are not directly involved in distance education need to pay some attention to this sub-field of education. First, while distance education still accounts for a small percentage of all adult and higher education, this percentage is growing very rapidly. Second, distance education is now affecting education at conventional institutions, for good or ill. (Archer, Garrison, & Anderson, 1999, is an examination of some disruptive effects that distance education might have at such institutions, coupled with some suggestions about how to deal with such disruptions.) Third, in the context of distance education educators can observe issues of control and responsibility for the educational transaction, unblurred by the excessive familiarity of the face-to-face setting. Many of these issues are thrown into stark relief against the background of the various technologies employed in distance education, and the educational design that is a prerequisite for employing those technologies effectively.

For the benefit of readers unfamiliar with distance education, we will begin this chapter with a definition of distance education, followed by some sketch descriptions of individuals engaged in various forms of distance education. We will then outline a conceptual framework that many educators have found to be an invaluable aid to understanding distance education. This framework will also serve as the starting point for a discussion of the concepts of instructional design and educational technology, with the underlying issues of responsibility and control, issues that are highlighted in the distance education context.

A Definition

Many scholars have published definitions of distance education. However, the one we find to be the best combination of comprehensiveness, clarity, and succinctness provides the following three defining criteria:

1. Distance education implies that the majority of educational communication between (among) teacher and student(s) occurs noncontiguously.
2. Distance education must involve two-way communication between (among) teacher and student(s) for the purpose of facilitating and supporting the educational process.
3. Distance education uses technology to mediate the necessary two-way communication. (Garrison and Shale, 1987, p. 11)

Examples of Distance Education

Example #1: Susan lives in a city where there are a number of educational institutions. However, she has three small children and can't afford to pay a baby-sitter very often, so is pretty well house-bound for a few years. She is using what free time she has, mostly in the evenings when the children are in bed, to pursue her lifelong ambition to become a writer. She has enrolled in a non-credit correspondence course in fiction writing offered by a college whose campus is located in another province. After the arrival of a box of books, audiotapes, and a course guide, Susan has begun writing the assignments described in the course guide and mailing them to the college. There the tutor who is handling this course writes comments and suggestions on her assignments and sends them back to Susan. Since this is a non-credit course, the tutor does not assign a grade.

Example #2: One evening a week Joan drives from her rural home to the local campus of a regional college in northern Canada. There she meets two other teachers who work in local public schools and who are also enrolled in the Master of Education program offered by a university whose campus is two hundred miles away. For two hours they, along with five other similar groups at other sites, communicate with their professor and the other students by means of a videoconference. They see the professor, or whichever student in the class is talking at the moment, on their television monitor. The motion on their screens is rather jerky because they are using what is called compressed video, which is much cheaper to transmit than the full motion video they are used to seeing in regular television programs. However, these students think this means of communication is an improvement over the older technology they have used during previous courses in the program. That technology was called audioteleconferencing. It was somewhat similar to the videoconferencing they are now using except that there was no visual contact. When they were using the audioconferencing system, they were able only to hear the voices of their professor and the students at the other sites.

Example #3: Bill is also enrolled in a course, the subject matter of which is the latest developments in software engineering. He lives in a city where there is a technical institute, a community college, and a university, all of which are quite near the office where he works for a large corporation and all of which offer courses in the content area he is interested in. But he travels a lot, and his schedule is very irregular, so he just can't fit in the regularly scheduled classes at those institutions. The course he is enrolled in is, in fact, offered by a private, for-profit training institution whose offices are located on the other side of the continent. However, the physical location of the headquarters of the institution doesn't really matter, because all the interaction in his course takes place via computer conference and file transfers over the Internet. Bill is able to work on his course from his office whenever he has a few spare minutes and from his home on weekends and evenings. He can even participate during his frequent business trips by connecting his laptop to the Internet from his hotel room. Once he has made this connection, he is able to read the postings that other students have made in the computer conference related to his course, and add his own comments. It is this flexibility, allowing him to access his course at any time, from any place, that led to Bill choosing this course rather than those offered by local institutions. This particular course doesn't lead to any certificate or degree, but that is fine with Bill since he already has all the educational credentials he needs. And the fact that this course is quite expensive doesn't concern him much either, since his company is cheerfully paying his tuition so that he can remain on the cutting edge of his fast-changing field.

These three adults are all in different life situations, and are engaged in adult or higher education for very different reasons. They do have in common at least one thing — they are all taking part in some sort of distance education. But the nature of the distance education they are taking part in is quite different for each of them, as even the brief paragraphs above should have made clear. And this is just a small sample of the many varieties of distance education that are taking place today.

The following section will provide a conceptual framework as an aid to understanding these and other forms of distance education.

A Conceptual Framework for Distance Education

Several scholars have noted that distance education can usefully be described as having occurred, historically, in three successive waves or generations. The first generation, most commentators agree, began with the development of efficient postal service in a number of countries early in the nineteenth century. The second generation began with the development of reliable telephone networks during the first half of the twentieth century. The third generation began with the creation of networks of computers during the last half of the twentieth century. Despite this historical progression, however, all scholars agree that the beginning of the second generation of distance education has not meant the disappearance of the first, nor has the development of the third wave of distance education meant the disappearance of the second. All three generations of distance education, in fact, are flourishing throughout the world, and are frequently employed in combination with one another in the same course.

The first and conceptually clearest statement of the "three generations" metaphor was formulated in Garrison (1985) and elaborated upon in Garrison (1989). It was recently updated by Archer (in press) to take into account the technological developments of the past decade, and to make more explicit the relationship between the different generations of distance education and the different types of educational transaction typical of each generation.

Tiffin and Rajasingham (1995), a perceptive book about adult education, has an entire chapter titled "Education is communication". We quite agree; as we have made clear throughout this book, all education, particularly collaborative constructivist education, is based on communication. For educators involved in the sub-field of distance education a central preoccupation has always been the means of communication that are used to bridge the physical gap between student(s) and teacher. It is not surprising, therefore, that Garrison (1985, 1989) based his classification of generations of distance education on successive changes in the dominant means of communication employed. And since Garrison takes as axiomatic that a true educational transaction must involve two-way communication between participants in the educational transaction, the boundaries between his "generations" are marked by changes in the primary technology for providing such two-way communication.

According to Garrison (1985, 1989) these primary technologies have been correspondence via the postal system for Generation 1 (see our Example #1 at the beginning of this chapter), teleconferencing in its various forms for Generation 2 (see Example #2), and communication processed by computers for Generation 3 (see Example #3). Other media, used for one-way communication only, frequently play a secondary role in enhancing distance education built around one of the primary, two-way media. Garrison refers to these as "ancillary media" (1985, pp. 239–240). This results in a conceptual scheme as follows (from Garrison, 1989, p. 50):

Distance Education Technologies
(Two-Way Communication)

1. Correspondence (First Generation)
    Message: Print
    Delivery Mode: Mail

2. Teleconferencing (Second Generation)
    Message: Audio/Video
    Delivery Mode: Telecommunications

3. Microprocessor Based (Third Generation)
    Message: Audio/Video/Alphanumeric
    Delivery Mode: Microprocessor

Ancillary Media
(*One-Way Communication*)

1. Print Material
2. Audio/Video Cassettes
3. Audiographics*
    — facsimile
    — slow-scan television
    — compressed video
    — telewriting
    — videotex
4. Laser Videodisc
5. Broadcast
    — radio
    — television

The three generations metaphor first outlined by Garrison (1985, 1989) was well received by the field of distance education, as it emphasizes the most significant changes that have occurred in the teaching/learning transaction as conducted at a distance. These changes have resulted from the introduction of new means of two-way communication between learner(s) and teachers — e.g. the introduction of group-based learning concurrent with the development of teleconferencing (Generation 2). However, during the decade and a half since Garrison (1985) first introduced this metaphor the need for some updating has become apparent. First, the names that Garrison (1985) gave to the generations now seem too narrow, too closely tied to specific technologies rather than types of technologies that have significant communication characteristics in common. Second, some relatively minor changes to the overall framework can allow the incorporation into the central framework of what Garrison (1985, 1989) puts somewhat to the side as "ancillary media". Third, some recent improvements to the two-way communication technologies used for distance education have enabled them to carry message types corresponding to all of the "meaningful learning activities" described in Figure 7.1 and Chapter 7 generally. These changes need to be emphasized within the conceptual framework.

The following modified form of Garrison's framework incorporates the changes discussed above. A more comprehensive discussion of this updated framework occurs in Archer (in press).

---

* May support two-way communication

The Conceptual Framework Updated

The updated framework (from Archer, in press) is outlined below:

1. Slow Asynchronous (Generation 1)
   Learning mode: individualized instruction
   Delivery mechanism: postal system
   Message types (two-way communication):
   — originally written language and still images
   — spoken language added by mailing of audiocassettes
   — moving images added by mailing of videocassettes

2. Synchronous (Generation 2)
   Learning mode: individualized or group
   Delivery mechanism: telecommunications systems (wired and wireless)
   Message types (two-way communication):
   — originally spoken language only
   — still images added by audiographics
   — written language added by audiographics and computer chat
   — moving images added by videoconferencing (various modes, some involving
     use of computers (desktop systems) and some not)

3. Fast Asynchronous (Generation 3)
   Learning mode: individualized (email) or group (computer conferencing)
   Delivery mechanism: telecommunications systems combined with networked
   computers (usually) or fax machines
   Message types (two-way communication):
   — originally written language (first networked computers)
   — still images added by graphics files and facsimile
   — spoken language added as audio files
   — moving images added as video files

This modification of Garrison's (1985, 1989) conceptual framework alters the
names of the three generations so as to highlight the nature of the crucial two-way
communication that occurs in each generation. The major distinction that is
highlighted is that between asynchronous communication (Generations 1 and 3),
in which there is a significant delay between the time a message is sent and the time
it is received, and synchronous communication (Generation 2), where there is no
significant delay. As noted previously (especially Chapter 7) presence or absence
of this delay is of great significance in the teaching learning transaction, as the delay
between a listening or reading activity and a response through talking or writing is
essentially the time available for reflection (see Figure 7.1).

A secondary distinction is the velocity of the two-way communication. Slow
two-way communication via the postal system was (and is) the basis of Generation
1 distance education. This slowness does, indeed, allow much time for reflection.
However, a delay of weeks between each question or statement and response

would mean that the equivalent of the many exchanges that take place during several months of a face-to-face course would take not years but decades. Therefore, from the very beginning of correspondence education there have been attempts to build feedback to anticipated learner questions into the package of printed materials provided to the learner, thus eliminating the long delays involved in mailing a question to a distant instructor and receiving a response via the postal system. This need to "build the instructor into the materials" was a major impetus for the growth of the craft and science of instructional design, discussed at length in a following section. (It should be noted that in recent decades many courses that are basically Generation 1 distance education have incorporated an element of Generation 2 distance education in the form of telephone tutoring, or an element of Generation 3 distance education in the form of email. Either of these eliminates the long delay between question and response that occurs in a strictly correspondence-based course.)

Generation 1 distance education was, until very recently, unquestionably the best-known form of distance education. One of its salient characteristics, which has made it beloved by many politicians, is that it permits great economies of scale through industrialized methods of producing standardized course packages. This characteristic is very important when the ultimate goal is to provide the greatest accessibility at the least cost. This has been, and is, the quite understandable goal of politicians faced with meeting unlimited demand for education with very limited means.

A second salient characteristic of Generation 1 distance education is the individualization of learning that it almost inevitably entails. In theory, it would be possible to conduct group-based learning by correspondence, with each participant mailing a copy of their question or comment to every other participant in the group. In practice, the long delays in transmission would result in multiple "crossings" of messages, which would make it very difficult to conduct a coherent discussion. This factor, combined with the sheer physical difficulty and expense of producing and mailing multiple copies of each contribution to the group discussion, have meant that group learning via correspondence is virtually unheard of. Educators who agree with the present authors that a collaborative constructivist model is the preferred form of learning will conclude that the individualized nature of Generation 1 distance education is a serious disadvantage.

Generation 2 distance education makes use of light-speed two-way communication via telecommunications systems, thereby solving the problem of the overly long delays that are characteristic of Generation 1. This form of distance education also allows for group learning, as a number of participants at several different sites can be connected for voice conversations, sometimes augmented by video transmissions. Generation 2 distance education has many of the positive transactional characteristics of face-to-face education, in that it permits collaborative constructivist approaches to learning in which responsibility and control are shared. It also has many of the negative characteristics of face-to-face education, in that participants must participate according to the schedule set by the institution, in contrast to the self-pacing enjoyed by the participant in Generation 1 distance education. Another somewhat negative characteristic is that the rapid-fire exchanges in synchronous, Generation 2 distance education, as in face-to-face education, may not allow sufficient time for the internal reflection necessary for the achievement of critical thinking.

Generation 3 distance education combines many of the strengths of Generations 1 and 2, making this form of distance education the first that is actually attractive enough to present a serious challenge to the previously unquestioned dominance of face-to-face education. In this type of distance education, participants type in their contributions to the discussion via a computer keyboard. These comments and questions are stored on a central computer, where they are accessible to everyone enrolled in the course. Participants are in control of when they will participate, as in Generation 1 distance education. However, the fact that communication takes place at light speed over telephone lines, rather than via the leisurely postal system, makes group learning possible. Messages are grouped under different "threads" or topics by software specially designed to support computer conferencing. While Generation 3 distance education was originally confined to text-based communication, recent developments in software now permit the inclusion of audio or video files in participants' contributions to asynchronous computer conferences. This is beginning to permit, in Generation 3 distance education, the same degree of "social presence" that is achieved through the synchronous voice and video communications in Generation 2. This most recent generation of distance education is now beginning to permit something approaching the broad-channel communication that is characteristic of a small face-to-face seminar. It is because of this combination of advantages that Generation 3 distance education is enjoying spectacular growth wherever the required infrastructure is in place — still largely restricted to the more developed countries. In these countries, face-to-face instruction at most post-secondary institutions is beginning to take on some features of Generation 3 distance education (web pages, computer conferences), suggesting an impending merger of these modes of education into what is now often referred to as "distributed learning" or "distributed education".

Despite the differences between the three generations of distance education, discussed above, they have in common that they entail a larger element of conscious instructional design than face-to-face education usually does, simply by force of the circumstance that the learners are distant from the instructor and communication between them is always more or less problematic. This is most obvious in Generation 1 distance education, in which the slowness of two-way communication via the postal system presents considerable difficulties. The communication problem in the distance education context, particularly in Generation 1, is one of the primary reasons for the emergence of the field of instructional design, discussed in the following section. Distance education, most obviously in Generations 2 and 3, is also heavily dependent on technologies of one kind or another. Instructional design has been closely associated with educational technologies throughout the twentieth century. This intertwined triad of distance education, educational technology, and instructional design is the subject of our next section.

The Role of Instructional Design in Education

Considerable planning precedes a successful educational learning experience. Traditionally, this process of planning has been largely the responsibility of teachers, at least within the macro-level parameters established by curricula set by government agencies. With the emergence of the first generation of distance education, however, this traditional locus of responsibility for the micro-level design of instruction began to be challenged. This, in turn, called into question traditional assumptions about the nature of the educational transaction.

Fundamental assumptions are made during the design process that determine the nature of the educational experience. Duffy and Jonassen (1991) state that "our theory of learning is implicit in our design" (p. 7). Conversely, design practices will shape approaches to teaching and learning. Therefore, instructional design may be the most important generic issue affecting the quality of the learning experience and its outcome. For this reason, it is imperative that we understand developments and issues surrounding instructional design. Some historical background will be useful at this point.

Background. As noted above, the field of instructional design has a long standing connection with distance education. In the early stages of the development of distance education, during the nineteenth century, the design of distance education materials was something of a craft, with practitioners learning from their own experience and from looking at materials developed by others that seemed to work well. However, a movement toward a more scientific approach to instructional design was perhaps inevitable with the technological and scientific advances we have experienced during the twentieth century. Given the enormous prestige of science, particularly behavioural psychology, during at least the first half of the twentieth century there were predictable pressures on educators to increase their credibility by adopting scientific methods. This led to a search for empirically based principles that could be generalized to all situations and ensure effective and efficient instruction. As a result of this search, what were formerly described as the goals of education evolved into "behavioural objectives", consistent with behavioural psychology. As a practical culmination of this evolution, programmed instruction was born in the 1950s. The ideal was a prescriptive and self-contained package of materials that attempted to standardize the learning process. In addition, the student was to become as independent of the teacher as possible. A logical niche for such teacher-independent materials, of course, was in Generation 1 distance education, where communication between teacher and students was slow, so materials that demanded little student-teacher interaction had obvious advantages.

The science of educational and instructional technology came to maturity in the 1960s and 1970s with instructional systems design (ISD). The development of this systematic, scientific approach to the design of the instructional process was linked to the surge in the prestige of and demand for distance education after the founding of the British Open University in 1969 (Jevons, 1987). The trend to instructional systems design was further advanced by early experiments in the 1960s and 1970s with computer-assisted instruction — essentially a transferral of programmed learning to the computer. This accelerated in the 1980s, as the advent of the microcomputer made computer technologies much more accessible (Shrock, 1991).

These developments created a role for the professional educational designer who employs scientific, objective approaches. This trend toward design specialists removes most of the design decisions from the teacher and the learning context. Professional educational designers use their technical knowledge to create instructional packages to be implemented by the teacher, usually without much thought as to the developing needs of the students and the variability of context. This prescriptive approach to design exerts considerable non-contingent control over the teaching and learning situation. Nunan (1983) argues that the designer's "intent is to exert control over the activities and participants in the classroom, and they justify this by appealing to theories and techniques which are 'superior' to those possessed by teachers" (p. 4).

Winn (1993) states that it "is generally understood that ID [instructional design] is a process by means of which the best instructional methods are selected to teach given outcomes under set conditions" (p. 16). Furthermore, the instructional designer uses prescriptive instructional theory to systematically and rigorously select instructional strategies. Such approaches are presumed to be valid and reliable. That is, they can be used without "further tinkering" in similar situations (Winn, 1993). The key concepts are that outcomes can be clearly and unambiguously defined, conditions are constant, and instructional theory and strategies are available to prescriptively design the teaching-learning process.

While professional ISD continues to flourish, concern and uneasiness with the field appears to be growing. Schiffman (1991) states that ambiguity shrouds the field and there is an undertone of criticism. The concern is the apparent excessive focusing of ISD on hardware, rigid and linear methods, and training; and, fundamentally, its behaviourist foundation. At the same time, Schiffman (1991) believes that these criticisms are unfair and unbalanced. To redress the balance he provides a moderate and reasonable perspective on the field. However, it still seems that ISD is most appropriately applied in training contexts. Moreover, this specialized field may offer little that can be transferred to an educational context involving the complex and ill-defined subject areas that are typical in adult and higher education.

Ill-defined content, by definition, introduces uncertainty in the educational process. Unfortunately, some have confused the need for educational planning with scientific predictability and standardization. The result is prescriptive linear design methods that do not serve educational contexts well. Under such circumstances, teachers and students have little opportunity to make decisions, and students are given little encouragement to assume responsibility for their learning. The alternative is to recognize the need for design and planning but understand that it cannot be divorced from the learning process. As Tripp (1991) states, design "is a dialogue with phenomena. It can be seen as a kind of social process of negotiation" (p. 2).

Designs or plans are seldom "specifications of fixed sequences of actions, but are strategies that determine each successive action as a function of current information about the situation" (Vera & Simon, 1993, p. 17).

Winn (1989) makes a crucial distinction with regard to the role of technology in education. He suggests that an often unstated implication of the role of technology in education is that it is to make instruction permanent. That is, it "should not be altered appreciably by the teachers who deliver it" (Winn, 1989, p. 37). This push for "teacher-proof materials" has resulted in a separation of design (often for preparation of materials for use with educational technologies) and implementation — i.e. use of materials in instruction. The problem is that the professional decision-making responsibility of the teacher has been seriously denigrated. Winn (1989) states that "Instruction designed for replicability has tended to be so cast in stone that it has not been able to adapt well to student needs and characteristics that become apparent only after students begin to interact with it" (p. 38). He goes on to say that one of the main reasons for the focus on replicability and not flexibility is that "design remains an activity driven largely by the assumptions of behavioral psychology" (p. 38).

When it comes to developing complex cognitive abilities in an educational context, technical design methods and prescriptions will seldom lead to such outcomes. The reason is that education is a complex and dynamic process that operates in ever-changing milieu of competencies and contingencies. In other words, education can only result from complex interactions that are not prescribed and controlled externally. The bottom line is that students' reactions to teaching cannot be predicted. Therefore, a new basis for designing and implementing teaching is demanded which integrates design and implementation in a flexible manner. As Winn (1989) argues, reintegrating instructional design with implementation represents "a total departure from the commonly acknowledged procedures of instructional design" (p. 41). Technical and behavioural orientations to design are inadequate for this purpose. Alternatively, cognitive–constructivist perspectives are beginning to influence instructional theory and design.

Emerging Paradigm

As noted above, instructional design continues to be heavily influenced by a behaviourist and technical view of education. In this paradigm, education is perceived as a process of transferring objective information, in whole, to the learner. Furthermore, effective instruction is simply dependent upon mastering and applying design procedures (Winn, 1990). These approaches to design may be justifiable in training contexts, but are difficult to justify in educational contexts.

Behavioural assumptions argue for prescriptive approaches to design and learning. Prescriptive instructional design strategies not only take the control and responsibility for learning from the student but also substantially remove the control and responsibility for teaching from the teacher. Design and implementation are separated and essentially determined by technologists who will not necessarily have much understanding of the contextual complexities. Notwithstanding the reluctance of instructional designers to abandon their traditional assumptions, there is growing pressure to reconsider how students approach learning and the nature of learning outcomes.

A collaborative constructivist approach to learning is a significant shift away from ISD and represents a distinctively different approach to design and implementation. As we have seen in previous chapters, a collaborative constructivist approach to learning is about individuals constructing meaning through a process of interpreting their experiences in a collaborative environment. It is a rejection of dualism in that it recognizes the existence of a social world while focusing on constructing personal meaning. It recognizes the external world but emphasizes that there is no single objective reality. Each individual is responsible for making sense of their experiences. These constructions will vary across individuals to the degree those individual experiences and interpretations are cumulatively different. That is not to say that each individual's reality is unique and cannot be shared (i.e. solipsistic). Collaborative constructivism is concerned with how individuals construct meaning and how the essence of this understanding can be validated and shared collectively.

Contextual complexity must be recognized and integrated into the educational transaction. That is, existing student, teacher, institutional and community knowledge, values, and beliefs must first be recognized and addressed. To accommodate some of the constructivist assumptions, Jonassen (1991) suggests several changes to instructional design. First, instructional "goals and objectives would be negotiated, not imposed" (p. 11). To engage students in negotiating meaning and validating knowledge necessitates that they have some control with regard to goals and objectives. Secondly, "Task and content analysis would focus less on identifying and prescribing a single, best sequence for learning" (p. 12). Instead, it would focus on discussion and cognitive strategies necessary for individual students to construct knowledge. Third, instructional treatments and learning activities would be prescribed to a lesser degree. Collaborative and contingent control of learning tasks and activities would facilitate student responsibility to construct meaning (i.e. internal control of mental processing). Fourth, evaluation "would become less of a reinforcement or control tool and more of a self-analysis tool" (p. 12).

It is not possible nor is it right to attempt to control everything that students learn in adult and higher education. That is not to say that collaborative constructivism is the answer to all instructional design problems. Certainly there will be situations where it may be appropriate to consider ISD; however, designers should also consider collaborative constructivist perspectives if meaningful learning and shared understanding is the goal. Teachers and designers may provide the educational parameters, "but in order to maximise individual learning, we may have to yield some control and instead prepare learners to regulate their own learning by providing supportive rather than intervening learning environments" (Jonassen, 1991, p. 13).

The key to a collaborative constructivist approach to education is to allow students to make decisions about their learning. This necessitates control over design during the implementation of instruction; otherwise, education becomes prescriptive and deterministic. The limits of the educational context must not be restricted to the degree that it artificially objectifies knowledge. Teachers and students must actively interpret, analyse and validate knowledge — preferably in a collaborative context.

Designing Situated Learning

Situated learning is consistent with a collaborative constructivist philosophy of learning. Situated learning is rooted in Dewey's (1916) philosophy that sees educationally worthwhile knowledge as that resulting from a "continuous reconstruction of experience" (p. 80). The quality of this educative experience is based upon cognitive (continuity) and collaborative (interaction) principles. The situated learning approach to education has also been influenced by Whitehead's (1929) concept of inert and robust knowledge. Inert knowledge can be recalled but not applied in a practical problem context. This is essentially the distinction made in previous chapters between reproductive and meaningful knowledge.

Situated learning is an approach that integrates the learning process with useful learning outcomes. Brown, Collins and Duguid (1989) challenge the separation of what is learned and how it is learned and used. Such approaches result in the learning of only abstract and decontextualized concepts, since they supply little opportunity to test and validate knowledge. How knowledge is constructed and applied will determine its meaningfulness and usefulness. Therefore, Brown, Collins and Duguid (1989) argue that situations "co-produce knowledge through activity. Learning and cognition ... are fundamentally situated" (p. 32).

When students are experiencing or applying knowledge in situated learning, the activities must be authentic. Brown, Collins and Duguid (1989) state that authentic activities are purposeful, coherent and meaningful and are "most simply defined as the ordinary practices of culture" (p. 34). Students must be able to understand the relevance and purpose of the learning activity, but it must also have the attributes of problems found in the social context beyond the classroom. That is, problems should reflect the complexity and ill-defined attributes of problems encountered in "real life", as well as the metacognitive and collaborative strategies used by competent adults to address such problems. Authenticity is vital to situated learning, but presents serious challenges to the design of educational activities.

The design of instruction in socially situated learning contexts presents paradoxical difficulties. The apparent paradox, according to Winn (1993), is that traditional instructional design "assumes that what people learn is relatively stable across the situations in which it is used" (p. 16) while proponents of situated learning argue that, since learning is contextually dependent, it is impossible to design instruction for all situations. The way out of this dilemma is simple, yet challenging. As Winn (1993) suggests, design and implementation need to be reunited and the teacher needs to become an integral part of the instructional system. The resulting designs "should be capable of a high degree of self-modification so that the design decisions made before implementation can be changed during instruction" (Winn, 1993, p. 18).

Streibel (1991) also recognizes a problematic relationship between instructional design and instructional practice. He states emphatically that what "*this* learner at *this* point in time and in *this* situation will make out of the learning situation cannot be predicted or even assumed to be understood by an instructional designer who is not part of the actual situation" (pp. 123–124). Streibel (1991) believes that instructional designs should not be used to control interactions but, instead, be used "as resources for future situated actions" (p. 125). That is, they should "only be used to orient future teachers or learners for situated learning and not prescribe how to teach or how to learn" (p. 125). This can best be accomplished through guiding principles that are adaptable to a variety of educational contexts. Designs should facilitate communication in, and reflection on, learning situations.

Young (1993) provides four critical tasks when designing situated learning. As one might expect, the first task is the selection of "situations that will afford the acquisition of knowledge that the teacher wishes each student to acquire" (Young, 1993, p. 46). While little research exists to guide this selection, some general principles can be suggested. They are to select relevant subject matter and authentic learning activities. Then have students recognize essential or key concepts in these complex, realistic problem spaces while progressing toward finer distinctions and variations. Instructional designs should start with fundamental concepts and the amount of detail should be kept to a minimum. In this way students have the time to integrate new concepts and, eventually, build complex knowledge structures based upon reflection and experience.

The second task is to construct the temporary scaffolding that will provide the support for students until they can assume greater responsibility for their learning. Young (1993) states that the "issues for instructional design, then, are what scaffolding to provide for each situated learning context and how quickly it can be removed as students move from novice to expert performance" (p. 47). This scaffolding can be provided by an advanced organizer which reveals links between concepts and with the learner's existing cognitive structure (Kember, 1991).

The third design task is to provide instructional support in developing methods and techniques for the teacher to interact knowledgeably and collaboratively with students. Teachers must diagnose conceptions and challenge misconceptions. This generally necessitates a degree of subject expertise and time. However, it must also be noted that other students may assume the teaching role and be facilitated by the learning environment. A common approach is to design extensive discussion opportunities. Collaboration to share control and responsibility is essential if the teacher is to assess individual perceptions or collaborative action. Since the task is enormous, teachers must encourage collaboration among cooperative groups of students (i.e. reciprocal learning).

The final design task concerns the role and nature of assessing situated learning. Young (1993) advises that as "the nature of instruction changes to be more collaborative, situated, and distributed in its sources of information, traditional means of assessment will quickly prove inadequate" (p. 48). Assessment is seen as integral to the teaching-learning transaction and concerned with developing cognitive strategies and depth of understanding. As we noted in Chapter 9, appropriate assessment is an essential component of successful situated learning.

Design and Judgement

From the perspective of teacher responsibility and effectiveness, situated actions represent a shift from theoretical, decontextualized knowledge to meaningful and relevant knowledge. The reality of designing instruction is that when "an instructor or learner gets down to the details of teaching or learning, the respective theories of instruction or learning are abandoned and the instructor or learner falls back onto his or her embodied skills in the situation" (Streibel, 1991, p. 126). Therefore, instructional designs should act only as resources for future context specific teaching and learning.

Nunan (1983) sees design as personal, local and adaptive as well as being integral to the teacher's role. From the perspective of curriculum content and Habermas' cognitive interests, Grundy (1987) states that:

> ... the criteria by which the quality of learning is to be judged are those relating to the degree of autonomy and equality experienced by members of the learning group. At no time, if the emancipatory interest is informing the action, are those judgements legitimately made by outsiders. It is the members of the learning community themselves who are to judge the validity and authenticity of their learning. (p. 139)

While this may represent the ideal, the point is made again that prescriptive instructional design conducted apart from the educational context has serious limitations with regard to meaningful knowledge construction in adult and higher education. It is argued that a competent and responsible teacher must make instructional decisions in context. But the question is, how does a teacher develop the situated knowledge necessary for competent action?

The removal of essential design decisions from the teacher removes the responsibility of judgement, and thereby of coping with the inherent unpredictability of students' learning processes. Archambault (1964) summarizes Dewey's thoughts on unpredictability in the curriculum as follows:

> The exact aims of instruction cannot be legislated, for they depend on a cluster of variables that are unique to a particular place and time. For a given situation, short-range aims must be relatively specific. Yet any school situation, since it is experimental in nature, has a quality of unpredictability. To try to specify, in exact detail,

> the precise knowledge that a student is to achieve, is to consider
> ends as remote, distinct, and separate from practical contingencies
> and the dynamic purposes of pupils. (p. xxiii)

The assumption of predictability is particularly troublesome in the sub-field of continuing professional development, if one views problems of professional practice as being ill-defined and not easily resolved by theoretical or technical knowledge (Schon, 1987). Professional practice is often characterized by its uniqueness, uncertainty, and conflicting normative value positions. Schon (1987) argues that most professional knowledge is contextually situated and, therefore, results from experience. He posits two forms of knowing: knowing-in-action (tacit knowledge), and reflection-in-action (rethinking tacit knowledge). The first is the direct result of experience, while the second is necessitated by a not readily solvable problem that precipitates a process of reflection. In any case, considerable professional knowledge and judgement is required.

In arguing for knowledge-in-action, Schon (1987) appears to reject theoretical knowledge as driving professional practice. However, theoretical knowledge should not be rejected outright. The position here is that theoretical knowledge can inform practice either directly or indirectly. As Fenstermacher (1987) states, "it is not a matter of having either the knowledge that Technical Rationality produces or the knowledge that Reflective Practice produces, but more a case of having both forms of knowledge, each informing the other" (p. 418). While we must certainly be aware of the indeterminate nature of professional educational practice, this does not mean that we can rely on tacit knowledge alone. It should be remembered from the second chapter that Dewey emphasized experience and reflective thought, in many ways not so different from Schon's formulation. However, Dewey would have rejected the dualism that Schon seems to imply in his description of professional practice. For Dewey (1938), there is a continuing dialectic between normative values and individual circumstances, while recognizing that the activity itself is the "chief carrier of control" (p. 56).

Design problems are often resolved in context by iteratively reflecting upon educational theory and practical knowledge as situations arise within the uncertain and complex teaching and learning transaction. Therefore, there are limitations in pre-planning an activity before it is in progress. As professional educators, we must have the opportunity and responsibility to reflect upon and shape design issues within the context of our teaching. The first step in making a design decision in context is to appreciate the nature of the problem. Given the collaborative nature of an educational transaction, control must be shared, which necessitates sustained communication.

Educational Technology and Communication

Technological infrastructure should follow from design considerations that reflect the appropriate balance between independent and collaborative approaches. Once design approaches are established, pragmatic (cost, availability) and educational factors will guide the selection of the communications technology.

Within a collaborative-constructivist paradigm, the essence of education is communication. Through communication instructional design and implementation are unified. In contrast, prescriptive instructional design removes control and responsibility from the teacher and students. It does this by reducing the scope and incentive for authentic two-way communication. On the other hand, integrated design and implementation encourages two-way communication as well as facilitating contextually based and collaborative decision making. One-way communication centralizes control while two-way communication distributes control. Educational technology can amplify either of these effects, depending on the type of communication it facilitates. Therefore, our understanding of educational technology must be consistent with our understanding of educational design.

Educators must understand what technology and media can and cannot bring to the educational enterprise. Clark (1983) argues that "media are delivery vehicles for instruction and do not directly influence learning" (p. 453). It is the underlying beliefs (ideals) regarding the aims of education that are the real determinants of the use of educational technologies (Blacker, 1993). Blacker (1993) suggests that educational value is determined not by technological devices per se, "but the basic assumptions motivating and enframing the instructional situation" (p. 193). Therefore, educators must be in control of how technology and media are integrated into the methodological design.

That is, technology must be understood from an educational perspective. Since education is essentially communication, then technology should be understood and judged in terms of how it facilitates and enhances the communication process. It cannot be judged just in terms of the access to information that it can provide but, instead, in terms of the opportunity it provides to share and negotiate meaning. This is the crucial criterion in classifying technology and media. Choice of educational media is closely linked to the choice between prescriptive, independent learning and collaborative, interdependent learning.

At this point, we need to clarify exactly what we mean by technology and media. Originally, "technology" referred to technical knowledge and systematic processes associated with practical matters. Recently, this word has been associated more with hardware and less with knowledge and process. The process or software component of technology should not be confused with the content or courseware of an educational activity. In other words, technology represents the tools (hardware) and techniques (software) that are employed for purposes of communication. One further distinction concerns the concept of media. Media, here taken to be a subset of hardware, are devices used to record and present information (one-way communication). Examples would be a book or a CD-ROM.

From an educational perspective, there is a need to provide some conceptual order to communications technologies. This can best be done by categorizing them according to their ability to record/present information, transmit information, or process information.

One group of communications technologies are media that simply record or present information — that is, there is no opportunity for corrective or informational feedback regarding the message. There is no opportunity for clarification or negotiation. Therefore, there is very little control on the part of the receiver, except for the choice between accepting the message as is or ignoring it. Typical examples of this sort of technology are print, audio and video tape or disk, broadcast radio and television, and databases. This group of one-way technologies are largely characterized as "ancillary media" in Garrison's (1985, 1989) conceptual model of distance education, as they generally cannot be used to carry the crucial two-way communication necessary for education to occur.

Among this type of non-interactive media, of special concern to educators is the seductive nature of broadcast television. Unfortunately, there is considerable confusion, even among some educators, between entertainment value and educational value. While television records processes exquisitely, it does not facilitate process. The result is that when television is used as an instructional medium, it is very difficult to get students to focus and take an active involvement in their learning. Moreover, broadcast television is very expensive; production and transmission costs for educational television are often unsustainable unless this medium can be used for very large classes. This sort of massification of education, of course, reinforces less than desirable teaching practices such as lecturing.

Another non-interactive medium that has managed to seduce some educators (and others) is the database, online or otherwise. Databases accessed through computer technology can provide an overwhelming amount of information. However, we must not confuse access to information with the construction of personal meaning and knowledge. As Suber (1991) states, "The ultimate question in education ... has never been access to information; it has always been wisdom or the capacity to judge information and build knowledge and action from it" (p. 70). When a large volume of information relevant to a particular field of study is available it is very difficult for students unfamiliar with that field of study to identify the key concepts and issues in the field without guidance and direction.

Databases do not provide that guidance. For this reason, the greatest potential for databases may be their permitting teachers to access current information when designing their courses. However, this will necessitate teachers' considering a wider range of material while designing learning activities around fewer essential concepts. Suber (1991) argues that "Enhanced access to information ... should cause teachers to reflect deeply on what they are trying to accomplish in the classroom" (p. 74). Enhanced access to information via databases may ultimately be a benefit to education, but the process of designing courses and teaching will not be easier.

Another category of communications technologies are those that have the capability to transmit information in a collaborative mode — i.e. they permit two-way communication. Examples of such technologies are audio and video based teleconferencing through various means of transmission (e.g. fibre optics, satellite). These technologies have the potential for "real-time" sustained communication both aurally and, in some cases, visually. The most significant application of these technologies has not been in the traditional classroom, but rather in the field of distance education, where their advent in the mid part of the twentieth century was of such significance that it signalled the birth of a second generation of distance education, as discussed in a previous section.

The final category of communications technologies are those that are capable of processing information. The effect on education of this type of technology is only just being realized. The computer, particularly in combination with telecommunication networks (e.g. the Internet) presents enormous possibilities for applications such as computer mediated communication (CMC). Locally operated (stand-alone) computer applications have the potential for providing individualized support and, in some applications, individual control over the learning process. However, it is computer mediated communication (CMC) via the Internet that has the potential to precipitate a significant transformation of adult and higher education. As noted previously, the advent of CMC signalled the birth of a third generation of distance education, a form of learning that is proving so attractive for many categories of students that it has the potential to precipitate a significant transformation of adult and higher education generally.

However, as Clark and Salomon (1986) have noted, one of the important lessons of research is that "no medium enhances learning more than any other medium regardless of learning task, learner traits, symbolic elements, curriculum, or setting" (p. 474). Therefore, it is important to consider the expense and convenience of the medium. Technologies or media merely set the stage; it is the nature of the educational activities or what students do that will have the significant influence on the quality of the learning. What the student does is, of course, the essence of instructional design. The focus must be on design and implementation of educational experiences. The crucial concern is how we as educators use technologies. For example, video images may be presented in a continuous and overwhelming flow of information or they can be presented on an interactive video disk, where the student can choose to watch just that material relevant to their particular purpose and ignore the rest. Another example is the use of computer assisted learning, which may be either prescriptive or self-directed.

Assuming the reasonableness of the previous discussion, it would seem that the key issues in selecting educational technologies are the educational goal, other interactive opportunities of the context, and the cost and convenience of available technologies. Once the educational goal or desired outcomes have been assessed, then the full contextual communication capabilities must be considered and appropriate technologies considered. Technology that simply provides more information, without appropriate processing and feedback opportunities, will not likely have a positive influence on the quality of the educational transaction. The cost and convenience of the technology must be considered along with its communication capabilities. Often, less expensive technologies prove as effective as more expensive technologies.

Conclusion

The evolution toward constructivist thinking in distance education, particularly Generations 2 and 3, has caused distance educators to re-examine instructional design (Shale & Garrison, 1994). This has been either precipitated or reinforced by cost-effective and ubiquitous advances in communications technologies, such as the spread of efficient postal service in the nineteenth century (Generation 1 distance education), the spread of efficient telephone networks in the first half of the twentieth century (Generation 2), and the development of the Internet in the last decades of the twentieth century (Generation 3). Therefore, it is essential that all educators, including distance educators, have clear educational principles and strategies that will shape approaches to design and guide the difficult judgements and decisions that are required in practice.

The complexity of the teaching-learning transaction does not lend itself well to technical and prescriptive approaches. Education will and should remain as much an art as it is a science. This balance must be carefully maintained. If technology means predictability and standardization, then a dangerous false sense of certainty is introduced into the educational process. Education is more than the uncritical assimilation of fragmented bits of information or inert knowledge. Education is as much the exploration and critical challenge of accepted orthodoxy as it is assimilating society's values and knowledge.

While communication technologies can significantly influence issues of responsibility and control, educators must be vigilant not to allow technology to dominate educational design and delivery. This is particularly true of powerful technologies such as the Internet. We should not confuse information access with educational communication and knowledge development. The Internet must be seen as more than a means of accessing information. However, education is about sustained communication and constructing knowledge. Ideally, the educational transaction involves sustained critical discourse; minimally, it involves reflective critical analysis and internal discourse.

The final chapter provides a brief systemic institutional perspective associated with the shift to responsible and meaningful approaches to learning.

11

A Systemic Perspective

The goal of the previous chapters was to provide a coherent perspective on the educational transaction. Emphasis was placed on the dynamic and reciprocal nature of a meaningful and worthwhile learning experience. This transactional perspective explored the interrelationship among the intentions of the participants, the actual learning activities, and the outcomes of an educational learning experience. It also recognized the uncertainties of knowing and the necessity of integrating personal needs and social standards. It focused on the complementary relationship between critical reflection and discourse when the purpose is to develop in individuals the capacity to be continuous learners.

A transactional view of teaching and learning is a systemic view of the educational process. It is a holistic frame of reference that attempts to provide a coherent understanding of the dynamic complexity of the interrelationships that influence behaviour in an educational context. Systems thinking is particularly useful in coping with complexity, and understanding transactional relationships from multiple perspectives. A systems perspective provides order, without which an educational transaction becomes difficult to fully appreciate, much less manage.

A systemic view of the teaching-learning transaction recognizes that teaching affects students' learning and that students' learning also affects teaching. Moreover, teachers and students need to be aware that each person influences, and is influenced by, their context. Senge (1990) explains that systems thinking "suggests that *everyone shares responsibility for problems generated by a system*" (Senge, 1990, p. 78). At the same time, he emphasizes that this does not mean that everyone exerts equal influence in shaping the system. To assume responsibility is to have the potential to exert influence.

Limits to Meaningful Learning

Change within a system, even when this change is in a positive direction, will inevitably be resisted by conservative forces and established power bases. It has been argued that change within higher and adult education to a deep and meaningful approach to teaching and learning is a worthwhile and even necessary innovation. Such an approach is a growing action that will inevitably be influenced by slowing actions. The forces that tend to impose limits to meaningful learning must be understood if growth is to occur.

According to Senge (1990), systems are influenced by growth (reinforcement) and stability seeking (balancing) feedback. Systems have implicit and explicit goals.

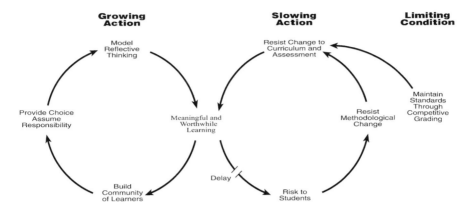

Figure 11.1: Limits to meaningful and worthwhile learning.

Stabilizing feedback attempts to maintain these goals and the status quo. Stabilizing processes are crucial in understanding change in systems. For example, if we wish to change the organization of the classroom, we must identify the stabilizing processes. Often these processes are embedded in the distribution of authority and control. Therefore, power relationships must be influenced in order for change to occur (Senge, 1990). Within the educational institution, the most influential power relationships limiting meaningful learning are embedded in the teaching-learning transaction.

Inevitably, innovations such as those described in this book will come up against the stabilizing forces of the existing educational system. Each teacher wishing to implement change will be faced with limits to growth. These stabilizing forces will be within the teachers themselves, students, colleagues and school administrators. It is, therefore, necessary to understand the stabilizing forces and identify points of influence or leverage. To clarify the structure of the teaching-learning transaction, a systems diagram has been created using Senge's (1990) limits to growth archetype (see Figure 11.1). The limits to growth are deemed appropriate because teachers typically reach limits to their growth and plateau. In higher education, the reason that growth eventually slows is due to a variety of competing responsibilities, pressures and structural contingencies. In adult education, with its focus on less formal learning experiences, growth is generally not as constrained.

The diagram consists of two loops corresponding to the growing and slowing processes in the typical classroom. The key themes and issues of this book are represented. In the centre we have the desired condition or goal of meaningful and worthwhile learning. Starting with the circle of growth, the key processes may include building a critical community of learners, providing choice, and encouraging students to assume responsibility for their learning. However, growth actions will inevitably be delayed due to stabilizing processes. Initially, students will perceive a risk of receiving lower grades. After all, students will likely have been successful in getting to where they are by approaching learning in a surface manner (i.e. assimilation and recall). Teachers will also resist change to the methods that they have grown comfortable with. Finally, those in authority will resist change to the curriculum (workload) and assessment procedures necessary for a meaningful approach to learning. Pressure will be exerted to "cover the curriculum" and provide a normal distribution of grades at the end of the term.

This brings us to the limiting condition that is typically an implicit goal or norm. In this scenario, the norm is that grading must be competitive in order to differentiate students and maintain standards. Therefore, since teachers are often unclear as to appropriate goals, it is natural that excessive amounts of content are presented in order to increase variability in student outcomes. The implicit assumption is that the quality of student learning is associated with workload and competition. This assumption is the fundamental limiting condition that must be addressed before long-term change can occur. The risk is that attention will be directed only to the symptoms. For example, approaches to teaching may change but assessment methods do not. This simply creates an incongruence that results in frustration for students and teachers. Naturally, students will resist such a change and try to revert back to a learning approach that will increase their chances for a good grade.

It is important to appreciate that there will always be new limits to growth — this is a never-ending process. Furthermore, addressing the fundamental conditions is a long-term approach that will require time for all involved in the educational process to develop a shared vision. Risk and effort are required to identify and define problems before widespread change can occur. Senge (1990) states that the "bottom line of systems thinking is leverage — seeing where actions and changes in structures can lead to significant, enduring improvements" (p. 114). We must see through the complexity to the underlying structures and find those points of influence if fundamental change is to occur in adult and higher education.

Fundamental change must consider the larger system. Notwithstanding that much can be accomplished within the classroom, education is a societal, and, therefore, a norm governed enterprise. It is these norms and organizational structures that fundamentally shape the educational process. Approaches to teaching and learning are not always freely arrived at. Although it is not the purpose here to critically assess the sociology of higher education institutions, organizational structures will influence the educational process. Organizational contingencies are most clearly evident in the size and scheduling of classes. There are also indirect cultural and political contingencies. That is not to say that organizational structures and norms are invariably dysfunctional. These structures do, however, represent real contingencies that must be addressed and leveraged to effect change.

Financial considerations may have a dominant influence upon how education is organized. That is, large classes may be a reality but this does not necessarily mean that teachers must abandon responsible and meaningful approaches to teaching and learning. It is possible for teachers to engage students meaningfully in large classes. It is assumed that even in highly bureaucratic educational organizations, there is considerable scope and opportunity for teachers to effect change in the classroom. Teachers in higher education do possess considerable autonomy and control within the classroom. Teachers must become aware of the possibilities and approaches that are available to them.

Teacher Development

Teaching in higher education is often undervalued. This is largely due to the imbalance that exists between teaching and research. For purposes of merit and promotion, research is normally valued more highly than teaching in universities. With regard to teaching development, Smith (1991) states that while most universities offer development support, as "a rule, the centres are small, with a permanent staff of one, and have very limited financial resources" (p. 58). These findings are consistent with an earlier study by Centra (1977) which suggests that not much has changed in the last twenty years. Two recommendations of the Smith (1991) report, among several, were that teaching proficiency should be demonstrated before faculty are hired, and funding for instructional development offices should be increased substantially to support pedagogical innovations.

However, changing teacher practices and the development of effective teachers will depend upon changing conceptions — not simply providing atheoretical technical advice regarding the latest technique. Sherman et al. (1987) suggest that experience is an important component of teaching excellence. At the same time, it is obvious that experience alone is not sufficient for excellence. For this reason, Sherman et al. (1987) focus on a developmental conception for understanding processes to improve teaching practice. The developmental conception reflects stages of increasing complexity with regard to teachers as educational decision-makers. They believe teachers must be in a collaborative environment that allows them to focus and reflect upon variables associated with excellence. In this way teachers can begin to develop a complex schema for teaching. Furthermore, metacognitive awareness and monitoring as well as remedial action are required for sophisticated thinking and the development of a complex schema associated with excellence in teaching.

There must be a connection between experience and teacher conceptions. Larsson (1987) suggests that teaching skills without an explanation of meaning leads to mystification. As a result, Larsson (1987) studied teachers' conceptions of their developmental skill in an adult education setting. The conceptions of teaching that emerged were based upon experience. Conceptions include a shift from teacher acts to student activities or thinking, establishing a repertoire of teaching practices, and a focus on essential concepts as opposed to transmitting a large quantity of facts.

Entwistle and Ramsden (1983) also argue for a "shift away from the concern with teaching techniques towards helping lecturers to understand the effects of their teaching on students' attitudes and approaches" (p. 211). Developing effective teaching will depend upon teachers' developing a clear insight into the effects of their beliefs and activities on student learning. And only in this context can the selection of methods and techniques be made with awareness.

Programs intended to foster teaching development must focus upon conceptions of teaching and learning as well as specific learning activities. It is not sufficient to provide technical skills without an appropriate framework to help interpret situations and guide decisions. Techniques are easily acquired; the challenge is understanding when to use them and in which contexts they are appropriate. The developmental perspective would also seem to suggest that effective teaching is a continuous change process and that a sharing, open climate is necessary in order to sustain it. Training may be important when starting a teaching career in adult or higher education but development must continue as a result of reflection upon experience. For this to happen the environment must be such that excellent teaching is demonstrably valued. Furthermore, institutional resources must provide opportunities for teachers to discuss and reflect upon what makes excellent teaching in particular contexts. Conceptions, however, must be sufficiently comprehensive and sophisticated as to allow teachers to make judgements about appropriate transactions that are consistent with desired and worthwhile outcomes.

The task of improving teaching in adult and higher education may seem overwhelming. When subjected to multiple demands (e.g. effective classroom teaching, graduate student supervision, research and service) too often we succumb to the temptation to just treat symptoms, rather than looking for basic, sustainable improvements. Ramsden (1992) suggests that the "truth is that the stresses placed on us form an entirely inadequate basis for enhancing the quality of teaching" (p. 3). There are no short-cuts or quick fixes. Nothing less than clarifying assumptions and developing an understanding of the teaching-learning transaction will do. If teaching is to be improved, treating symptoms will not do it. In the long term, the most efficient and certainly effective approach will be to address the values, beliefs and understanding of the teaching-learning transaction by teachers within the context of their practice.

Final Thoughts

Much of the discussion in previous chapters has been around the themes of responsibility and control, which constitute a transactional perspective of teaching and learning in adult and higher education. Responsibility and control are essential conditions for meaningful and worthwhile learning. Responsibility and control merge to ensure continued learning characterized by the critical and self-directed pursuit of constructing personal meaning and worthwhile (i.e. valid) knowledge structures. Both teacher and learner must address responsibility and control concerns, although they will be manifested differently in the context of these two different roles.

As educators we must be sure that learning experiences are constructive and lead to continuous learning — that is, that we have facilitated students to become critical and self-directed learners. This is accomplished when individuals have learned to learn. Learning how to learn should be an integral part of learning what to learn.

Ryle (1967) argues that one responsibility of a teacher is "to get his [her] pupils to advance beyond their instructions and to discover new things for themselves, that is, to get them to think things out for themselves" (p. 107). To think for oneself is to assume responsibility for constructing meaning and confirming that meaning through discourse and action. Critical thinking necessitates that students risk confronting their misconceptions and assume responsibility for constructing meaningful knowledge.

Thinking is precipitated by uncertainty. If teachers make learning prescriptive and predictable, then students will have little reason to think for themselves. Thinking in complex and ill-structured domains is about making reasoned judgements and constructing coherent knowledge structures. Critical thinking includes creative/intuitive processes as well as logically deductive processes. However, those of us in higher education should feel uneasy at the fact that college seniors do not typically demonstrate the "habits of mind" characterized by critical or reflective thinking (King & Kitchener, 1994). Thinking and the methods that facilitate it are about quality of learning — not only quantity of curriculum covered.

Critical thinking is at the centre of meaningful and worthwhile learning. The reason is that critical thinkers are responsible self-directed learners. Furthermore, self-directed learning can only exist in an educational context where choice is valued and encouraged. Self-directed and continuous learning thrive in a climate of freedom and choice; that is, a climate in which there is the security to speak honestly and openly. However, with this freedom comes responsibility. Another freedom is the existential freedom of Rogers and the cognitive autonomy realized in the emancipation interest of Habermas (1971). It is openness to new ideas and an awareness of one's own thoughts and ways of thinking. This communicative and reflective educational ideal has been termed collaborative constructionism.

The ultimate responsibility of a teacher is to create the conditions and climate where thinking is valued and collaboratively facilitated. Responsible teachers communicate to students their responsibility in thinking and learning as well as the standards by which learning outcomes will be judged. Responsible teachers also share their own beliefs and methods. Through the explicit modelling of their own thought processes they reflect an authenticity and commitment to the facilitation of thinking and continuous learning. Reflection, collaboration and modelling are the invariables of responsible teaching. Within this framework each teacher must construct his or her own meaningful framework to inform their professional judgements while considering the contingencies of their particular context.

It has been assumed that the fundamental goal of education is to facilitate the construction of meaningful and worthwhile learning — during the process of which cognitive abilities and dispositions are being developed to ensure continuous learning. Knowledge is neither certain nor static; therefore, meaningful and worthwhile learning is a continuous search. The goal is for each student to become a critical and self-directed learner — to continue to learn how to learn. The only way this can reasonably be accomplished is by integrating reflective thinking and critical discourse. In this way, teachers and students take responsibility and control for the educational experience, and ultimately, the quality of the learning outcomes.

References

Anderson, J.R. (1983). *The Architecture of Cognition*. Cambridge, MA: Harvard University Press.

Andrews, J., Garrison, D. R., & Magnusson, K. (1996). The teaching and learning transaction in higher education: A study of excellent professors and their students. *Teaching in Higher Education, 1*(1), 81–103.

Applebee, A.N. (1984). Writing and reasoning. *Review of Educational Research, 54*, 577–596.

Apps, J.W. (1991). *Mastering the Teaching of Adults*. Malabar, Florida: Krieger.

Archambault, R.D. (1964). Introduction. In R.D. Archambault (Ed.), *John Dewey on Education* (pp. xiii–xxx). Chicago: University of Chicago Press.

Archer, W. (in press). Distance education for adults. In D.H. Poonwassie & A. Poonwassie (Eds.), *Choosing Adult Education*, Canadian Educators' Press.

Archer, W., Garrison, D.R., & Anderson, T. (1999). Adopting disruptive technologies in traditional universities: Continuing education as an incubator for innovation. *Canadian Journal of University Continuing Education, 25*(1), 13–30.

Ausubel, D.P., Novak, J.D., & Hanesian, H. (1978). *Educational Psychology: A Cognitive View* (2nd ed.). New York: Holt, Rinehart and Winston.

Bandura, A. (1977). *Social Learning Theory*. Englewood Cliffs, N.J.: Prentice-Hall.

Bandura, A. (1986). *Social Foundations of Thought and Action: A Social Cognitive Theory*. Englewood Cliffs, N.J.: Prentice-Hall.

Barnes, C.P., & Ellner, C.L. (1983). The present perspective. In C.L. Ellner & C.P. Barnes (Eds.), *Studies of College Teaching* (pp. 13–27). Lexington, MA: Lexington Books.

Bastick, T. (1982). *Intuition: How We Think and Act*. New York: John Wiley & Sons.

Beauchamp, L., Haughey, M., & Jacknicke, K. (1992). Coming back to the question. In M.S. Parer (Ed.), *Developing Open Learning Courses* (pp. 321–346). Churchill, Australia: Monash University.

Bereiter, C. (1992). Referent-centred and problem-centred knowledge: Elements of an educational epistemology. *Interchange, 23*, 337–361.

Bereiter, C., & Scardamalia, M. (1987). *The Psychology of Written Composition*. Hillsdale, New Jersey: Lawrence Erlbaum.

Biggs, J.B. (1987). *Student Approaches to Learning and Studying*. Melbourne, Australia: Australian Council for Educational Reseach.

Biggs, J. (1988). Approaches to learning and to essay writing. In R.R. Schmeck (Ed.), *Learning Strategies and Learning Styles* (pp. 185–228). New York: Plenum.

Blacker, D. (1993). Allowing educational technologies to reveal: A Deweyan perspective. *Educational Theory, 43*, 181–194.

Bowden, J. (1988). Achieving change in teaching practices. In P. Ramsden (Ed.), *Improving Learning: New Perspectives* (pp. 255–267). London: Kogan Page.

Bowers, K.S., Regehr, G., Balthazard, C., & Parker, K. (1990). Intuition in the context of discovery. *Cognitive Psychology, 22*, 72–110.

Brockett, R.G., & Hiemstra, R. (1991). *Self-Direction in Adult Learning: Perspectives on Theory, Research, and Practice*. London: Routledge.

Brook, P., & Garrison, D.R. (1995). Design of the first session: Faculty preferences. *Canadian Journal of University Continuing Education, 21*(1), 29–44.

Brookfield, S. (1985). Analyzing a critical paradigm of self-directed learning: A response. *Adult Education Quarterly, 36*, 60–64.

Brookfield, S.D (1986). *Understanding and Facilitating Adult Learning*. San Francisco: Jossey-Bass.

Brookfield, S.D. (1987a). *Developing Critical Thinkers*. San Francisco: Jossey-Bass.

Brookfield, S.D. (1987b). Eduard Lindeman. In P. Jarvis (Ed.), *Twentieth Century Thinkers in Adult Education* (pp. 119–143). London: Croom Helm.

Brookfield, S.D. (1990a). *The Skillful Teacher*. San Francisco: Jossey-Bass.

Brookfield, S.D. (1990b). Using critical incidents to explore learners' assumptions. In J. Mezirow (Ed.), *Fostering Critical Reflection in Adulthood* (pp. 177–193). San Francisco: Jossey-Bass.

Brookfield, S.D. (1995). *Becoming a Critically Reflective Teacher*. San Francisco: Jossey-Bass.

Brown, J., & Duguid, P. (1996). Universities in the digital age. *Change, 28*(4), 10–19.

Brown, A.L., & Palincsar, A.S. (1987). Reciprocal teaching of comprehension strategies: A natural history of one program for enhancing learning. In J.D. Day & J.G. Borkowski (Eds.), *Intelligence and Exceptionality: New Directions for Theory, Assessment, and Instructional Practices* (pp. 81–132). Norwood, NJ: Ablex.

Brown, A.L., & Palincsar, A.S. (1989). Guided, cooperative learning and individual knowledge acquisition. In L.B. Resnick (Ed.), *Knowing, Learning, and Instruction* (pp. 393–452). Hillsdale, N.J.: Lawrence Erlbaum.

Brown, J.S., Collins, A., & Duguid, P. (1989). Situated cognition and the culture of learning. *Educational Researcher, 18*(1), 32–42.

Bruner, J. (1990). *Acts of Meaning*. Cambridge, MA: Harvard University Press.

Buchmann, M., & Floden, R.E. (1992). Coherence, the rebel angel. *Educational Researcher*, 4–9.

Butler, D.L., & Winne, P.H. (1995). Feedback and self-regulated learning: A theoretical synthesis. *Review of Educational Research, 65*, 245–281.

Candy, P.C. (1989). Constructivism and the Study of Self-direction in Adult Learning. *Studies in the Education of Adults, 21*, 95–116.

Candy, P.C. (1991). *Self-Direction for Lifelong Learning*. San Francisco: Jossey-Bass.

Candy, P., Harri-Augstein, S., & Thomas, L. (1985). Reflection and the self-organized learner: A model of learning organizations. In D. Boud, R. Keough & D. Walker (Eds.), *Reflection: Turning Experience into Learning* (pp. 100–116). London: Kogan Page.

Carr, W., & Kemmis, S. (1986). *Becoming Critical: Education, Knowledge and Action Research*. London: The Falmer Press.

Centra, J.A. (1977). Faculty development practices. In J.A. Centra (Ed.), *Renewing and Evaluating Teaching* (pp. 49–56). San Francisco: Jossey-Bass.

Chickering, A.W., & Gamson, Z.F. (1987). Seven principles for good practice in under-graduate education. *AAHE Bulletin, 39*(7), 3–7.

Chickering, A.W., & Gamson, Z.F. (1991). Appendix A: Seven principles for good practice in undergraduate education. In A.W. Chickering & Z.F. Gamson (Eds.), *Applying the Seven Principles for Good Practice in Undergraduate Education* (pp. 63–69). San Francisco: Jossey-Bass.

Chipman, S.F., & Segal, J.W. (1985). Higher cognitive goals for education: An introduction.

In J.W. Segal, S.F. Chipman & R. Glaser (Eds.), *Thinking and Learning Skills Volume 1: Relating Instruction to Research* (pp. 1–19). Hillsdale, NJ: Lawrence Erlbaum.

Christensen, C.R., & Hansen, A.J. (1987). *Teaching and the Case Method*. Boston: Harvard Business School.

Clark, H.H., & Brennan, S.E. (1991). Grounding in communication. In L.B. Resnick, J.M. Levine & S.D. Teasley (Eds.), *Perspectives on Socially Shared Cognition* (pp. 127–149). Washington, DC: American Psychological Association.

Clark, R.E. (1983). Reconsidering research on learning from media. *Review of Educational Research, 53*, 445–459.

Clark, R.E., & Salomon, G. (1986). Media in teaching. In M.C. Wittrock (Ed.), *Handbook of Research on Teaching* (3rd ed.) (pp. 464–478). New York: Macmillan Publishing.

Cohen, E.G. (1994). Restructuring the classroom: Conditions for productive small groups. *Review of Educational Research, 64*, 1–35.

Corno, L. (1989). Self-regulated learning: A volitional analysis. In B.J. Zimmerman & D.H. Schunk (Eds.), *Self-Regulated Learning and Academic Achievement: Theory, Research, and Practice* (pp. 111–141). New York: Springer-Verlag.

Corno, L. (1993). The best-laid plans: Modern conceptions of volition and educational research. *Educational Researcher, 22*(2), 14–22.

Corno, L. (1994). Student volition and education: Outcomes, influences, and practices. In D.H. Schunk & B.J. Zimmerman (Eds.), *Self-Regulation of Learning and Performance: Issues and Educational Applications* (pp. 229–251). Hillsdale, NJ: Lawrence Erlbaum.

Corno, L., & Rohrkemper, M.M. (1985). The intrinsic motivation to learn in classrooms. In C. Ames & R. Ames (Eds.), *Research on Motivation in Education Volume 2: The Classroom Milieu* (pp. 53–90). Orlando: Academic Press.

Crooks, T.J. (1988). The impact of classroom evaluation practices on students. *Review of Educational Research, 58*, 438–481.

Curry, L. (1990). *Learning Styles in Secondary Schools: A Review of Instruments and Implications for their Use*. (ERIC Document Reproduction No. ED 317 283).

Daley, B.J., (1999). Novice to expert: An exploration of how professionals learn. *Adult Education Quarterly, 49*, 133–147.

D'Angelo, E. (1971). *The Teaching of Critical Thinking*. Amsterdam: B.R. Gruner.

Dart, B. (1998). Teaching for improved learning in small classes. In B. Dart & G. Boulton-Lewis (Eds.), *Teaching and Learning in Higher Education*. (pp. 222–249). Melbourne: ACER.

Dart, B., & Boulton-Lewis, G. (1998). *Teaching and Learning in Higher Education*. Melbourne: ACER.

Dewey, J. (1902). *The Child and The Curriculum* (7th printing, 1963). Chicago: Phoenix Books, The University of Chicago Press.

Dewey, J. (1916). *Democracy and Education* (4th printing, 1964). New York: Macmillan.

Dewey, J. (1933). *How We Think* (rev. ed.). Boston: D.C. Heath.

Dewey, J. (1938). *Experience and Education* (7th printing, 1967). New York: Collier.

Dewey, J. (1959). My pedagogic creed. In J. Dewey (Ed.), *Dewey on Education* (pp. 19–32). New York: Teachers College, Columbia University. (Original work published 1897)

Dewey, J. (1967). Psychology. In J. A. Boydston (Ed.), *John Dewey: The Early Works, 1882–1898 Vol. 2* (pp. 204–213). Carbondale: Southern Illinois University Press. (Original work published 1887.)

Dewey, J. (1969a). Plan of organization of the university primary school. In J. A. Boydston (Ed.), *John Dewey: The Early Works, 1882–1898 Vol. 5* (pp. 224–243). Carbondale: Southern Illinois University Press. (Original work published 1895.)

Dewey, J. (1969b). The present position of logical theory. In J. A. Boydston (Ed.), *John Dewey: The Early Works, 1889–1892, Vol. 3* (pp. 125–141). Carbondale: Southern Illinois University Press. (Original work published 1891.)

Dewey, J. (1981). Experience and nature. In J.A. Boydston (Ed.), *John Dewey: The Later Works, 1925–1953, Vol. 1*. Carbondale: Southern Illinois University Press. (Original work published 1925.)

Dewey, J. (1984a). Qualitative thought. In J. A. Boydston (Ed.), *John Dewey: The Later Works, 1925–1953 Vol. 5* (pp. 243–262). Carbondale: Southern Illinois University Press. (Original work published 1930.)

Dewey, J. (1984b). The public and its problems. In J.A. Boydston (Ed.), *John Dewey: The Later Works, 1925–1953, Vol. 12* (pp. 1–527). Carbondale: Southern Illinois University Press. (Original work published 1938.)

Dewey, J., & Childs, J.L. (1981). The underlying philosophy of education. In J.A. Boydston (Ed.), *John Dewey: The Later Works, 1925–1953, Vol. 8* (pp. 77–103). Carbondale: Southern Illinois University Press. (Original work published 1933.)

Dixon, N.M. (1985). The implementation of learning style information. *Lifelong Learning, 9*(3), 16–18, 26.

Donald, J.G. (1985). The state of research on teaching effectiveness. In J.G. Donald & A.M. Sullivan (Eds.), *Using Research to Improve Teaching* (pp. 7–20). San Francisco: Jossey-Bass.

Duffy, T.M., & Jonassen, D.H. (1991). Constructivism: New implications for instructional technology. *Educational Technology, 31*(5), 7–12.

Dworkin, M.S. (1959). John Dewey: A centennial review. In J. Dewey (Ed.), *Dewey on Education* (pp. 1–18). New York: Teachers College, Columbia University.

Eble, K.E. (1988). *The Craft of Teaching* (2nd ed.). San Francisco: Jossey-Bass.

Elias, J.L., & Merriam, S. (1980). *Philosophical Foundations of Adult Education*. Malabar, Florida: Robert E. Krieger.

Ellner, C.L., & Barnes, C.P. (1983). The context. In C.L. Ellner & C.P. Barnes (Eds.), *Studies of College Research* (pp. 1–11). Lexington, MA: Lexington Books.

Entwistle, N. (1981). *Styles of Learning and Teaching*. Toronto: John Wiley.

Entwistle, N. (1998). Approaches to learning and forms of understanding. In B. Dart & G. Boulton-Lewis (Eds.), *Teaching and Learning in Higher Education* (pp. 72–101). Melbourne: ACER Press.

Entwistle, A., & Entwistle, N. (1992). Experiences of understanding in revising for degree examinations. *Learning and Instruction, 2*, 1–22.

Entwistle, N., & Marton, F. (1994). Knowledge objects: understandings constituted through intensive academic study. *British Journal of Educational Psychology, 64*, 161–178.

Entwistle, N.J., & Ramsden, P. (1983). *Understanding Student Learning*. London: Croom Helm.

Entwistle, N., & Tait, H. (1990). Approaches to learning, evaluations of teaching, and preferences for contrasting academic environments. *Higher Education, 19*, 169–194.

Erwin, T.D. (1991). *Assessing Student Learning and Development*. San Francisco: Jossey-Bass.

Evans, T., & Nunan, T. (1992). Creating a course on research in distance education. In M.S. Parer (Ed.), *Developing Open Learning Courses* (pp. 167–182). Churchill, Australia: Monash University.

Ewert, G.D. (1991). Habermas and education: A comprehensive overview of the influence of Habermas in educational literature. *Review of Educational Research, 61*, 345–378.

Feldman, K.A. (1976). The superior college teacher from the students' view. *Research in Higher Education, 5*, 243–288.

Feldman, K.A. (1988). Effective college teaching from the students' and faculty's view: Matched or mismatched priorities? *Research in Higher Education, 28*, 291–344.

Fenstermacher, G.D. (1987). A reply to my critics. *Educational Theory, 37*(4), 413–421.

Fenstermacher, G.D., & Soltis, J.S. (1992). *Approaches to Teaching* (2nd ed.). New York: Teachers College Press.

Finke, R.A., Ward, T.B., & Smith, S.M. (1992). *Creative Cognition: Theory, Research, and Applications*. Cambridge, MA: MIT Press.

Fisher, C.G., & Grant, G.E. (1983). Intellectual levels in college classrooms. In C.L. Ellner & C.P. Barnes (Eds.), *Studies of College Research* (pp. 47–60). Lexington, MA: Lexington Books.

Fraser, K. (1996). *Student Centred Teaching: The Development and Use of Conceptual Frameworks* (Green Guide No 18). Australian Capital Territory: HERDSA.

Fulwiler, T. (1987). *Teaching with Writing*. Portsmouth, NH: Boynton/Cook.

Furedy, C., & Furedy, J.J. (1985). Critical thinking: Toward research and dialogue. In J.G. Donald & A.M. Sullivan (Eds.), *Using Research to Improve Teaching* (pp. 51–69). San Francisco: Jossey-Bass.

Gamson, Z.F. (1991). A brief history of the seven principles for good practice in undergraduate education. In A.W. Chickering & Z.F. Gamson (Eds.), *Applying the Seven Principles for Good Practice in Undergraduate Education* (pp. 5–12). San Francisco: Jossey-Bass.

Garrison, D.R. (1985). Three generations of technological innovation in distance education. *Distance Education, 6*, 235–241.

Garrison, D.R. (1990). Perceived control and the decision-making process to participate in adult education: An explication of Rubenson's recruitment paradigm. *Adult Education Research Conference Proceedings*, Athens, Georgia.

Garrison, D.R. (1991). Critical thinking and adult education: A conceptual model for developing critical thinking in adult learners. *International Journal of Lifelong Education, 10*, 287–303.

Garrison, D.R. (1992). Critical thinking and self-directed learning in adult education: An analysis of responsibility and control issues. *Adult Education Quarterly, 42,* 136–148.

Garrison, D.R. (1993). An analysis of the control construct in self-directed learning. In H.B. Long (Ed.), *Emerging Perspectives of Self-Directed Learning* (pp. 27–43). Norman, OK: Oklahoma Research Center for Continuing Professional and Higher Education of the University of Oklahoma.

Garrison, D.R. (1997a). Computer conferencing: The post-industrial age of distance education. *Open Learning, 12*(2), 3–11.

Garrison, D.R. (1997b). Computer conferencing and distance education: Cognitive and social presence issues. *Proceedings of the 18th ICDE World Conference*, Pennsylvania State University, June.

Garrison, D.R., & Anderson, T. (2000). *Transforming and enhancing university teaching: Stronger and weaker technological influences*. In T. Evans & D. Nation (Eds.), *Changing University Teaching: Reflections on Creating Educational Technologies*. London: Kogan Page.

Garrison, D.R., & Brook, P. (1991). *What Adult Students Say about the First Session*. Unpublished manuscript.

Garrison, D.R., & Brook, P. (1992). Getting it right the first session. *Adult Learning, 3*(6), 25–26.

Garrison, D.R., & Shale, D.G. (1987). Mapping the boundaries of distance education: Problems in defining the field. *The American Journal of Distance Education, 1*(1), 7–13.

Garrison, D.R., & Shale, D. (1990). *Education at a Distance: From Issues to Practice.* Malabar, Florida: Krieger.

Garrison, J. (1997). *Dewey and Eros: Wisdom and Desire in the Art of Teaching.* New York: Teachers College Press.

Gergen, K.J. (1985). The social constructivist movement in modern psychology. *American Psychologist, 40,* 266–275.

Glaser, R. (1984). Education and thinking: The role of knowledge. *American Psychologist, 39*(2), 93–104.

Glaser, R., & Silver, E. (1994). Assessment, testing, and instruction: Retrospect and prospect. In L. Darling-Hammond (Ed.), *Review of Research in Education* (Vol. 20, pp. 393–419). Washington, DC: American Educational Research Association.

Glasersfeld, E. von (1989). Cognition, construction of knowledge, and teaching. *Synthese, 80,* 121–140.

Goldberg, P. (1983). *The Intuitive Edge: Understanding and Developing Intuition.* Los Angeles: Jeremy P. Tarcher Inc.

Gordon, H. (1988). Learning to think: Arendt on education for democracy. *The Educational Forum, 33*(2), 49–62.

Gow, L., & Kember, D. (1993). Conceptions of teaching and their relationship to student learning. *British Journal of Educational Psychology, 63,* 20–33.

Grundy, S. (1987). *Curriculum: Product or Praxis.* London: The Falmer Press.

Habermas, J. (1971). *Knowledge and Human Interests* (J.J. Shapiro, Trans.). Boston: Beacon Press. (Original work published 1968.)

Habermas, J. (1984). *The Theory of Communicative Action: Vol. 1* (T. McCarthy, Trans.). Boston: Beacon Press. (Original work published 1981.)

Halpern, D.F. (1984). *Thought and Knowledge: An Introduction to Critical Thinking.* Hillsdale, NJ: Lawrence Erlbaum.

Hannaway, J. (1992). Higher order skills, job design, and incentives: An analysis and proposal. *American Educational Research Journal, 29,* 3–21.

Harrington, H.L., & Garrison, J.W. (1992). Cases as shared inquiry: A dialogical model of teacher preparation. *American Educational Research Journal, 29,* 715–735.

Hergenhahn, B.R. (1988). *An Introduction to Theories of Learning* (3rd ed.). Englewood Cliffs, N.J.: Prentice Hall.

Hodgson, V. (1984). Learning from lectures. In F. Marton, D. Hounsell & N. Entwistle (Eds.), *The Experience of Learning* (pp. 90–102). Edinburgh: Scottish Academic Press.

Howe, M.J.A. (1987). Motivation, cognition and individual achievements. In E. de Corte, H. Lodewijks, R. Parmentier & P. Span (Eds.), *Learning and Instruction: Volume 1* (pp. 133–146). Oxford: Pergamon Press.

Jarvis, P. (1988). Knowledge and learning in adult education. In C.E. Warren (Ed.), *Adult Education Research Conference Proceedings* (pp. 163–168). Calgary: The University of Calgary.

Jevons, F. (1987). Distance education and campus-based education: Parity of esteem. In P. Smith and M. Kelly (Eds.), *Distance Education and the Mainstream: Convergence in Education* (pp. 12–23). London: Croom Helm.

Jonassen, D.H. Objectivism versus constructivism: Do we need a new philosophical paradigm? *Educational Technology Research and Development, 39*(3), 5–14.

Joughin, G. (1992). Cognitive style and adult learning principles. *International Journal of Lifelong Education, 11,* 3–14.

Kagan, D.M. (1992). Implications of research on teacher belief. *Educational Psychologist, 27,* 65–90.

Kal, V. (1988). *On Intuition and Discursive Reasoning in Aristotle*. New York: E.J. Brill.

Kanfer, R. (1989). Conative processes, dispositions and performance: Connecting the dots within and across paradigms. In R. Kanfer, P.L. Ackerman, & R. Cudeck (Eds.), *Abilities, Motivation, and Methodology* (pp. 375–388). Hillsdale, NJ: Lawrence Erlbaum.

Kanfer, R., & Ackerman, P.L. (1989). Motivation and cognitive abilities: An integrative/aptitude treatment interaction approach to skill acquisition. *Journal of Applied Psychology*, 74, 657–690.

Kaye, T. (1987). Introducing computer-mediated communication into a distance education system. *Canadian Journal of Educational Communication*, 16(2), 153–166.

Kelly, M. (1990). Course creation issues in distance education. In D.R. Garrison & D. Shale (Eds.), *Education at a Distance: From Issues to Practice* (pp. 77–99). Malabar, Florida: Krieger.

King, P.M., & Kitchener, K.S. (1994). *Developing Reflective Judgement*. San Francisco: Jossey-Bass.

Kintsch, E. (1993). Principles of instruction from research on human cognition. In J.M. Spector, M.C. Polson & D.J. Muraida (Eds.), *Automating Instructional Design: Concepts and Issues* (pp. 23–42). Englewood Cliffs, NJ: Educational Technology Publications.

Kleinfeld, J. (1992). Learning to think like a teacher: The study of cases. In J.H. Shulman (Ed.), *Case Methods in Teacher Education* (pp. 33–49). New York: Teachers College Press.

Knowles, M. (1975). *Self-Directed Learning*. New York: Association Press.

Kulik, J.A., & Kulik, C.C. (1979). College teaching. In P.L. Peterson & H.J. Walberg (Eds.), *Research on Teaching: Concepts, Findings, and Implications* (pp. 70–93). Berkeley, California: McCutchan.

Kurfiss, J.G. (1988). *Critical Thinking: Theory, Research, Practice and Possibilities*. Washington, DC: Office of Educational Research and Improvement. (ERIC Document Reproduction Service No. ED 304 041.)

Kusnic, E., & Finley, M.L. (1993). Student self-evaluation: An introduction and rationale. In J. MacGregor (Ed.), *Student Self-Evaluation: Fostering Reflective Learning* (pp. 5–14). San Francisco: Jossey-Bass.

Lachman, R., Lachman, J., & Butterfield, E. (1979). *Cognitive Psychology and Information Processing: An Introduction*. Hillsdale, N.J.: Lawrence Erlbaum. (See Phillips & Soltis.)

Lakomski, G. (1991). Critical theory. In K. Marjoribanks (Ed.), *The Foundations of Students' Learning* (pp. 317–326). Oxford: Pergamon.

Lang, H., McBeath, A., & File, J. (1994). *Teaching: Strategies and Methods for Student-Centered Instruction*. Toronto: Harcourt Brace.

Larsson, S. (1983). Paradoxes in teaching. *Instructional Science*, 12, 355–365.

Larsson, S. (1987). Learning from experience: Teachers' conceptions of changes in their professional practice. *Journal of Curriculum Studies*, 19, 36–44.

Lave, J. (1991). Situating learning in communities of practice. In L.B. Resnick, J.M. Levine, S.D. Teasley (Eds.), *Perspectives on Socially Shared Cognition* (pp. 63–82). Washington, DC: American Psychological Association.

Lefrancois, G.R. (1972). *Psychological Theories and Human Learning: Kongor's Report*. Monterey, CA: Brooks/Cole.

Lindeman, E.C. (1926). *The Meaning of Adult Education* (4th printing, 1989). Norman, Oklahoma: The University of Oklahoma.

Lipman, M. (1991). *Thinking in Education*. Cambridge: Cambridge University Press.

Long, H.B. (1989). Self-directed learning: Merging theory and practice. In H.B. Long (Ed.), *Self-Directed Learning: Merging Theory and Practice* (pp. 1–12). Norman, Oklahoma:

Research Center for Continuing Professional and Higher Education of the University of Oklahoma.

Long, H.B., & Redding, T.R. (1991). *Self-Directed Learning Dissertation Abstracts 1966–1991*). Norman, Oklahoma: Research Center for Continuing Professional and Higher Education of the University of Oklahoma.

Loving, C.C. (1997). From the summit of truth to its slippery slopes: Science education's journey through positivist-postmodern territory. *American Educational Research Journal, 34*, 421–452.

Lutkenhaus, P., Bullock, M., & Geppert, U. (1987). Toddlers' actions: Knowledge, control, and the self. In F. Halisch & J. Kuhl (Eds.), *Motivation, Intention, and Volition* (pp. 145–161). New York: Springer-Verlag.

Marchese, T. (1998). Disengaged students II. *Change, 30*(3), 1.

Marsick, V.J. (1990). Case Study. In M.W. Galbraith (Ed.), *Adult Learning Methods: A Guide for Effective Instruction* (pp. 225–246). Malabar, Florida: Krieger.

Marton, F. (1992). Phenomenography and "the art of teaching all things to all men". *Qualitative Studies in Education, 5*, 253–267.

Marton, F., & Ramsden, P. (1988). What does it take to improve teaching? In P. Ramsden (Ed.), *Improving Learning: New Perspectives*. London: Kogan Page.

Marton, F., & Saljo, R. (1976). On qualitative differences in learning: I — Outcome and process. *British Journal of Educational Psychology, 46*, 4–11.

McCarthy, T. (1978). *The Critical Theory of Jurgen Habermas*. Cambridge, MA: The MIT Press.

McPeck, J.E. (1981). *Critical Thinking and Education*. Oxford: Martin Robertson.

McPeck, J.E. (1990a). *Teaching Critical Thinking: Dialogue and Dialectic*. New York: Routledge.

McPeck, J.E. (1990b). Critical thinking and subject specificity: A reply to Ennis. *Educational Researcher, 19*(4), 10–12.

Merriam, S.B., & Caffarella, R.S. (1991). *Learning in Adulthood: A Comprehensive Guide*. San Francisco: Jossey-Bass.

Meyer, J.H.F., & Muller, M.W. (1990). Evaluating the quality of student learning. I — an unfolding analysis of the association between perceptions of learning context and approaches to studying at an individual level. *Studies in Higher Education, 15*, 131–153.

Meyers, C. (1986). *Teaching Students to Think Critically*. San Francisco: Jossey-Bass.

Meyers, C., & Jones, T.B. (1993). *Promoting Active Learning: Strategies for the College Classroom*. San Francisco: Jossey-Bass.

Mezirow, J. (1981). A critical theory of adult learning and education. *Adult Education, 32*, 3–24.

Mezirow, J. (1985). A critical theory of self-directed learning. In S. Brookfield (Ed.), *Self-Directed Learning: From Theory to Practice* (pp. 17–30). San Francisco: Jossey-Bass.

Mezirow, J. (1990). Conclusion: Toward transformative learning and emancipatory education. In J. Mezirow (Ed.), *Fostering Critical Reflection in Adulthood* (pp. 354–376). San Francisco: Jossey-Bass.

Mezirow, J. (1991). *Transformative Dimensions of Adult Learning*. San Francisco: Jossey-Bass.

Mezirow, J. (1994). Understanding transformation theory. *Adult Education Quarterly, 44*, 22–224.

Mezirow, J. (1998). On critical reflection. *Adult Education Quarterly, 48*, 185–198.

Moran, J.J. (1997). *Assessing Adult Learning: A Guide for Practitioners*. Malabar, Florida: Krieger.

Murray, H.G. (1991). Effective teaching behaviors in the college classroom. In J.C. Smart (Ed.), *Higher Education: Handbook of Theory and Research Volume VII* (pp. 135–172). New York: Agathon.

Nickerson, R. S. (1991). Some observations on the teaching of thinking. In R.F. Mulcahy, R.H. Short & J. Andrews (Eds.), *Enhancing Learning and Thinking* (pp. 3–9). New York: Praeger.

Noddings, N., & Shore, P.J. (1984). *Awakening the Inner Eye: Intuition in Education*. New York: Teachers College Press.

Nunan, T. (1983). *Countering Educational Design*. London: Croom Helm.

Olson, D.R. (1977). From utterance to text: The bias of language in speech and writing. *Harvard Educational Review, 47*, 257–281.

Pajares, M.F. (1992). Teachers' beliefs and educational research: Cleaning up a messy construct. *Review of Educational Research, 62*, 307–332.

Parer, M.S. (1992). *Developing Open Learning Courses*. Churchill, Australia: Monash University.

Pask, G. (1988). Learning strategies, teaching strategies, and conceptual or learning style. In R.R. Schmeck (Ed.), *Learning Strategies and Learning Styles* (pp. 83–100). New York: Plenum.

Passmore, J. (1972). On teaching to be critical. In F.R. Dearden, D.H. Hurst & R.S. Peters (Eds.), *Education and the Development of Reason* (pp. 415–433). London: Routledge & Kegan Paul.

Paul, R. (1990). *Critical Thinking*. Rohnert Park, CA: Sonoma State University.

Perkins, D.N. (1981). *The Mind's Best Work*. Cambridge, Massachusetts: Harvard University Press.

Perkins, D. (1986). On creativity and thinking skills: A conversation with David Perkins. *Educational Leadership, 43*(8), 12–18.

Perry, W. (1970). *Forms of Intellectual and Ethical Development in the College Years*. New York: Holt, Rinehart & Winston.

Peters, R.S. (1972). On teaching to be critical. In F.R. Dearden, D.H. Hurst & R.S. Peters (Eds.), *Education and the Development of Reason* (pp. 209–229). London: Routledge & Kegan Paul.

Phillips, D.C., & Soltis, J.F. (1985). *Perspectives on Learning*. New York: Teachers College Press.

Pintrich, P.R. (1989). The dynamic interplay of student motivation and cognition in the college classroom. In M.L. Maehr & C. Ames (Eds.), *Advances in Motivation and Achievement: Motivation Enhancing Environments* (pp. 117–160). Greenwich, Connecticut: Jai Press.

Pintrich, P.R. (1990). Implications of psychological research on student learning and college teaching for teacher education. In W.R. Houston (Ed.), *Handbook of Research on Teacher Education* (pp. 826–857). New York: Macmillan.

Pintrich, P.R., & DeGroot, E.V. (1990). Motivational and self-regulated learning components of classroom academic performance. *Journal of Educational Psychology, 82*, 33–40.

Pratt, D.D. (1981). The dynamics of continuing education learning groups. *Canadian Journal of University Continuing Education, 8*(1), 26–32.

Pratt, D.D. (1984). Teaching adults: A conceptual framework for the first session. *Lifelong Learning, 7*(6), 7–9.

Prawat, R.S. (1991). The value of ideas: The immersion approach to the development of thinking. *Educational Researcher, 20*(2), 3–10, 30.

Prawat, R.S. (1992). Teachers' beliefs about teaching and learning: A constructivist perspective. *American Journal of Education, 100*(3), 354–395.

Prawat, R.S. (1993). The value of ideas: Problems versus possibilities in learning. *Educational Researcher, 22*(6), 5–16.

Prawat, R.S. (1997). Problematizing Dewey's views of problem solving: A reply to Hiebert et al. *Educational Researcher, 26*(2), 19–21.

Prawat, R.S. (1998). Current self-regulation views of learning and motivation viewed through a Deweyan lens: The problems with dualism. *American Educational Research Journal, 35*, 199–224.

Prawat, R.S. (1999). Dewey, Peirce, and the learning paradox. *American Educational Research Journal, 36*, 47–76.

Prosser, M., & Trigwell, K. (1998). Teaching in higher education. In B. Dart & G. Boulton-Lewis (Eds.), *Teaching and Learning in Higher Education* (pp. 72–101). Melbourne: ACER Press.

Ramsden, P. (Ed.). (1988a). *Improving Learning: New Perspectives*. London: Kogan Page.

Ramsden, P. (1988b). Context and strategy: Situational influences on learning. In R.R. Schmeck (Ed.), *Learning Strategies and Learning Styles* (pp. 159–184). New York: Plenum.

Ramsden, P. (1992). *Learning to Teach in Higher Education*. London: Routledge.

Ramsden, P., & Entwistle, N.J. (1981). Effects of academic departments on students' approaches to studying. *British Journal of Educational Psychology, 51*, 368–383.

Rando, W.C., & Menges, R.J. (1991). How practice is shaped by personal theories. In R.J. Menges & M.D. Svinicki (Eds.), *College Teaching: From Theory to Practice* (pp. 7–14). San Francisco: Jossey-Bass.

Resnick, L.B. (1987). *Education and Learning to Think*. Washington, DC: National Academy Press.

Resnick, L.B. (1989). Introduction. In L.B. Resnick (Ed.), *Knowing, Learning, and Instruction* (pp. 1–24). Hillsdale, N.J.: Lawrence Erlbaum.

Resnick, L.B. (1991). Shared cognition: Thinking as social practice. In L.B. Resnick, J.M. Levine, & S.D. Teasley (Eds.), *Perspectives on Socially Shared Cognition* (pp. 1–20). Washington, DC: American Psychological Association.

Resnick, L.B., & Klopfer, L.E. (1989). Toward the thinking curriculum: An overview. In L.B. Resnick & L.E. Klopfer (Eds.), *Toward the Thinking Curriculum: Current Cognitive Research* (pp. 1–18). 1989 Yearbook of the Association for Supervision and Curriculum Development.

Resnick, L.B., & Resnick, D.P. (1992). Assessing the thinking curriculum: New tools for educational reform. In B.R. Gifford & M.C. O'Connor (Eds.), *Changing Assessments: Alternative Views of Aptitude, Achievement and Instruction* (pp. 37–75). Boston: Kluwer.

Richardson, V. (1994). Constructivist teaching: Theory and practice. *Teaching Thinking and Problem Solving, 16*(6), 1, 3–7.

Roderick, R. (1986). *Habermas and the Foundations of Critical Theory*. London: Macmillan.

Rogers, C.R. (1969). *Freedom to Learn*. Columbus, Ohio: Charles E. Merrill.

Rogoff, B. (1990). *Apprenticeship in Thinking: Cognitive Development in Social Context*. New York: Oxford University Press.

Rowntree, D. (1975). Two styles of communication and their implications for learning. In J. Baggaly, H. Jamieson, & H. Marchant (Eds.), *Aspects of Educational Technology: Volume VIII: Communication and Learning* (pp. 281–293). London: Pitman.

Rowntree, D. (1977). *Assessing Students*. London: Harper & Row.

Rubenson, K. (1987). Participation in recurrent education: A research review. In H.G. Schutze & D. Istance (Eds.), *Recurrent Education Revisited — Modes of Participation and Financing* (pp. 39–67). Paris: Organization for Economic cooperation and Development.

Ruggiero, V.R. (1984). *The Art of Thinking: A Guide to Critical and Creative Thought*. New York: Harper & Row.

Ryan, R.M., Connell, J.P., & Deci, E.L. (1985). A motivational analysis of self-determination and self-regulation in education. In C. Ames & R. Ames (Eds.), *Research on Motivation in Education Volume 2: The Classroom Milieu* (pp. 13–51). Orlando: Academic Press.

Ryle, G. (1967). Teaching and training. In R. S. Peters (Ed.), *The Concept of Education* (pp. 105–119). New York: Humanities Press.

Saljo, R. (1979). *Learning in the Learner's Perspective: Some Common Sense Conceptions* (Report No. 76). Molndal, Sweden: University of Goteborg.

Saljo, R. (1991). Introduction: Culture and learning. *Learning and Instruction, 1*, 179–185.

Salk, J. (1983). *Anatomy of Reality: Merging of Intuition and Reason*. New York: Columbia University Press.

Salomon, G. (1992). The changing role of the teacher: From information transmitter to orchestrator of learning. In F.K. Oser, A. Dick & J. Patry (Eds.), *Effective and Responsible Teaching: The New Synthesis* (pp. 35–49). San Francisco: Jossey-Bass.

Schiffman, S.S. (1991). Instructional system design: Five views of the field. In G.J. Anglin (Ed.), *Instructional Technology: Past, Present, and Future* (pp. 102–116). Englewood, CO: Libraries Unlimited.

Schmeck, R.R. (1988a). An introduction to strategies and styles of learning. In R.R. Schmeck (Ed.), *Learning Strategies and Learning Styles* (pp. 3–19). New York: Plenum.

Schmeck, R.R. (1988b). Strategies and styles of learning. In R.R. Schmeck (Ed.), *Learning Strategies and Learning Styles* (pp. 317–347). New York: Plenum.

Schon, D.A. (1983). *The Reflective Practitioner: How Professionals Think in Action*. New York: Basic Books.

Schon, D.A. (1987). *Educating the Reflective Practitioner*. San Francisco: Jossey-Bass.

Seixas, P. (1993). The community of inquiry as a basis for knowledge and learning: The case of history. *American Educational Research Journal, 30*, 305–324.

Senge, P.M. (1990). *The Fifth Discipline: The Art & Practice of the Learning Organization*. New York: Doubleday.

Shale, D., & Garrison, D.R. (1994). Instructional design in distance education. Paper presented at the Canadian Association for Distance Education, Vancouver, June.

Shavelson, R.J. (1992). New roles for teachers and students. In F.K. Oser, A. Dick & J. Patry (Eds.), *Effective and Responsible Teaching: The New Synthesis* (pp. 31–34). San Francisco: Jossey-Bass.

Sheffield, E.F. (Ed.) (1974). *Teaching in the Universities: No One Way*. Montreal: McGill-Queen's University Press.

Sherman, T.M., Armistead, L.P., Fowler, F., Barksdale, M.A., & Reif, G. (1987). The quest for excellence in university teaching. *Journal of Higher Education, 48*, 66–84.

Shrock, S.A. (1991). A brief history of instructional development. In G.J. Anglin (Ed.), *Instructional Technology: Past, Present, and Future* (pp.11–19). Englewood, CO: Libraries Unlimited.

Shuell, T.J. (1986). Cognitive conceptions of learning. *Review of Educational Research. 56*, 411–436.

Shulman, J.H. (1992). Toward a pedagogy of cases. In J.H. Schulman (Ed.), *Case Methods in Teacher Education* (pp. 1–30). New York: Teachers College Press.

Siegel, H. (1988). *Educating Reason: Rationality, Critical Thinking, and Education*. New York: Routledge.

Singer, D.L., Astrachan, B.M., Gould, L.J., & Klein, E.B. (1975). Boundary management in psychological work with groups. *Journal of Applied Behavioural Science, 11*, 137–176.

Smith, D.G. (1983). Instruction and outcomes in an undergraduate setting. In C.L. Ellner & C.P. Barnes (Eds.), *Studies of College Research* (pp. 83–116). Lexington, MA: Lexington Books.

Smith, S.L. (1991). *Report: Commission of Inquiry on Canadian University Education*. Ottawa: Association of Universities and Colleges of Canada.

Sorcinelli, M.D. (1991). Research findings on the seven principles. In A.W. Chickering & Z.F. Gamson (Eds.), *Applying the Seven Principles for Good Practice in Undergraduate Education* (pp. 13–25). San Francisco: Jossey-Bass.

Spear, G.E., & Mocker, D.W. (1984). The organizing circumstance: Environmental determinants in self-directed learning. *Adult Education Quarterly, 35*, 1–10.

Spiro, R.J., Coulson, R.L., Feltovich, P.J., & Anderson, D.K. (1988). Cognitive flexibility theory: Advanced knowledge acquisition in ill-structured domains. *The Tenth Annual Conference of the Cognitive Society Proceedings* (pp. 375–383). Hillsdale, NJ: Lawrence Erlbaum.

Stalker, J. (1993). Voluntary participation: Deconstructing the myth. *Adult Education Quarterly, 43*, 63–75.

Sternberg, R.J. (1988). A three facet model of creativity. In R.J. Sternberg (Ed.), *The Nature of Creativity* (pp. 125–147). New York: Cambridge University Press.

Sternberg, R.J. (1994). PRSVL: an integrative framework for understanding mind in context. In R.J. Sternberg & R.K. Wagner (Eds.), *Mind in Context* (pp. 218–232). New York: Cambridge University Press.

Stewart, D.W. (1987). *Adult Learning in America*. Malabar, Florida: Robert E. Krieger.

Stewart, W.J. (1988). Stimulating intuitive thinking through problem solving. *The Clearing House, 62*(4), 175–176.

Store, R., & Armstrong, J. (1981). Personalizing feedback between teacher and student in the context of a particular model of distance education. *British Journal of Educational Technology, 2*(12), 140–157.

Streibel, M.J. (1991). Instructional plans and situated learning. In G.L. Anglin (Ed.), *Instructional Technology: Past, Present and Future* (pp. 117–132). Englewood, CO: Libraries Unlimited.

Suber, P. (1991). How teachers teach, how students learn: Teaching in a blizzard of information. *Proceedings of a National Forum on Teaching and Technology at Earlham College* (pp. 67–74). Ann Arbor, Michigan: Pierian Press.

Taylor, C.W. (1988). Various approaches to and definitions of creativity. In R.J. Sternberg (Ed.), *The Nature of Creativity* (pp. 99–123). Cambridge: Cambridge University Press.

Tennant, M. (1988). *Psychology and Adult Learning*. London: Routledge.

Thayer-Bacon, B.J. (1993). Caring and its relationship to critical thinking. *Educational Theory, 43*, 323–340.

Thomas, A.M. (1991). *Beyond Education: A New Perspective on Society's Management of Learning*. San Francisco: Jossey-Bass.

Thomas, L.F., & Harri-Augstein, E.S. (1985). *Self-Organized Learning: Foundations of a Conversational Science for Psychology*. London: Routledge & Kegan Paul.

Tiffin, J., & Rajasingham, L. (1995). *In Search of the Virtual Class: Education in an Information Society*. London: Routledge.

Tobin, K. (1983). The influence of wait-time on classroom learning. *European Journal of Science Education, 5*(1), 35–48.

Torrance, E.P. (1988). The nature of creativity as manifest in its testing. In R.J. Sternberg (Ed.), *The Nature of Creativity* (pp. 43–75). Cambridge: Cambridge University Press.

Tough, A. (1971). *The Adult's Learning Projects.* Toronto: Ontario Institute for Studies in Education.

Tripp, S.D. (1991). Two theories of instructional design. Paper presented at the Annual Conference of the Association for Educational Communications & Technology, February, Orlando.

Vera, A.H. & Simon, H.A. (1993). Situated action: A symbolic interpretation. *Cognitive Science, 17,* 7–48.

Vroom, V. (1964). *Work and Motivation.* New York: John Wiley.

Weinstein, M. (1993). Critical thinking: The great debate. *Educational Theory, 43*(1), 99–117.

Weisz, J.R. (1983). Can I control it?: The pursuit of veridical answers across the life-span. In P.B. Baltes & O.G. Brim (Eds.), *Life-Span Development and Behavior* (pp. 233–300). New York: Academic Press.

White, E.M. (1993). Assessing higher-order thinking and communication skills in college graduates through writing. *The Journal of General Education, 42,* 105–122.

White, J.P. (1972). Creativity and education: A philosophical analysis. In F.R. Dearden, D.H. Hurst & R.S. Peters (Eds.), *Education and the Development of Reason* (pp. 132–148). London: Routledge & Kegan Paul.

Whitehead, A.N. (1929). *The Aims of Education.* Cambridge: Cambridge University Press.

Wiener, N. (1956). *The Human Use of Human Beings: Cybernetics and Society.* Garden City, NY: Doubleday.

Winn, W. (1989). Toward a rationale and theoretical basis for educational technology. *Educational Technology Research & Development, 37*(1), 35–46.

Winn, W. (1990). Some implications of cognitive theory for instructional design. *Instructional Science, 19(1),* 53–69.

Winn, W. (1993). Instructional design and situated learning: Paradox or partnership? *Educational Technology, 33*(3), 16–21.

Winne, P.H. (1995). Inherent details in self-regulated learning. *Educational Psychologist, 30,* 173–187.

Wittrock, M.C. (1991). Models of heuristic teaching. In K. Marjoribanks (Ed.), *The Foundations of Students' Learning* (pp. 73–87). Oxford: Pergamon.

Wlodkowski, R.J. (1985). *Enhancing Adult Motivation to Learn.* San Francisco: Jossey-Bass.

Young, M.F. (1993). Instructional design for situated learning. *Educational Technology Research & Development, 41*(1), 43–58.

Young, R.E. (1990). *A Critical Theory of Education: Habermas and Our Children's Future.* New York: Teachers College Press.

Index